ORDINARY ETHICS IN CHINA

ORDINARY ETHICS IN CHINA

EDITED BY CHARLES STAFFORD

LONDON SCHOOL OF ECONOMICS MONOGRAPHS ON SOCIAL ANTHROPOLOGY

Volume 79

B L O O M S B U R Y
LONDON • NEW DELHI • NEW YORK • SYDNEY

Bloomsbury Academic

An imprint of Bloomsbury Publishing Plc

50 Bedford Square	175 Fifth Avenue
London	New York
WC1B 3DP	NY 10010
UK	USA

www.bloomsbury.com

First published 2013

British Library Cataloguing-in-Publication Data
A catalogue record for this book is available from the British Library.

ISBN: HB: 978-0-8578-5459-9
PB: 978-0-8578-5460-5

Library of Congress Cataloging-in-Publication Data

Ordinary ethics in China / edited by Charles Stafford.
p. cm. — (London school of economics monographs on social anthropology; volume 79)
Includes bibliographical references and index.
ISBN 978-0-85785-459-9 (alk. paper) — ISBN 978-0-85785-460-5 (alk. paper) — ISBN 978-0-85785-811-5 (alk. paper) — ISBN 978-0-85785-810-8 (alk. paper) 1. Ethnology—China.
2. Ethics—China. 3. China—Moral conditions. 4. China—Social life and customs. I. Stafford, Charles.
GN635.C5O85   2013
306.0951—dc23   2012033162

Typeset by Apex CoVantage, LLC, Madison, WI, USA.
Printed and bound in Great Britain

CONTENTS

ACKNOWLEDGEMENTS

This volume is the product of a workshop held at the London School of Economics in May 2009 on the topic of 'Ordinary ethics in China today'. The funding for this event was provided by the Asia Research Centre at the LSE, and we are very grateful for this generous support. During the workshop, we benefited greatly from the insightful contributions of Harriet Evans, James Laidlaw, Michael Lambek, Erik Mueggler and other participants.

ACKNOWLEDGEMENTS

INTRODUCTION

CHAPTER I

ORDINARY
ETHICS IN CHINA TODAY

Charles Stafford

This book is a reflection on 'ordinary' moral and ethical life in contemporary China. That is, the contributors focus as much or more on
everyday questions of morality and ethics as on China's dramatic collective histories (in which, of course, moral questions have been writ
large) or on the explicit moral philosophies of specialists (of which, of
course, there are many in China). How, for example, are schoolchildren
judged to be 'good' or 'bad' by their peers? What, if anything, do sons
and daughters owe their parents? Is it acceptable to be jealous when
one's neighbours, for example, in a rural community, become wealthy?
If a person moves overseas, what are the ethics of him holding onto or
letting go of the values he grew up with? Should the wrongs of the past
be forgotten or dealt with now?

In the case of China, such questions—and the answers to them—
have obviously been shaped by the (sometimes turbulent) social and historical contexts against which they have been posed and by the weight
of various Chinese traditions. But here we strive to approach them on a
human scale. More specifically, we approach them from an anthropological perspective, based on participation in the flow of everyday life
while carrying out fieldwork in Chinese communities.

Of course, anthropologists have long been interested in moral life,
for example, in the rules that govern children's behaviour with respect
to their elders (see Westermarck 1906: 597–628). Indeed, most of what
anthropologists focus on in their research—family life, public rituals,

the distribution of resources, and so forth—is at least implicitly, and often explicitly, tied to moral judgement, that is, to the views of ordinary people about the 'goodness' or 'badness' of given states of affair. It is arguably difficult, however, for us to avoid conceiving such judgements in *aggregate* terms: for instance, to avoid concluding that the residents of a particular Chinese village or town, or even Chinese people as a whole, 'think' or 'believe' that the elderly should be cared for by the young, and that a Chinese son who fails to care for his ageing parents 'will be seen to be' bad. Anthropologists obviously know that characterizations of these kinds—statements about widely distributed understandings of moral rules—don't, on their own, tell us what individuals really *do* think about a particular rule, nor what actions they will take with respect to it, nor how new circumstances may cause the rules to be rewritten. Ethnographic accounts typically focus precisely on such matters. Still, the notion of morality as collective consensus is hard to resist. As James Laidlaw observes, anthropologists sometimes even write as if the aggregate view of goodness *is* actually good (Laidlaw 2002, cf. Laidlaw 2010).

This is where ethics comes in. Although making a sharp distinction between morality and ethics is not easy, the philosopher Bernard Williams reminds us that these terms do have different origins (Williams 1985; see also Laidlaw 2002; Zigon 2008; Lambek 2010). The term 'morals' (from Latin) relates to questions of custom, social expectation and rule whereas 'ethics' (from Greek) has more to do with individual character—and with the active attempts people make to do what is, or could be, right. Using a different language, we could say that morality is instantiated in structure (e.g. in rules of behaviour for persons in given structural positions) whereas ethics is instantiated in agency (e.g. in the attempts these persons make to negotiate moral rules/ frameworks). Obviously, these terminologies are specific to particular traditions of thought, and could be endlessly problematized. But the simple point here—that is, the reason for saying that *ethics* is the subject of our book—is to draw attention to the role of reflection, judgement and agency in moral life and, by implication, to shift away from overly rule-oriented (thereby consensualist) perspectives on moral personhood. While in some of the chapters that follow the terms 'morality' and 'ethics' are used interchangeably, our emphasis throughout is on the agentive side of moral life, that is, on 'ethics' in the Greek sense.

What, then, do we mean by describing certain ethical situations and practices as *ordinary*? This usage comes from the recent, highly thought-provoking work of Michael Lambek, who notes, among other things: (*a*) that being subject to ethical potentials and demands is an ordinary part of the human condition; (*b*) that ethical life is therefore observable not only in exceptional circumstances—such as 'moral dilemmas' of the kind that evoke explicit (often specialist) commentary—but also in routine and everyday ones; and (*c*) that routine ethical circumstances are often dealt with via tacit understandings and the micro processes of everyday life (e.g. via passing linguistic exchanges) rather than via explicit philosophizing, theory building or decision-making (Lambek 2010).

Much could be said about Lambek's approach, which draws extensively on philosophy and linguistics as well as anthropology, but here I wish to note one way in which the emphasis in this volume differs somewhat from his. Lambek follows Aristotle in conceiving ethics primarily as 'a dimension of action' rather than 'an aspect of thought'. He also broadly follows Bourdieu in highlighting the extent to which ethical judgements rely on implicit, 'embodied' understandings of how things are, as opposed to explicit, conscious reflection. The exceptions to this are, for the most part, exceptional: ethics typically becomes explicit or conscious—and thus 'non-ordinary'—when someone breaks a rule, or because a particular issue has become 'hotly contested', or when a movement of some kind starts to promote moral/ethical revival, and so on (Lambek 2010: 2; see also Zigon 2008). The case studies in this book, however, highlight the fact that explicit ethical reflection, explicit discussion of ethical matters and explicit judgement and decision-making in relation to ethical demands are *also* 'ordinary' aspects of human life (a point I return to later). Furthermore, the content of explicit ethical deliberation is often very rich—indeed, arguably richer than the content of the implicit or 'embodied' morality we acquire as a result of enculturation (see Stafford 2010). In short, although ethics is clearly a 'dimension of action' in which implicit understandings are crucial, ethics is also—routinely, ordinarily—the subject of explicit and conscious deliberation.

***

As it happens, a large number of articles and books within the anthropology of China subfield—perhaps even the majority of them—focus on cases where explicit grappling with moral and ethical problems is in the foreground. One thinks, for instance, of Margery Wolf's classic account of the tensions in a Taiwanese farm family, *The House of Lim* (1960), or of Mayfair Yang's work on 'the art of social relationships' during the post-Mao era of economic reforms (Yang 1994), or of the more recent studies by Vanessa Fong (2004) and Andrew Kipnis (2011) of the pressures children and young people face within China's intensely competitive educational system. In all of these books, ordinary people are heard talking—quite a lot—about the ethical quandaries they and others encounter. Other books that focus specifically on moral transformations in contemporary China have come from Xin Liu (2000), Ellen Oxfeld (2010), Arthur Kleinman et al. (2011) and of course from Yunxiang Yan (2003, 2009). Yan's highly influential writings, based primarily on his long-term fieldwork in rural Heilongjiang, examine recent processes of 'individualization' which, he argues, have radically transformed popular Chinese understandings of moral personhood. The individuals and communities Yan describes are genuinely struggling—again, often explicitly—with new moral demands and possibilities.

So where does our book fit into this crowded field? In brief, our approach is characterized by two things. The first, as already noted, is a bias towards what could be called 'ordinary' rather than exceptional ethical circumstances. While necessarily taking account of China's collective histories, we generally adopt a small-is-beautiful approach in which the routine, everyday and highly personal aspects of ethics are stressed (somewhat along the lines of Wolf 1960; Oxfeld 2010). Even the chapters in this book that most directly link ethics to large-scale historical and politico-economic determinants do so via stories of the quotidian and the personal. The second thing that characterizes our approach is an interest in broadly 'psychological' questions—although what this means varies considerably between the sections of the book and between the individual chapters:

- Section 1 deals with moral/ethical issues linked to learning, childhood and youth. Here we provide accounts of children at school, children moving between home and school, rural youth moving to cities in search of work and overseas migrants raising their children and grandchildren in new (non-Chinese) environments. In all of these case studies, questions of *learning* and child development are in the foreground.

- Section 2 deals with ethical action in situ, and especially the question of how adults in rural communities *think* about and ultimately *judge* their own actions and those of the people around them. How forgiving should we be of the failings of others? Can we avoid others resenting our circumstances and criticizing our actions? Against which standards should an individual's life as a whole be evaluated? What is the ideal type of family to have, and to strive for?
- Section 3 deals with cases in which technologies and/or 'techniques' of various kinds mediate ethical life—specifically in relation to everyday experience, to patterns of governance, to the inculcation of morality and to health. The broader issue that emerges in this section is thus the materialization of ethics and the relationship of this to our everyday *understandings* of it—including our *emotional* reactions to moral/ethical quandaries when we are confronted by them.

The book ends with an Afterword by Yunxiang Yan in which he provides a penetrating analysis of the cultural, historical and political changes that set the background to the micro-ethnographies of ethics found in the preceding chapters. In particular, Yan frames his discussion around the ethics of the 'striving individual', a post-Mao phenomenon he finds exemplified in virtually all of our case studies. Indeed, readers who are not familiar with China's modern history, and with the post-Mao landscape, might find it worth starting with Yan's chapter—although it is also worthwhile, I would suggest, to start by reading the ethnographic chapters on their own terms first before turning to Yan.

In any case, because he does an excellent job of situating the volume historically and in relation to existing debates in anthropology and other fields, in the remainder of this introduction I will focus primarily on exploring the narrative thread that brings our case studies together, taking each of the three sections in turn. At the end, drawing on our findings, I will make a few suggestions regarding further research on ordinary ethics.

SECTION 1: CHILDHOOD, YOUTH AND ETHICAL TRAJECTORIES

Where do our ideas about morality and ethics come from? And where, exactly, do we put them into practice? In the case of contemporary China, schools are assumed to function not only as crucial sites for moral instruction but also as sites where morality plays itself out. Indeed, being a 'good' Chinese child has become synonymous, to a remarkable extent, with achieving success *in* school. Unfortunately, however, the competitiveness of China's educational system makes success in these terms highly elusive—with the result that schooling generates as many ethical dilemmas, for parents and children alike, as it notionally clarifies or resolves through instruction (see Fong 2004; Kipnis 2011).

So what is it like to be a Chinese schoolchild today? In approaching this question, Chih-yuan Wang carried out research in two radically different Beijing primaries: a semi-legal one for the children of migrant workers and an elite one affiliated with a top university. One might expect students at the elite school to be typical overachievers, driven to succeed at any cost. However, Wang counters this expectation, providing a vivid account of a disruptive fourth-grade pupil. Wu Hao is a joker and classroom bully who is not doing well in his studies. Most students try to avoid him when they can—but is he 'bad'? In fact, the teachers at his school (which is more liberal than most in educational philosophy) prefer to call such students disruptive and noisy rather than labelling them bad as such. And as Wang shows, at least one teacher is sympathetic to Wu Hao's circumstances: as a 'thin and feeble' kindergarten student he was bullied in the past. Moreover, in this system the blame for misbehaviour and underachievement is felt to rest as much with the teachers as with the pupils.

The case of Wu Hao thus raises the question of moral responsibility, a theme that emerges repeatedly in the studies in this book. For example, in Hui Zhang's study of envy, or 'red eye', in a rural community (Chapter 7), it is suggested that those who *provoke* envy because of their wealth are more blameworthy than those who *feel* it. The former are held responsible for the—socially disruptive—emotions they generate in the latter. To return to Wu Hao's case, Wang suggests that the response of teachers to his misbehaviour is, in the end, largely pragmatic rather than moralistic: above all, this boy is a managerial headache. The other students, however, *do* hold him responsible for his actions, blaming Wu Hao (not his parents or teachers) for what he does. Still, they acknowledge that there are good things about him too. Wang reports that other children 'recognized [him] as a boy full of ideas and tricks and they admitted . . . that they sometimes join Wu Hao's games [such as "Gun Fight" and "The Game of Provoking Li"] out of interest and curiosity'.

The obvious but important point here is that even relatively 'simple' moral evaluations—is this child good or bad?—are often nuanced. Part of being ethical, we might say, is allowing ourselves or perhaps even *forcing* ourselves to be nuanced and generous in evaluating others. This is an issue I will come back to in a moment.

While Wang's chapter is based on research carried out in an elite school in Beijing, James Johnston starts at a very different position within China's educational hierarchy, in rural Anhui. Here most children and young people are in the early stages of an inevitable—and ethically loaded—migration: down from remote, supposedly 'low quality', mountain villages towards more 'advanced' towns and cities below in search of education and employment. Places like Beijing are a distant dream for most. In this setting Johnston describes two moralities that sit uncomfortably alongside each other: a centripetal one in which the obligation is to stay at home, and a centrifugal one in which the obligation is to leave in pursuit of success. The conjunction of these moralities creates, he suggests, a complex 'moral geography' in the area around and beyond Nishui, the site of his fieldwork.

One of the notable complications here is that many children in Nishui actually spend little time with their parents, because they live most days of the week at schools away from home and/or because their parents have migrated away from home for work. As a result, Johnston observes, 'it is common for children in Nishui to see one or both parents only once a year or sometimes even less'. Given these circumstances, children's attachments to their natal families and communities can hardly be taken for granted, and indeed family relationships in Nishui are defined as much by separation as by anything else. Two points might be said to follow from this. The first is that the ethics of handling togetherness, when it occurs, might be expected to be of considerable importance. The expression of love and mutual dependency via subtle turns of phrase, the drawing out of moments of departure, and so on might really *matter* here (Stafford 2000). A second point, as Johnston stresses, is that the ethical relations between individuals are in many respects materialized and/or 'externalized' in and around Nishui. That is, the physical spaces through which children and adults move in order to 'show' that they are being good, as well as the material objects linked to parent–child attachments and separations (e.g. train ticket stubs), themselves become part of an ethical narrative. As already noted, this

9

ORDINARY ETHICS IN CHINA

question of the materialization of ethics will be explored further in the section on technology.

Johnston's chapter focuses on movement away from the (remote) countryside and on the ethical issues this provokes. I-chieh Fang's chapter deals with some of the same issues but from the perspective of the big cities where rural migrants arrive. More specifically, Fang conducted fieldwork among young, mostly female, workers in a Shenzhen electronics factory, and here she focuses in particular on the question of their marriage strategies. As one might expect, rural migrants are thought to go through a process of learning and growing—a kind of 'rite of passage'—as they move to cities and start working. In spite of the physical (and sometimes emotional) intimacy of factory life, Fang found that young migrants live in a world filled, as they see it, with untrustworthy strangers. People change jobs frequently, fabricate CVs, borrow money under false pretences, and so forth. Indeed, one of the most interesting aspects of Fang's chapter—in terms of everyday ethics—is her account of relations that seem at once strikingly close and strikingly distant (this situation may be usefully compared with the 'virtual' parent–child relationships of Johnston's Anhui case study).

According to Fang, the key life strategy for girls in the factory is to find a romantic partner. Parents no longer exercise total control over marriage plans, and Fang's informants are mostly free to choose the partner they like. It is also taken for granted that they will have premarital sex. As this suggests, the moral landscape of Chinese courtship and marriage has changed greatly (see Yan 2003). However, Fang suggests that the responsibility—to use that word again—that follows from having the 'freedom to choose' puts young women into a moral panic of sorts, not least because their lives remain constrained by traditional gender values. They *must* marry, after all, and virtually all of them will do so in order to avoid the moral censure of others (for a comparative perspective on this, see Allerton 2007). Fang suggests, moreover, that many of them actually 'yearn for intimacy', having lived separately from their parents during childhood in the countryside. They know that marriage will enhance their status and even their power, and that a 'good marriage' will, in effect, prove to the world that they are good too. Nevertheless, finding the perfect match—someone who will provide them with emotional and financial security in a world filled with untrustworthy strangers—is not an easy matter.

Although Eona Bell's contribution deals with a number of issues taken up in the first three chapters—childhood, schooling, parent–child relations, migration and work—the context of her project was very different. She studied Hong Kong Chinese parents who are bringing up (or who have brought up) their children in Edinburgh, Scotland. Also, while the other chapters are written primarily from the perspectives of children and young people, Bell's is framed from the perspective of adults as they look back at childhood and the decisions they have made with regard to family life.

When migrants settle for the long term in a new country—one with a different set of values but also, crucially, different institutional arrangements—ethical questions emerge. Would it be best for all concerned to leave the children behind, that is, in Hong Kong with their grandparents? If the children move to Scotland will they lose their Chineseness? If this happens, what, if anything, can be done about it? Some of the issues Bell's informants face relate specifically to the catering trade (with its unsociable hours) in which many of them have been employed. In theory, they might keep their children with them in the evenings—'behind the counter' or 'under the cooker' at takeaways and restaurants—and sometimes do so. However, in a Scottish context in which children are not expected or allowed to work this can be problematic. Might the parents be reported for child cruelty? The children could instead be left at home, but there are dangers in this arrangement as well. One of Bell's informants told her that when left alone as a child, she and her brother were 'under strict instructions not to open the curtains in case the neighbours saw'. Such children sometimes slipped out to visit friends in the evenings, taking turns answering the telephone to report (to their parents) that everyone was safely at home.

These may seem minor, even trivial, details: parents sorting out childcare arrangements in light of work demands, children deciding to what extent they dare 'deceive' their parents in order to have fun. And yet—to return to the question of ordinary ethics—such details surely comprise the substance of moral and ethical relations, as they are lived. When asked twenty or thirty or forty years after the fact to reflect on their childhoods, these are precisely the details that emerge in the narratives of Bell's informants.

SECTION 2: ETHICAL ACTION AND MORAL EVALUATION IN RURAL COMMUNITIES

The chapters by Johnston, Fang and Bell deal not only with childhood but also with ethics 'on the move', that is, against the background of migration for schooling and/or work. The next four chapters deal primarily with ethics in situ and especially with the question of moral evaluation as it unfolds among adults living in close-knit rural communities. Through what social and psychological processes are people and their actions judged good or bad?

My own chapter is built around ethnographic vignettes involving one family in Liaoning province, north China. Again, the scenes observed are everyday ones: a meal is organized for an outside guest, an interaction takes place with a local teacher, a bit of minor gossip about neighbours is shared. In relation to all of these things, implicit and explicit moral evaluations emerge. For instance, a local teacher who barges into a meal is not necessarily deserving of respect (most people feel that local teachers, and the schools in which they teach, are very inadequate); and yet he is *given* respect. One possible reason for this, I suggest, is that people in small, rural communities know perfectly well why most of those they interact with are as they are. It is easy to be critical of others, of course, but in such communities what might be called the 'knowledge conditions for generosity' (i.e. knowledge of explanations for the weaknesses and failings of others) are typically in place.

I relate this fact to recent discussions of morality and ethics in the disciplines of psychology and philosophy. One finding of psychologists, to put it simply, is that we tend on the whole to be generous in judging our own actions—taking all mitigating factors into account—and relatively harsh in judging the actions of others. However, in rural communities (unlike the urban settings in which most psychological research has been conducted) knowledge of others is typically quite extensive. So the cognitive effort required to be generous is not, after all, very great. Moreover, this question of generosity or forgiveness may be linked to culturally specific types of 'determinism'—that is, to theories which hold that what happens is determined by one or more external causes and thus not (necessarily) the fault of any given agent. Needless to say, in spite of knowing a lot about why people are bad or inadequate, and in spite of the application of various excuses for behaviour (including

Chinese versions of determinism), the people I met *do* continue to judge, blame and criticize those around them. Following the philosopher Peter Strawson (2008), I suggest that the tension between laying blame and being generous and forgiving is a crucial one in everyday ethical experience.

The issue of judging others is also the topic of Hui Zhang's chapter. She deals specifically with a well-known problem from China's post-Mao era: how should we react when people around us become successful and wealthy? In Zhang's fieldwork community in rural Hebei, certain families received significant windfall payments thanks to mining activity in the region. There was resentment about this in some quarters and unhappiness about transactions in which a number of families lost out. How should situations of this kind be dealt with? Is it acceptable to feel envious of others and, in some cases, to go a step further and *act* on this envy?

As Zhang makes clear, the ethics of envy—and 'envy avoidance'—in modern China are highly complex (see also Zhang 2010). One key point, already noted, is that it is considered a kind of social sin to provoke envy in others; this is actually said to be worse than feeling envious oneself. In Zhang's fieldwork community, it is said that successful individuals can (and should) avoid provoking resentment by maintaining good 'social relations' (*renyuan*) with those around them. As one of her informants puts it,

> If you know how to behave, there won't be any problem with 'red eye' [i.e. with malicious envy]. Be generous to others, and even if you rake in lots of money they won't mind. Otherwise you are inviting jealousy and hatred.

This theory of good *renyuan* as the solution to the problem of envy sometimes fails, however. And if a person is very proper in his relations with others and these others still express malicious envy towards him, then the blame, according to Zhang's informants, may in fact shift back to the enviers. In short, it can be read as a sign that these people are 'low quality' (*suzhi di*)—otherwise they would see the propriety of the successful person's behaviour and not resent his or her fortunate circumstances.

Hans Steinmüller's chapter also deals with moral evaluation in the countryside; however, his starting point is in some respects the opposite of Zhang's. Zhang is interested in situations where success breeds (or doesn't breed) envy. Steinmüller is interested in cases where failure—or at least the inability to live up to certain demands and expectations— breeds irony. People in the community of Bashan, where he carried out fieldwork, are exhorted to be successful, to have good families, to be upright citizens and so on. Steinmüller provides accounts of three men whose life experiences (including through the period of high Maoism and its aftermath) are strikingly different and who stand in very different positions vis-à-vis exhortations to virtue and excellence. They sometimes find themselves in positions of 'situational irony', that is, in situations that are inherently ironic. And they and their neighbours sometimes use 'rhetorical irony'; in other words, they comment on themselves and the world around them in explicitly ironic language.

Steinmüller points out that irony is a means of commenting on the disjuncture between what should be done and what is actually possible and on the fissures between (sometimes competing) moral frameworks. At times, the demands of Chinese moral discourses, including those coming from the state and its institutions, are so overwhelming that failure is likely. Moreover, one may 'fail' because it is impossible to meet two incompatible demands at the same time (e.g. from one's own family and from the state). Irony acknowledges this and opens up the possibility of reflection on moral frameworks in general. Of course, through sharing with others, including one's neighbours, the tendency to use distancing language when talking about official discourses, an ethical community of sorts may also be created. Within this community, joking—however obliquely—about how things are becomes an ethical act. Ironic distancing sometimes relates, of course, to serious topics, including the extent to which the Chinese state can or should spell out what everyone must do. But irony is also part of the flow of everyday life and of ordinary interactions with others.

In the final chapter in this section, Daniel Roberts focuses on the living and working arrangements of families in the Zhejiang village of Wangcun and how these are evaluated depending on their circumstances and composition. In attempting to be good and to maintain 'harmonious relationships', Roberts suggests, people adopt a range of strategies. He refers to these respectively as the large family, dispersed family, and concentrated family strategies. Roberts concludes that each of these arrangements may generate its own internal contradictions and also that 'very different strategies can be chosen and/or praised based on competing priorities and circumstances'. One important circumstance, in the community of Wangcun, is that most families received windfall payments (cf. the discussion of windfalls in Zhang's chapter) to compensate for the loss of agricultural land—but were then allowed to keep their land for agricultural purposes. As a result, their priorities have shifted away from immediate economic need to such things as emotional well-being. Perhaps more to the point, the response of families to these payments may be seen as indicative of their broader strategies. Large families invested in corporate property of a kind, dispersed families invested in educating their children and concentrated families invested in starting business ventures to be run by family members. So while it may be true that some key priorities of Chinese kinship remain unchanged (e.g. 'maintaining harmony'), it is also true, as Roberts explains, that many things have changed quite fundamentally—including the contexts in which life strategies and actual outcomes are evaluated.

One feature of Roberts's chapter deserves mention here because it relates to the question of how much people really *think* (consciously, deliberatively) about ethics: he includes extended passages of direct speech taken from interviews with informants. As one might expect, some of this is formulaic. An older man tells Roberts, for example, that one's sons or daughters should, ideally, possess 'the moral excellence of the Chinese people'—a stock phrase. But informants also talk spontaneously, often passionately, about such issues as the ethics of support for the elderly. This spontaneous talk is evidence of two things: (*a*) that most people have rather worked out and explicit theories about how people are meant to behave, many of which draw directly on, or at least refer to, Confucian ideals discourses (see the Afterword by Yan in this book); (*b*) that in China there are widely distributed—again explicit—understandings of the range of practical arrangements through which kinship and other moral obligations actually can and/or should be met. Note, however, that the gap between how things should be and how they really are is sometimes wide (as discussed in Steinmüller's chapter and in this one as well) and that this gap is a topic of more or less endless, spontaneous ethical commentary among our Chinese informants.

SECTION 3: TECHNOLOGY, TECHNIQUES
AND THE MATERIALITY OF ETHICS

As noted earlier, Johnston's chapter raises interesting questions about
the materialization of ethics: the departure of the young from villages
in Anhui is part of a moral geography in which, among other things,
the actual physicality of the landscape matters (to 'go down from the
mountains' is, in effect, to succeed). Indeed, physical spaces and material objects play a salient role in many of our case studies. Fang tells us,
for instance, about the sharing of beds by 'isolated' migrant workers in
the—incredibly crowded—factory dormitories of Shenzhen. For Bell's
informants in Edinburgh, the physical layout/requirements of takeaway
businesses have an impact on the childcare arrangements made by parents. For people in Zhang's Hebei field site, the question of provoking
envy in others is closely linked to the question of showing (or hiding)
wealth in material form.

The chapters in this third and final section pursue this question of
materiality more explicitly, examining cases where technologies and/or
'techniques' of various kinds directly mediate and transform ethical
practices and understandings. Francesca Bray makes important analytical comments with respect to this. Her most general point is simply that
technology matters, sometimes a great deal, for ethics. In the modern
world, we clearly live and work in spaces filled with technological artefacts. Further to this, however, Bray poses a question about the direction
and focus of technology studies:

> Is it only the high-tech innovations of recent decades, like the Inter-
> net or 'assisted reproduction', that deserve our attention, or should
> simple, mundane technologies like the light bulb or the *kang* [tradi-
> tional heated bed] figure more systematically in our studies of how
> people express values and construct moral personhood?

Bray reminds us that although we tend to associate technology with new-
ness and modernity, the reality is that technology and material culture—
as well as *change* in technology/material culture—have been features
of Chinese life for a very long time. This is a point she has illustrated
beautifully in her previous work, which shows how changes to productive and reproductive technologies were central to a deep transformation
in the ethics of gender in late imperial China (Bray 1997). Finally, Bray

suggests that a focus on technology ('even' of the mundane sort) can help us, as anthropologists, make connections across analytical fields that might otherwise be treated separately:

> Whether high- or low-tech, the investigation of technological practices offers a privileged field for integrating materialist and interpretive analysis, and for linking what Raymond Williams dubbed 'structures of feeling' to political economy.

This, in fact, is the ambition of Gonçalo Santos's chapter. He focuses on what might be called a traditional 'technique of moralization' and links this both to intimate family life and to the wider political economic landscape against which it plays out. Santos describes a fundraising auction organized by a local temple in the community of Harmony Cave, in northern Guangdong, where he conducted fieldwork. Here local people bid for small decorative mirrors (material culture artefacts) on which 'words of virtue' have been painted. Briefly, during the Harmony Cave auction, Santos's friend Bright Gold submitted bids he could not live up to—thus leading to public controversy. One element in the story is Bright Gold's own (apparently shifting) analysis of the ethics of what he has done. He cannot accept that his actions have been wrong and instead calls into question the legitimacy of the temple committee and the whole practice of auctioning words of virtue. This is still meant to be a Communist society, after all, and he (as someone brought up in the Maoist era) contemplates paying his dues with spirit money rather than cash, as an act of ironic defiance against 'superstitions'. In the end, however, his family beg him not to embarrass them publicly and he subsequently manages to purchase the mirror.

Of course, rituals are material practices, involving real temples, real financial transactions and—in this case—real decorative mirrors. These mirrors (and more specifically, the words of virtue painted on them) are auctioned and thus play a role in the production and circulation of a moral standard in the local community. In a Durkheimian sense, this is a socially sanctioned 'technique of moralization'. And yet (as in the cases described by Steinmüller, Roberts and others), the setting of a moral standard in Harmony Cave, and making it 'real' through material means, does not ensure that people such as Bright Gold will live up to it, or even want to do so. They may actively challenge and contest the way things are. Along the way, complex emotional ties to others (in this case, Bright Gold and his closest relatives) help shape their actions, thus playing a central role in the production of given ethical outcomes.

Stephan Feuchtwang, in considering retrospective evaluations of the Great Leap Forward campaign (1959–61), takes us back to the starting point of this Introduction. There I noted that, in spite of China's dramatic collective histories, our main focus in this book would be on the everyday experiences that constitute 'ordinary' ethical life. However, the subsequent chapters have illustrated that the shadow of history is never far away in China—be it the history of Confucianism (with its ongoing impact on schooling, even very 'modern' schooling); the history of mass migration in the post-Mao reform era (which leads, among other things, to the arrival of young women in Shenzhen factories); or the history of repeated state initiatives in modern China (which may cause ordinary people to take particular stances, including the stance of ironic detachment, when yet more initiatives come along). As Feuchtwang observes, 'Everyday judgments of action and everyday actions themselves are historically saturated' (again, see Yan's Afterword for an exegesis of this).

But in what sense does the particular ethical/historical case examined by Feuchtwang—the Great Leap Forward—relate to *technology*? Most obviously, it is in the sense that the Great Leap was an attempt to place scientific socialist principles into effect on a grand scale, including technical solutions to problems of agricultural and industrial production. Moreover, the campaign was realized through revolutionary 'techniques of governance' which (with the knowledge of many, if not all, concerned) formally kept the reality of declining production from higher authorities. From the point of view of ethics, what is perhaps most striking is Feuchtwang's account of the human psychology that helped push this process towards its outcome. He observes that the emotion of shame— including the shame of individuals at their own real or perceived lack of revolutionary ardour—was a crucial factor. More specifically, local cadres had to report that production was surging ahead, lest they be shamed for their 'failed enthusiasm'. Meanwhile, as famine took hold, they faced the unspeakable (and to some extent still unspoken) shame of allowing local children and elderly people to die. As Feuchtwang observes, to be ethical in recalling these circumstances today may involve being *tactful*, at least sometimes, about the ethical dilemmas faced by cadres and others in the past. This, of course, takes us back to fundamental questions of responsibility, blame, understanding and forgiveness.

Jing Shao and Mary Scoggin deal in their contribution with a more recent crisis that nevertheless echoes the Great Leap Forward in certain respects: the one following the recent spread of HIV infections in central China as a result of the commercial harvesting of human plasma. This crisis—which has many explicitly technological/scientific dimensions to it—has produced its own highly complex ethical landscape. Here shame, fear, coercion and even irony and sarcasm play their parts. Are the victims to be blamed for what has befallen them? What does it mean to become ill via particular routes (e.g. through selling plasma for cash) rather than others? What are the scientific/technical means through which the infection is diagnosed and dealt with, and what are the ethical implications of using, or withholding, these means? On what terms could people infected with HIV (many of them living in the countryside and lacking resources) become a community and work together to fight injustice? As their probing questions suggest, Shao and Scoggin are interested not only in medical issues and medical technologies, in the narrow sense, but also in broader issues of public ethics and political economy. And yet their ethnography of the blood contamination scandal shows ethics playing itself out very much at a human scale: via shared (and also often competing) understandings and via micro processes of human interaction, including those tied to the practice of ethnographic research itself.

***

Of course, the case studies in this book raise questions that I have not touched on here and which will be taken up by individual authors in their own chapters and/or by Yunxiang Yan in his Afterword. Before concluding, however, I would like to make a few comments related to the themes I've already outlined, in order to point readers in directions that, in my view, deserve further research.

CHILD DEVELOPMENT AND THE INVENTION OF ETHICS

Obviously, moral and ethical judgements come from somewhere, and most anthropologists take it for granted that socialization and enculturation play a crucial role in this regard. That is, we *learn* to be ethical, and both the process and the content of ethical learning are culturally specific. In recent years, however, psychologists and others have criticized this 'blank slate' view, providing evidence that our moral judgements—including, for example, feelings of disgust when we observe something 'wrong'—are shaped and constrained by evolved cognitive mechanisms (for a clear and succinct overview of recent work in the psychology of morality, see Haidt and Kesebir 2010). Meanwhile, anthropologists of childhood (including Toren 1999) have sharply criticized the 'acquisition' view of socialization: that children simply pick up, through instruction and general absorption, existing cultural models, including ideas related specifically to morality and ethics. Cultural transmission, these scholars suggest, is in fact an uncertain process in which children create/transform knowledge as much as they absorb it. Even in highly stable, traditional societies—where one might think cultural transmission should be straightforward—children do not 'become their parents' in any simple sense.

Regarding modern China, two further points might be added. The first is that (as noted earlier) parent–child separation is a key feature of contemporary Chinese childhood. This is strikingly so for children such as those studied by Johnston in rural Anhui and migrants from the countryside such as those studied by Fang in Shenzhen—many of whom are/ were 'children left behind'. But it is also true for many urban Chinese children such as those studied by Wang in Beijing and for the children of global migrants such as those studied by Bell in Edinburgh. Home remains a key site of moral inculcation for many, and parent–child relations undoubtedly continue to frame ethical personhood in a deep sense. Nevertheless, the ordinariness of parent–child separation surely increases the opportunities for children and young people to write their own scripts and to learn as much or more from each other as they learn from their elders. The second point is that many Chinese children live in worlds radically unlike the worlds in which their parents and grandparents grew up. Unsurprisingly, they sometimes have greater expertise than their elders when it comes to the question of how things work now.

This leads to a conundrum. We are interested in the question of how children acquire a moral/ethical sense from the adults around them and from the general cultural environment in which they live. But there is good evidence for the view that children have a significant 'moral sense' regardless of the cultural environment in which they live and that, in any case, they learn as much or more via their own experiences, and from other children, as they do from adults. For these and other reasons, the empirical study at the micro level of child development, youth culture and schooling—as in the China-based studies by Yan (2003) and Fong (2004) and the contributions to this volume by Wang, Johnston, Fang and Bell—can be of real value. Such studies illuminate not only the transmission and practice of, but also the *invention* of, ordinary ethics in new social environments.

I might add that although the child-focused chapters in this book do not, for the most part, engage directly with the psychological litera-ture on moral learning, psychologists and anthropologists clearly have a great deal to learn from each other when it comes to the study of child development in general and children's moral/ethical development in par-ticular. Some of the topics psychologists are currently studying, such as the role of imagination in the development of moral frameworks and understandings, and the processes whereby children give 'deference' to authority figures (Harris 2000), are directly relevant to the questions of ordinary ethics addressed in this volume.

ETHICAL JUDGEMENT

I noted earlier that judgements of relatively simple ethical situations may in fact be quite nuanced—citing the children in Wang's chapter who dislike their disruptive classmate Wu Hao (he is extremely annoy-ing) and yet are struck by his genius for inventing games. By the end of Section 3, readers will have encountered a number of illustrations of this tendency, including

- the Shenzhen factory girls in Fang's study who manage to tolerate, even praise, supposedly 'bad' behaviours once these are put into context;
- the Hubei farmers in Steinmüller's study who lace their moral com-mentaries with irony (and thus with shades of grey);
- the Fujianese villagers in Feuchtwang's study who are tactful con-cerning the responsibilities of those who were unable to save their dependents during the Great Leap famine.

What are we to make of these cases? We could, on the one hand, say it is *surprising* that people, including very young children, manage to be so nuanced and balanced and tolerant and subtle and tactful in their moral judgements. And yet, on the other hand, the accumulation of such examples—they are found in more or less every chapter of this book—might lead one to the opposite conclusion, namely that it is the most ordinary thing in the world, even automatic, for humans to make sophisticated moral judgements. Not only this, we appear to find it easy to *articulate* these judgements and to explain them in detail when asked. This suggests that we are explicitly thinking about ethical issues before we are questioned about them (e.g. by anthropologists) and that ethics cannot therefore be entirely based on implicit, unconscious understandings of how the world works.

Of course, there is a difference between the formulaic recitation of moral values one sometimes encounters in fieldwork (e.g. 'In China, we defer to our elders') and the nuanced, reflective working through of ethics one *also* sometimes encounters in fieldwork—either as this occurs spontaneously in everyday life or as it takes place under prompting. To go back to the 'morals' versus 'ethics' contrast I drew at the outset: if morals are taken-for-granted moral rules, then the articulation of such rules often seems hopelessly crude compared to the real-world understandings that people apply to ethical practice in ordinary life and can articulate when asked (see Stafford 2010).

What is perhaps really surprising, then, is when our normal, spontaneous making of nuanced (and articulable) ethical judgements is suspended and we instead make crude and predictable judgements based on inherited moral codes. Why does *this* happen? As I discuss in my chapter, there may be a cognitive preference for the simplicity of the latter (i.e. for the simplicity of black and white judgements based on moral codes). Or, as Peter Strawson has suggested, we may have a *need* to judge—it may be a prerequisite for social life as we know it. That is, we cannot always just diminish the responsibility of others by giving them the (nuanced) benefit of the doubt. A more typically anthropological explanation would be that society obliges us to make harsh judgements some of the time and in particular that our ability to punish wrongdoing, thus upholding social norms, depends on it. In any case, the tension between laying blame and being generous and forgiving—partly through being nuanced in our judgements of others—is surely a crucial one in everyday ethical experience and deserves further study by anthropologists.

HISTORICIZATION AND MATERIALIZATION OF ETHICS

I began this Introduction by stressing the 'ordinary' aspects of ethical life in contemporary China. Our intention in this volume has been to resist putting *too* much stress on the collective and historical side of things—thereby leaving a bit more space for the individual, reflective, agentive dimensions of ethical practice. And yet, as my overview of Section 3 suggests, and indeed as all the chapters might be said to suggest individually, history is never far away in China, or at least it is rarely far from the minds of our informants. The implications of this are laid out forcefully by Yunxiang Yan in his Afterword.

So let me take a different tack. If we assume the 'historical saturation' of ethical life in China, it may help—if we want to remain focused on ordinary ethics—to bear in mind several different ways in which history unfolds. First, although the fact of this is sometimes overlooked, history is intrinsically linked to micro processes surrounding learning and child development. Obviously, children are *in* history. More crucially, however, they *make* history as they acquire and produce knowledge (including historical knowledge) about the world around them. Second, if history—including moral history—is a narrative (which is surely right), such narratives are heavily shaped by the psychological constraints and biases of the humans who construct and communicate them. As I've just been noting, we have the ability to construct highly complex models and judgements, but, in certain circumstances, the bias is against doing just that. The psychological factors behind this deserve attention, but so too do the biographical factors which lead given agents to respond to the key narratives around them in particular ways, sometimes struggling to be ethical, and to think critically, when an easy, non-reflective morality is on offer. Third, to return to Francesca Bray's contribution, history and historical change—again, including change to ethical practice—unfolds as much in material form as at the level of 'ideas' and 'values'. This is perhaps especially obvious in the post-Mao era of technological change, but everyday life in China has always, of course, been 'material'—that is, linked to processes of living and working surrounded by (historically defined) artefacts of different kinds. As Bray observes, mundane artefacts, such as light bulbs and beds, may have profound implications vis-à-vis ethical personhood.

Interestingly, this materialized/artefactual ethics is a considerable focus of attention and interest for ordinary people in China. As has often been pointed out, when it comes to the morality of kinship, many people in China appear to worry as much about the practical side of things (how to give actual support and nurturance, e.g. in the form of food) as they do about the ideas side of things. And when it comes to religion, many people appear to focus on practical activities—building the temples, doing the rituals—worrying as much or more about these matters as they worry about 'belief' (cf. the debate on orthopraxy and orthodoxy initiated by James L. Watson and summarized in Sutton 2007). To make a crude distinction between ideas and practice would, of course, be an analytical mistake, and it would be wrong to caricature Chinese people as hard-nosed pragmatists uninterested in ideas. But the simple point here is that the material world clearly matters a great deal when it comes to ordinary ethics. Moreover, in China as elsewhere, people *think* a great deal (consciously, explicitly) about this material world—creating it, transforming it, communicating through it, learning from it (see Hutchins 1995). As Bray suggests, to bring material culture consistently into the frame is therefore a good way of transcending the material/ideal divide in our consideration of ethical personhood.

REFERENCES

Allerton, C. (2007), 'What Does It Mean to Be Alone?', in R. Astuti, J. Parry and C. Stafford (eds), *Questions of Anthropology*, London School of Economics Monographs on Social Anthropology no. 76, Oxford: Berg.

Bray, F. (1997), *Technology and Gender: Fabrics of Power in Late Imperial China*, Berkeley: University of California Press.

Bray, F. (2008), 'Constructing Intimacy: Technology, Family and Gender in East Asia', *East Asian Science, Technology and Society*, 2: 151–65.

Fong, V. (2004), *Only Hope: Coming of Age under China's One-child Policy*, Stanford, CA: Stanford University Press.

Haidt, J., and Kesebir, S. (2010), 'Morality', in S. Fiske et al. (eds), *Handbook of Social Psychology,* 5th ed., Hoboken, NJ: Wiley.

Harris, P. (2000), *The Work of the Imagination*, Oxford: Blackwell.

Hutchins, E. (1995), *Cognition in the Wild*, Cambridge, MA: MIT Press.

Kipnis, A. (2011), *Governing Educational Desire: Culture, Politics and Schooling in China*, Chicago: Chicago University Press.

Kleinman, A., et al. (2011), *Deep China: The Moral Life of the Person*, Berkeley: University of California Press.

Laidlaw, J. (2002), 'For an Anthropology of Ethics and Freedom', *Journal of the Royal Anthropological Society*, 8/2: 311–2.

Laidlaw, J. (2010), 'Agency and Responsibility: Perhaps You Can Have Too Much of a Good Thing', in M. Lambek (ed.), *Ordinary Ethics: Anthropology, Language and Action*, New York: Fordham University Press.

Liu, X. (2000), *In One's Own Shadow: An Ethnographic Account of the Condition of Post-reform Rural China*, Berkeley: University of California Press.

Oxfeld, E. (2010), *Drink Water, but Remember the Source: Moral Discourse in a Chinese Village*, Berkeley: University of California Press.

Stafford, C. (2000), *Separation and Reunion in Modern China*, Cambridge: Cambridge University Press.

Stafford, C. (2010), 'The Punishment of Ethical Behaviour', in M. Lambek (ed.), *Ordinary Ethics: Anthropology, Language and Action*, New York: Fordham University Press.

Strawson, P. (2008 [1974]), *Freedom and Resentment and Other Essays*, London: Routledge.

Sutton, D. L. (2007), 'Ritual, Cultural Standardization, and Orthopraxy in China: Reconsidering James L. Watson's Ideas', *Modern China*, 33/1: 3–21.

Toren, C. (1999), *Mind, Materiality and History: Explorations in Fijian Ethnography*, London: Routledge.

Westermarck, E. (1906), *The Origin and Development of the Moral Ideas, Vol. 1*, London: Macmillan.

Williams, B. (1985), *Ethics and the Limits of Philosophy*, London: Fontana.

Wolf, M. (1960), *The House of Lim: A Study of a Chinese Farm Family*, New York: Prentice Hall.

Yan, Y. (2003), *Private Life under Socialism*, Stanford, CA: Stanford University Press.

Yan, Y. (2009), *The Individualization of Chinese Society*, Oxford: Berg.

Yang, M. (1994), *Gifts, Favors and Banquets: The Art of Social Relations in China*, Ithaca, NY: Cornell University Press.

Zhang, H. (2010), 'Windfall Wealth and Envy in Three Chinese Mining Villages', PhD dissertation, London School of Economics and Political Science.

Zigon, J. (2008), *Morality: An Anthropological Perspective*, Oxford: Berg.

PART I

CHILDHOOD, YOUTH AND ETHICAL TRAJECTORIES

CHAPTER 2

RIGHT OR WRONG? A *TAOQI* STUDENT IN AN ELITE PRIMARY SCHOOL IN BEIJING

Chih-yuan Wang

A well-known central concern of Confucianism is the process of *zuo ren*, that is, being or becoming a person. This process is meant to entail the moral development of the individual from an inferior to a superior status and is characterized by the fulfilment of one's inner potential. Schooling, especially elementary schooling, is viewed as a crucial foundation for later moral development. According to neo-Confucianists, the period between the ages of seven and fourteen is especially important in this regard, a vital turning point for young children:

> Young students during the period of elementary learning were viewed as closer to the ways of the inferior man than to the self-disciplined behaviour of the superior man. They were, after all, immature and could not yet be trusted to do what was right on their own; as such they required a scaffolding of regulations and rules to guide their behaviour within proper bounds until they developed internal means for self-direction. (Saari 1990: 35)

Though Confucianism was condemned during the May Fourth movement of 1919 and later during the Cultural Revolution of the 1960s, the legacy of constant worry over children's moral development arguably remains prevalent in China. This constant worry was, moreover, apparently intensified by the implementation of the one-child policy in the 1980s, at around the same time that the post-Mao economic reforms were being introduced. It seems the combination of economic change and the one-child policy have transformed the power structure in Chinese families quite radically (cf. Yan 2003). Members of the single-child generation, born into a better standard of living than their parents, are described as 'little emperors' by the mass media. In the 1980s, Chinese psychologists, educationists and journalists worried that parents and grandparents would drown the little emperors with love. Anthropologists noted that the public was also anxious about the future of the spoiled generation (Jing 2000). Nevertheless, in the 1990s there emerged more and more evidence to counter the 'little emperor' anxiety. The psychological status and development of urban singletons were arguably no different from those of children with siblings (Falbo et al. 1996). Still, the condemnation of singletons by parents, teachers and educational officials reaffirmed, in effect, the Chinese ideology that children should display unselfishness and show consideration and deference towards others, especially elders (Wu 1996).

As Vanessa Fong has noted, although single children generally enjoy the love of parents and grandparents, they also bear the pressure of being the 'only hope' of their elders (Fong 2004). In my fieldwork, I found that the single children of the Beijing upper-middle class I met were, indeed, the only hope of their parents and grandparents. In order for their children to succeed in a competitive, exam-oriented society, middle-class parents in Beijing would use any means necessary to send their children to a particular primary school as the foundation for entrance to a good high school and a top university. Top primary schools in Beijing are famous for their outstanding academic performance and strict discipline. In schools of this kind, we might expect to find a collection of truly outstanding, highly disciplined children.

BACKGROUND TO RESEARCH

From December 2006 to June 2007, I carried out field research in what I refer to as EPS (meaning 'elite primary school'), a prestigious state school affiliated to a top-ranking university located in central Beijing. I also carried out some months of fieldwork in a school for the children of migrant workers, but I will not refer to that research in this chapter. As an elite institution, EPS is a typical provider of education to the upper-middle class in Beijing. It has about 1,800 students and about 100 teaching and administrative staff. Despite being a state school, it is not open to every family in Beijing but only to those who are rich and well connected. One-third of the students are children of the staff of the school and the university, and another third come from families working for the government or for companies that donate huge amounts of money to EPS every year. The remaining places are open to wealthy and well-connected families. At the time of my fieldwork, these people had to pay an entrance fee of at least 60,000 renminbi (about £6,000) for their children to attend EPS; I understand that the charge is now significantly higher.[1]

As is the case with other top primary schools in Beijing, EPS is renowned for its academic standards. The parents I interviewed believed that their children would have a much better chance of attending the best junior high schools after attending EPS, and they were happy with the teaching and discipline there. The principal once boasted to me about the quality of teaching at EPS, saying that EPS would only hire very experienced teachers or young teachers who had graduated from the best universities. Meanwhile, the high academic standards meant a heavy workload and perennial pressure for the teachers working there; it was not unusual to see them with long faces on campus. One teacher complained to me that EPS simply would not accept any student failing an exam: teachers had to work overtime to help failing students, without extra pay. Still, although EPS prioritized exams and grades just like other elite primary schools, it had a relatively lenient attitude towards discipline. Students were required to wear their school uniforms only on Mondays and Wednesdays, and they did not have to sit in tight formation in class, as was expected at other well-known primary schools in Beijing. Perhaps this was because the principal had a background in psychology and also because the parents in EPS were overwhelmingly middle class and influenced, through a variety of routes, by Western educational philosophies.

THE CASE OF WU HAO

Towards the end of 2006, after some preliminary research, I was finally able to enter the classrooms in EPS and meet the students of Class 5, Grade 4. On the very first day of my arrival in the classroom, Wu Hao was the first student to walk up to me and show an interest. He asked me who I was, what I was doing there, and where I was from. When he found out that I came from Taiwan and was doing my PhD research in his class, he instantly told me, 'Teacher, Taiwan cannot declare its independence [from China]—if you do so we will send out the troops!' I was so stunned by this bold and direct reply that I did not know what to say. In order to hide my embarrassment, I smiled and asked him, 'How do you know about that? Do you watch the programme "Two Sides of the Taiwan Strait" on TV every night?'[2]

Wu Hao was one of the bluntest and rudest students I met in Beijing. Later I learned that he was well known to school teachers of all grades, but not for good reasons, and he was a controversial figure among his classmates as well. Out of curiosity, I decided to get to know him better by chatting and playing with him during breaks. Fortunately, Wu Hao would talk to me, and sometimes he more or less forced me to join in his games. He would ask me to walk him home after school, and he would take the opportunity to ask me to buy some snacks for him from the food stores just outside the school. In order to be friendly, I would sometimes buy him something. In exchange, he would sometimes share secrets and rumours about the school or his classmates. To some extent, Wu Hao was my best friend at EPS, and we maintained a good relationship throughout my stay there.

Wu Hao comes from a relatively humble family compared with his classmates. His grandfather is a retired physical education teacher at the university to which EPS is affiliated, and indeed that was the reason Wu Hao was able to attend the school. His father was a taxi driver, and his mother worked in a supermarket as a cashier. As a taxi driver, Wu's father did not have fixed working hours. If a job required a trip to another province, he might have to leave home for up to a week. On the other hand, he might stay at home for several days if there was no work at hand. Wu Hao's mother was a typical supermarket worker with a meagre income and long working hours. Most days she would work for up to ten hours, and every two days she had to work until 10.00 in the evening. Furthermore, she had to work one day each weekend. Wu Hao's father explained to me that he knew about the problems with Wu Hao's behaviour and about his difficulties in school, but he and his wife were too busy to take care of him, that is, to *guan* (control) and to discipline him. Moreover, Wu Hao's father believed that being healthy was more important for a child than just being good at studying.

Although both Wu Hao and his father suggested to me that they did not spend enough time together, it is certainly not possible for me to say conclusively that Wu Hao's bad behaviour was caused, in some straightforward way, by his family background and parenting. What I can say, however, is that Wu Hao, as a mischievous student, did not quite fit into the contemporary Chinese school system; or to be precise, I should say he did not quite fit into his school.

SCHOOL AS AN INSTITUTION FOR DISCIPLINE

In the popular view, a good primary school is one which will take responsibility for monitoring children's academic performance and help its students enter good high schools (Kipnis 2009, 2011; Fong 2004; Lau and Yeung 1996). Meanwhile, primary school is also an institution for discipline, a place where children learn how to behave themselves in society. In other words, a primary school teaches not only 'knowledge' (*zhishi*), but also 'codes of proper behaviour' (*xingweiguifan*), as well as the substance of 'how to be a person' (*zuoren de daoli*). Teachers should be models of the good person; students, for their part, are expected to cultivate good habits for living and should more generally show that they are of superior 'quality' (*suzhi*).

Wu Hao never fit into EPS because he never paid attention to his studies and it seemed that he never worried about his future. He was only interested in playing and in watching TV. It was difficult for him to focus on class teaching, and the only classes he liked were the science-related ones—which, as it happens, are not included in the junior high school entrance exams. It was not uncommon to see him grounded in the classroom during breaks, being forced to complete his unfinished homework. Wu Hao did not fit into EPS because he disturbed class order, violated school rules, and caused a good deal of trouble for all concerned. He was a frequent visitor to the tutor's office and the deputy principal's office because of his behaviour. Another relatively naughty student in Wu Hao's class once commented to me that 'you basically find him involved in *all* the mischief and trouble'.

Good students (*hao xuesheng*) are, in simple terms, good at learning and good at obeying rules. They are recognized as good by their teachers. Clearly, Wu Hao did not belong to this category. However, in my experience the teachers in EPS never called troublesome students like Wu Hao 'bad' (*huai*) as such. A student's mental health and dignity was a sensitive issue at EPS: teachers had to avoid stigmatizing or labelling them. Instead, the teachers would address such students as 'mischievous' (*taoqi*), or as 'problematic' (*wenti xuesheng*), or as 'individual' (*gebi xuesheng*)—meaning they were out of the ordinary. The terms *tao* and *nao* are often used when talking about such students. *Tao* describes children who are mischievous and hard to control. *Nao* has the meaning of noisy, as in 'a noisy disturbance' (*nao shi*). Even the other students in Wu Hao's class would not use the word 'bad' to describe their naughty classmates. They would say that these *taoqi* classmates were beyond the control of teachers, that no one could discipline them. Wu Hao was recognized to be one of the three most *taoqi* students in his class, both by class teachers and students. And he was also well known to the deputy principals and to the head teacher of the fourth grade as a student who was 'without rules or discipline' (*meiguiju*).

The Chinese terms for discipline include *guan* and *guanjiao*. It is very common to hear teachers or parents talking about *guan haizi* ('to discipline or control a child'). The word *guan* has several meanings in Chinese: to restrict, to teach, to care about, to consider; and *jiao* means to pass on knowledge and teach. Hence the term *guanjiao* means 'to teach through control and discipline'. During my time at EPS, teachers often told me that the aim of order and discipline in the school is to 'help students cultivate good habits'. Though there has been a long debate in various Confucian schools about the original nature of man being either good or evil, the teachers I met in EPS tended to embrace a somewhat subtle version of the negative perspective. As a teacher once told me, 'To play is a child's nature, it is not right to let them play but it is also not right to over-*guan* [control] them.' It is the teacher's duty to transform spoiled children into capable, disciplined and well-mannered students—but this can be done sensitively (cf. Tobin et al. 1989).

TEACHERS' IMPRESSIONS OF WU HAO

For most teachers, Wu Hao was a student in need of *guanjiao*. The Chinese teacher (who also taught Morality and Society to Wu Hao's class) could not hide his aversion towards him. Expressing his disapproval of Wu Hao's unruly behaviour, he said,

In China [here he was explaining the specifically Chinese way of thinking about such problems], if we [the teachers] spoil him [Wu Hao], he will become a man against society in the future. Playing or fooling around all day long, the student will not succeed; this will ruin his whole family.

But this teacher failed to change Wu Hao, so far as I know. The students told me that Wu Hao's behaviour in Chinese class never changed, and the teacher let him do whatever he wanted so long as he was not making too much noise.

Wu Hao's class tutor[3] in the fourth grade was Ms Li, a math teacher with a first degree in psychology who was doing her part-time master's degree during my stay. In spite of the trouble caused by Wu Hao, Ms Li had a positive opinion of him compared to other *taoqi* students in the class. I was quite surprised about this: I presumed she would want to get rid of this troublemaker. Ms Li told me, however, that although Wu Hao was mischievous in school, 'he is a sincere child' (*hen zhen de haizi*). His naughty but forthright behaviour made Wu Hao a lovable student in Ms Li's eyes. She told me that although Wu Hao behaved like a bully, he never abused his strength, nor did he really hurt any student intentionally. She also defended Wu Hao by telling me that he was a thin and feeble boy in kindergarten and was the victim of another bully. However, after he rapidly gained a lot of weight, the prey became the predator.

While Ms Li liked this naughty but sincere student, Ms Luo, Wu Hao's class tutor when he moved up to the fifth grade, had quite a different opinion of him.[4] Ms Luo did not like Wu Hao and found him troublesome. The fifth year of primary school is tense, with a heavy workload: teachers and students alike can feel the pressure building up. Wu Hao disliked homework, and his lack of motivation for study increased Ms Luo's already heavy workload. She complained to me that Wu Hao did not apply his mind to study, and this worried her a lot. To make it worse, Ms Luo did not see the bright side of Wu Hao but regarded him simply as a mischief-maker. She told me about an incident in which one student (who had an emotional disorder) had a severe quarrel with the science teacher in class. Out of rage, the student even pounded his desk and shouted at the science teacher. This was seen by Wu Hao, who could not wait to tell everyone what had happened in science class. What annoyed Ms Luo was that Wu Hao praised the student to the others: 'He's really got balls, he dared to pound his desk in front of the science teacher!' Ms Luo commented that Wu Hao was the type of student who loves to be boisterous and never tired of causing trouble.

Though he claimed to be afraid of no one in class or at school, there were still some teachers Wu Hao did not want to come across on the school campus, let alone meet in their offices. The teachers Wu Hao feared most were Ms Sha, a retired teacher but still active at EPS; Ms Wang, the deputy principal; and Mr Yu, a teacher in charge of the sport facilities. Actually, when I asked students whom they feared most in school, they all gave the names of these three teachers. Students even give them a joint nickname by putting their surnames together to make the word 'ShaYuWang', which is pronounced similarly to 'Shark King', a pun. Ms Sha and Ms Wang were in charge of student discipline, school order and health and safety issues; hence, they would stop and rebuke anyone breaching school rules. When Wu Hao walked around campus, he would avoid being seen by them, especially during the long break after lunch. I witnessed how Wu Hao took fright at catching sight of Ms Sha and Ms Wang and then tried to hide from them during a game at break time. When I talked with Ms Sha about Wu Hao and other *taoqi* students, she complained that these children were spoiled by their parents at home and then brought their bad habits into school. According to Ms Sha, unless Wu Hao's parents changed their parenting style and supported the teachers in their work, Wu Hao would not get rid of his *taoqi* behaviour.

In this volume, Stafford raises the question of how we judge other people's actions. It is interesting to note that at EPS, most teachers tended, in the end, to blame Wu Hao's parents rather than attribute his naughtiness to his own person or personality. On the other hand, classmates were prone to believe that it was something in Wu Hao's character itself leading him to behave in such a way.

INTERACTION WITH CLASSMATES

As a *taoqi* student, Wu Hao was not popular among his classmates. Actually, most students told me that they did not like him. This was partly because of his habits and behaviour but also, it seems, because the teachers had labelled him a bad student. My first impression of Wu Hao was that he was a bully. Perhaps this was too strong an accusation, but he was certainly quite rude and mean towards his classmates in my experience. Wu Hao's seat was always at the back of the classroom, and he had no one sitting next to him. Each student has his or her own desk and chair, and in order to accommodate forty-five students in the limited space, some students had to join their desks to another classmate's. Hence, most students had a classmate sitting next to them, and teachers were prone to arrange it so that a boy was sitting next to a girl. Considering his performance in class, class tutors let Wu Hao stay alone at the back of the classroom, hoping he would not disturb his classmates. Also, the students told me that they would prefer not to sit close to Wu Hao because he always demanded a large space to stretch his body and scatter his belongings. He would shout or push others away if they entered his territory. I observed him pushing the chair of the classmate in front of him to maximize his own space.

Among the fourth-grade students, I noticed there was a clear boundary between girls and boys; boys tended to have their own groups, while girls would play with girls. However, I noticed that during the breaks, Wu Hao would not join any male group and the boys did not want to play with him either. Sometimes, he had to play with the girls. Though he had two little boys in class as his entourage, Wu Hao seemed marginalized. I once asked the other boys why they would not play with Wu Hao, and they told me that he was so fat and so slow in ball games that no one wanted to be his teammate. Further, he would cheat or breach rules in ball games, and this obviously annoyed the others. I noticed that Wu Hao did not like admitting defeat or losing a game: he would try by all means to be the winner in a game. And of course sometimes he would cheat or deny another's success in order to win. For the boys, it seemed, Wu Hao was a habitual cheat and deserving of his reputation.

I had experienced his cheating many times as well when playing with him in school. During a class break, he produced a marble from his pocket, and he proposed to play a simple game with me. The game was played on a desk; we faced each other across the desk and used pencil boxes as guards and strikers to push the marble. If the marble rolled over the edge of the desk on your side, you lost a point. I played the simple game with Wu Hao quite seriously. It was a battle to and fro, as we exchanged the lead several times. And I noticed that Wu Hao felt frustrated and annoyed when I scored more points than he did. In the end, he put a hand on my pencil box, threw the ball to me and announced that he had won the game. In order to annoy him, I claimed I had won the game and accused him of cheating, and Wu Hao just kept saying, 'I won.'

But perhaps I exaggerate a little about Wu Hao's friendship predicament: he never worried about finding someone to play with. There were at least three boys who might play with him, sometimes, and he never seemed to find it embarrassing to play with girls. Wu Hao even told me that he sometimes visited one classmate's home and played with another classmate on the university campus during the weekend or long holidays.

While some boys would play with him, most girls in the class did not like him, saying they found him 'rude' and annoying. According to the girls, Wu Hao would 'pick on someone for fun when there's nothing else to do'. Along these lines, I witnessed Wu Hao bossing others around in the classroom during cleaning time. All students have to take part in cleaning the classroom once a week: the forty-five students are divided into five groups and each group has to clean the classroom on a designated day. Each group has a team leader in charge of team members to make sure they finish their cleaning responsibilities before leaving school. I saw Wu Hao shouting at his teammates, even when he was not the team leader. He would command others to do their jobs, and they then had to report to him when they completed their assigned tasks. If Wu Hao was not happy with their performance, he would ask them to redo it. Also, he would yell at a team member if he or she dared not to do the cleaning task. The students complained to the class tutor about Wu Hao's attitude during cleaning time, but Wu Hao never changed his 'management' style, so far as I know.

Wu Hao told me that yelling at his teammates made him feel 'majestic, authoritative' (*you weiyan*) and that he wanted his classmates to be afraid of him. In Chinese writing class, Wu Hao and Yan (another *taoqi* student) would not do their writing but instead patrol the classroom to ensure order. The two of them would walk around to ensure no one was talking or playing but writing his or her essay. The Chinese teacher could not control these two *taoqi* students, so he just allowed them to keep order in class. In order to fulfil their duty, Wu Hao and Yan would yell at a classmate or knock his or her desk to remind him or her to get back to work. They might chat with their own best friends or whoever they chose while they were on duty. Sometimes, the students would complain to the Chinese teacher that Wu Hao and Yan distracted them from writing. What the two students did was more like harassment than order and control. Wu Hao and Yan admitted to me that they really enjoyed being the men in power in Chinese writing class. They both enjoyed abusing their power, it seems, telling classmates what to do and what not to do at their discretion.

As a dominant figure in the class, Wu Hao was quite proud of himself. He and two other *taoqi* students coincidentally each told me about their 'ranking' in the class order when I interviewed them separately. Wu Hao said he was number one in the class, which meant that he feared no one and no one in the class could beat him. Yan, for his part, told me that he was the number two: only Wu Hao could beat him. Some students told me that they would try to avoid fighting with Wu Hao, and some told me that they had been hit by Wu Hao in a fight. During my stay at EPS, Wu Hao at least twice damaged the backpacks of two classmates who irritated him, and I witnessed at least one instance when he hit a classmate's head. Some girls complained to me that they could not report Wu Hao to the class tutor because the tutor could only reprimand Wu Hao, which in reality had no effect at all. Further, once they reported Wu Hao to the class tutor, Wu Hao would be angrier and take revenge on them afterwards.

PLAYING AND CAUSING TROUBLE IN SCHOOL

Despite his rude behaviour and bully-like characteristics, Wu Hao had some notable strengths: he was creative and good at inventing new games. Perhaps Wu Hao devoted all his energy to games and playing instead of studying. Even his classmates recognized Wu Hao as a boy full of ideas and tricks, and they admitted to me that they might sometimes join Wu Hao's games out of interest and curiosity. When playing, Wu Hao seldom thought about the requirement of discipline in school, so he sometimes got himself and the classmates who played with him into trouble. During my stay at EPS, I used to join the games and play with the students during the breaks, which was a very effective means of getting close to these ten-year-old students. I also joined in games separately with Wu Hao.

One game Wu Hao proposed was called Gun Fight, a modified form of Hide-and-Seek. It was a game allegedly invented by Wu Hao and which some girls and boys liked to join in. The rules of the game were very simple, and it could be played by any number of participants. The participants were divided into two groups: the runners and the seekers. Runners had thirty seconds to find a corner to hide in. The seekers then had to find and capture all the runners before the end of the break; otherwise the seekers would lose. Unlike Hide-and-Seek, in this game running fast is a huge advantage, whether one is escaping the seekers or attempting to catch runners. Also, once a runner was captured he or she would be asked to give information about other runners' hiding places, and sometimes the captured runners would volunteer to help catch those still hiding. More girls wanted to play Gun Fight with Wu Hao than I expected. In total more than ten people played this game, and we played it during the long breaks for a whole week. I was a runner as well as a seeker in the game, and I quite enjoyed playing this with the students as they led me to explore all the secret corners on campus.

It was against school regulations to run within school buildings, however, especially in corridors and stairways. Hence it was better not to play Gun Fight around the fourth-grade classroom to avoid being caught by the class tutor and other teachers. Also, the offices of the principals were located at the same floor of the fourth-grade classrooms, so it would be unwise to mess around there. One boy once warned me not to play the game with Wu Hao because it might get me into trouble. He told me that he and other boys used to play this game with Wu Hao during second and third grades; however, they got caught and reprimanded by the teachers several times because of running inside.

But when I played the game with Wu Hao and teamed up with him, I realized how smart and sly this child was. I witnessed how he gave out orders to other seekers when playing as a seeker: he would tell them to guard the entrances of the building he was going to search. When he played as a runner, Wu Hao loved to team up with Xin-lin because she was fast. The two of them had a preferred secret corner on campus, and they would normally hide there first and then move secretly to other places to avoid being tracked down. What intrigued me was that Wu Hao would ask Xin-lin to look to see if there was any sign of a seeker; meanwhile, he would keep a distance from Xin-lin. In other words, he was using Xin-lin as bait; and if Xin-lin was spotted by a seeker, Wu Hao would abandon her and run away himself. In the game of Gun Fight,

Wu Hao demonstrated a natural talent for leadership but also his sly and mischievous nature.

Wu Hao would take any opportunity to amuse himself in school. He told me that he used to play a game called 'The Game of Provoking Li' during first and second grade. Li was one of Wu Hao's best friends, and they would visit each other's home during the weekends. According to Wu Hao, Li was very sensitive to physical touch by others: he would react strongly to anyone who accidentally bumped into him, and he would hit back if anyone tried to hit him. Hence, Wu Hao used to encourage other classmates to join him in irritating Li by hitting him and then running away. They would hit Li and then run in different directions and enjoy watching Li's angry and frustrated face. When I confirmed this with Li, he told me that he used to be sensitive to others' provocations but now he was more tolerant of it.

Apart from teasing classmates, Wu Hao was a unique student who was not afraid to express his opinion. During my stay at EPS, I witnessed the re-election of student representatives for *daduiwei*, the highest cadres for fourth-grade students. At that time, Chen Yu was current *daduiwei*, and she wanted to serve a second term. Though she tried her best to win her classmates' support, Wang Lu defeated her badly. No one was willing to vote Chen Yu into a second term, and later I learned that she was disliked by her classmates: even Wu Hao was more popular than her. During the class discussion time, I saw Wu Hao shouting loudly in support of Wang Lu and booing Chen Yu when she gave her election speech. Wu Hao never hid his aversion to Chen Yu. Wu Hao once boasted to me that he had waged an 'anti-Chen campaign' in third grade too. This campaign was sanctioned and supported by most classmates but aroused the class tutor's intervention.

WU HAO'S IDEA OF SCHOOL AND OF HIMSELF

When I asked Wu Hao about his opinion of school regulations, he complained to me that school was too strict on children's play, saying, 'What can a kid do? We're not allowed to play basketball, not allowed to play football, not allowed to run in the corridor, everything is banned: what can we do?' He further commented, 'The school wants me to sit in the classroom chatting like girls do, don't they?' One reason I liked Wu

Hao was because he was an honest boy, never shy about expressing his distaste for what he did not like. Wu Hao admitted to me that he knows what school rules are and what teachers' expectations are, but he just does not follow them. Also, he totally agreed that it is morally wrong to beat someone up or to bully a classmate.

Wu Hao justified himself by telling me that he never really touched his classmates, he would just threaten them. Moreover, Wu Hao claimed that if he hit someone, it would be someone who had irritated him first. He told me, 'When you think I was bullying someone, it was not bullying; it was retribution, revenge for the person who had irritated me.' Further, he defended himself and told me that he would react belligerently only if someone offended him first. He once said to a classmate accusing him of using brutal force, 'If you had never irritated me, I would not hit you, and anyway I have never really hit you. If I *really* hit you, how come you are still here?' He claimed to be a sincere person, unlike his classmates. Wu Hao told me that he was not a selfish person because he would buy snack food for his friends sometimes and he had given 10 renminbi to a beggar on the street.

'HAO' STUDENT AND 'TAO' STUDENT

The teachers, tutors and principals I met at EPS seemed to have rather standard ideas about what is right and what is wrong and about proper and improper behaviour in school. 'Naughty' and 'troublesome' students are hard to control. These children have their own opinions and are not afraid to express them.

I would suggest, however, that many of the good students actually hold quite similar ideas about school and about discipline as those held by the *taoqi* students—but their self-image and self-expectation restrain them from causing trouble. In a discussion of the traditional view of Chinese childhood, Saari (1990) points out that a child was not born a filial, civilized, well-educated person. This meant that 'Conformity to group expectations had to be learned, and most Chinese children, like children elsewhere, were imperfect learners' (Saari 1990: 235). Moreover, he suggests, 'The inner resistance [i.e. of the child to the surrounding moral order] was predicated upon splitting the self into an inner secret self and an outer public one' (Saari 1990: 117). Perhaps this notion of 'inner resistance' can help explain, to some extent, the double face of good students and the discontent of naughty students such as Wu Hao, as I observed these things at EPS. Some psychologists suggest that self-image and self-expectation propel people into moral activities. However, it cannot explain why those *taoqi* students failed to comply with school rules, because Wu Hao thought of himself as unselfish and, in fact, a just figure (though perhaps not in a traditional way).

The naughty students I met, not least Wu Hao, have notably strong personalities: it is hard for them to embrace an idea without first voicing scepticism. Their outspokenness presents a direct threat to school teachers and causes trouble every day. On the other hand, the so-called good students tend to be flexible, empathetic, considerate but also soft-spoken and obedient. Perhaps the difference between being a good student or a *taoqi* student lies not in accepting or rejecting the school's ideas, but rather in having the personality traits that lead given students (i.e. good or *taoqi* ones) to behave in certain ways.

The fourth-grade students' understanding of discipline and their daily behaviour raises the issue of how children learn rules or norms, of course. Understanding rules and knowing how to reason from social norms is one thing, but how to put these things into practice is another. The schoolchildren know what the standard norms are, but this does not mean they behave accordingly. Those smart but naughty students know the school rules and the teachers' expectations perfectly well, but still they behave in their own way. So perhaps in order to know about children's understanding of discipline and morality, it is better to ask why most students follow rules and behave themselves in school, rather than asking why the naughty ones do not follow rules and do not behave themselves. They all have it in themselves, I want to suggest, to be like Wu Hao.

NOTES

1. This fee was generally referred to as a 'contribution' and EPS would not give parents a receipt for the money. Indeed, the principal denied the existence of such payments, but their existence was an open secret.
2. This is a television programme that focuses on cross-strait relations.
3. Each class has a class tutor who is in charge of class students' daily life in school and responsible for their academic performance.
4. I returned to EPS in April 2008, when Wu Hao and his class then were in fifth grade.

REFERENCES

Falbo, T., Poston, D. L., and Feng, X.-t. (1996), 'The Academic, Personality, and Physical Outcomes of Chinese Only Children: A Review', in S. Lau (ed.), *Growing up the Chinese Way: Chinese Child and Adolescent Development*, Hong Kong: The Chinese University Press.

Fong, V. L. (2004), *Only Hope: Coming of Age under China's One-child Policy*, Stanford, CA: Stanford University Press.

Jing, J. (2000), 'Introduction: Food, Children, and Social Change in Contemporary China', in J. Jing (ed.), *Feeding China's Little Emperors*, Stanford, CA: Stanford University Press.

Kipnis, A. (2009), 'Education and the Governance of Child-centred Relatedness', in G. Santos and S. Brandtstadter (eds), *Chinese Kinship: Contemporary Anthropological Perspectives*, London: Routledge.

Kipnis, A. (2011), *Governing Educational Desire: Culture, Politics and Schooling in China*, Chicago: Chicago University Press.

Lau, S., and Yeung, P. P. W. (1996), 'Understanding Chinese Child Development: The Role of Culture in Socialization', in S. Lau (ed.), *Growing up the Chinese Way: Chinese Child and Adolescent Development*, Hong Kong: The Chinese University Press.

Saari, J. L. (1990), *Legacies of Childhood: Growing up Chinese in a Time of Crisis, 1890–1920*, Cambridge, MA, and London: Council on East Asian Studies, Harvard University.

Tobin, J. J., Wu, D. Y. H. and Davidson, D. H. (1989), *Preschool in Three Cultures Japan, China and the United States*, New Haven, CT, and London: Yale University Press.

Wu, D. Y. H. (1996), 'Parental Control: Psychocultural Interpretations of Chinese Patterns of Socialization', in S. Lau (ed.), *Growing up the Chinese Way: Chinese Child and Adolescent Development*, Hong Kong: The Chinese University Press.

Yan, Y. (2003), *Private Life under Socialism*, Stanford, CA: Stanford University Press.

CHAPTER 3

FILIAL PATHS AND THE ORDINARY
ETHICS OF MOVEMENT

James Johnston

FILIAL PATHS

'It can be tough to make parents happy,' I complained to Chu Zhenghong, a final-year student at Anqing Teachers College in Anhui. 'They tell me they want me to finish my PhD quickly and find a good job, yet they are insisting that I travel back to spend the holiday with them.' It was early autumn 2008, and I had returned to the college where I had spent a term before going to do fieldwork in the Dabieshan Mountains to the west of the city. I was telling Chu how my Chinese parents-in-law were putting pressure on me to return for National Day. After I spent eighteen months away from China and missed the Chinese New Year celebrations, they told me it was important that we were all together for this festival before my wife and I returned to Britain.

The dilemma I faced as to how best to satisfy my parents-in-law was familiar to Chu Zhenghong. He and most of his fellow students are faced with similar questions about when it is right to leave one's parents in order to make a success of one's life and bring prosperity to one's family, and when it is right to remain with one's parents to fulfil one's filial obligation to attend to and care for them. In this chapter, I explore this moral dilemma, demonstrating how it is central to parent–child relations in rural China. Taking the mountain village of Nishui in Anhui as my example, I examine how from a young age the ordinary movements of children around the spaces of the village become morally inflected and how the children learn that movements in certain directions are more desirable than others. In this context, decisions about when and where to move, such as when it is appropriate to leave parents and when it is appropriate to return to parents, are in a sense ethical dilemmas about how one should behave as a dutiful child.

Certainly most of the students at Anqing Teachers College were returning home during the week's break from classes. I had seen many students dragging their bags from the dormitories to the main roads and flagging down buses that would take them homeward. But not all the students were leaving. In early January each year, the national exam for entry to postgraduate degree courses would take place, and for ambitious students this exam was of great significance. For some students in their final year, including Chu Zhenghong, the pressure of preparing for this exam was too great to return home and the extra study time was more valuable than time spent with their families.

Anqing Teachers College is not a prestigious university. Most of the students come from the countryside. While they may have outperformed most of their peers in their villages, many students will still feel disappointed not to have achieved the grades required to attend more celebrated universities in grander cities. Though few are enthusiastic about the prospect, most of the students at Anqing Teachers College are expected to become teachers; and indeed, after graduation most graduates will return to their home counties and become teachers in middle schools close to where they were born. While those with money, connections or good fortune may find other routes to jobs in the cities, postgraduate study is seen as the best way to guarantee students an alternative and more desirable future: that of a prosperous and urban lifestyle.

Success in the exam for postgraduate study means the opportunity to attend a more distinguished university, improve job prospects and earning potential and establish oneself as a permanent urban resident. It was this hope that kept Chu Zhenghong and other students away from their families during the holiday, sacrificing time spent with their family for long days studying in the library. Chu was from Nishui, the village where I had done my fieldwork. We talked about relations between children and parents in the village, and I asked him what his parents thought about him not returning home during the holiday. He was adamant that his parents agreed with him that study was the priority. He pointed out that his parents had sacrificed a great deal for the sake of his education, paying out a considerable amount of money on the fees and living expenses for school and university. They always encouraged him to work hard to get into the best school or university even if this meant living farther away and seeing his parents less often. He had made sacrifices too. He had not lived at home permanently since he was twelve years old, and he had been expected to work hard, sacrificing his own opportunities for leisure. He even blamed his studying for damaging his eyesight. The reward for all this sacrifice was the promise of better prospects and opportunities (*chulu*, lit: 'paths out') which would allow him to avoid the hardship and bitterness of village life that his parents had endured.

However, Chu thought my situation was different. He told me it was my filial duty (*xiaodao*) to obey and to go and be with my parents-in-law. He would certainly return to stay with his parents during the Chinese New Year following the exam in January, but I would not be able to do so; therefore, I must go now regardless of my research.

I decided to follow his advice, but on my last evening in Anqing, I went out for dinner with Wu Jian and his friend Pan Hui. Wu, a charismatic young lecturer in the English Department, had graduated from Anqing Teachers College himself a few years before, placing near the top of his class. He had hoped to go on to become a diplomat but failed to make the grades in the exam for postgraduate study. While he waited to re-sit the exam the following year, Anqing Teacher's College offered him a teaching job. After a couple of years, he gave up on the plan to become a diplomat and concentrated on building up a career in the university, earning a supplementary income giving private classes to middle school students.

Wu was originally from a village in the east of Anhui. His parents had been peasants, though for a while they attempted to go into business breeding chickens. The business failed and his parents were left in great financial difficulty. His job in the university gave Wu the finances and the contacts to relocate his parents from their village to Anqing, where they lived together in a flat in the city centre. During dinner on my last night in Anqing, I talked to Wu and his friend about the competing pressures of education and spending time with family. I joked that Wu seemed to be the perfect son: he had succeeded in education and moved to the city, and by bringing his parents with him, he was still able to see them every day. He was not so sure that his situation was ideal. He did not particularly want to remain in Anqing; he still wanted to travel more, visit foreign countries and become a celebrated English teacher, all of which would likely take him farther from his parents. Indeed, in 2010 he not only moved out of the flat he shared with his parents to live in a new flat with his fiancée, he also took part in an academic exchange programme spending a semester teaching in the USA. So where does this leave his parents? He still loves them and will always try to take care of them, he tells me, but this does not mean he can always be with them.

Wu's friend, Pan Hui, was a local Anqing resident who had been at college with Wu and had returned to visit his family for the National Holiday. After getting into a postgraduate course, Pan was now working in the wealthy port city of Ningbo. We were talking about the chaotic scenes from earlier in 2008 when the New Year holiday coincided with the worst weather in decades in central and southern China. Snow had led to trains being cancelled, and thousands of people had been left waiting in the cold outside train stations. Pan Hui ridiculed the obsession with returning home at New Year that led to hundreds of millions of people moving around China during the 'Spring Mobilisation' (*chunyun*):

Is it unfilial [*buxiao*] not to return home for the New Year if you haven't been able to buy train tickets or because you haven't got enough money or enough time? That's ridiculous!

Confucius instructed us to be filial and told us we should not travel far from where our parents live, but this was on the basis of different practical circumstances. At that time, when sons grew up, they built new homes on land in their father's village and each son farmed a portion of the father's land. When they married, they took a wife from a neighbouring village. Of course, in those circumstances, it was one's filial duty to stay with your parents.

But how about now? Take me, for instance. I had the misfortune of being born in a small town in Anhui—don't even mention those children born in villages—the economy is grim and there are few prospects. From when we are young, we are instilled with the importance of doing well in our exams in order to go to university and leave the countryside. This is the righteous path [*zhengdao*]. If you are unable to leave and stay at home then this is shameful. After twenty years of suffering, I finally have work on the coast, but again this idea of 'filial obligation' [*xiaodao*, lit: 'the path of filial obligation'] forces me to go home. My boss only gives me seven days holiday and everybody knows the difficultly of obtaining train tickets, so why go home?

I'm not saying that once you have work it's alright to forget one's family. But I don't want people to be pressured into things by cultural traditions that haven't kept up with modernization. It's alright to return home for New Year, but it isn't something that we must do.

It seems that being a good child in China is not straightforward. Discussions, such as those I had with Chu Zhenghong, Wu Jian and Pan Hui, about the pressures experienced by children trying to satisfy their parents while also trying to lead their own lives were not unusual. Indeed, the topic came up frequently, often triggering emotional reflections on the difficult ethical choices children must make. The difficulty did not lie in any moral ambiguity. On the contrary, children were frequently lectured about what was required of them and criticized when parents felt they had strayed from the correct path. The dilemma faced by those trying to be good children was that what was required of them by their parents was contradictory, both pushing them away and pulling them back.

The conflicting demands made by parents on children are clear in the words of Pan Hui. For twenty years, his parents pressed him to work hard to escape from the village and to make a good life in the city. He describes this behaviour as following the 'righteous path' (*zhengdao*). As Pan explains, rural parents demand that their children study hard at school so they can succeed in education, go to the city and bring prosperity to the family. In this context, to be a good child means doing well at school. However, each step in the ladder of educational success takes them away from their family, towards China's developed cities primarily on the east coast. In encouraging the education of their children, rural parents are pushing their children away, encouraging them to aspire to a lifestyle that is alien to their rural villages.

Yet, as Pan found, this centrifugal morality sits uncomfortably alongside a centripetal morality which ties children to or brings them back towards their home. For Pan, this moral expectation to return was part of the 'path of filial obligation' (*xiaodao*), which forced him to return home after he had finally escaped. According to this alternative centripetal morality, to be a good child it is necessary to provide not only material support to one's parents, which a successful but absent child might be able to offer, but also affective support. To do this, children should be close to one's parents and grandparents so that they can attend to them, keep them company and care for them as they grow old. Such behaviour is a child's moral duty in recognition of all the elder generations have done. This centripetal morality of attachment to home is taught explicitly both in the home and the classroom, and it is learned implicitly in the course of daily life described so effectively by Stafford (1999, 2000, 2003). The grip of this morality is strong, and the prospect of an aged parent alone in the village is both painful and shameful for a child.

It is not possible to follow the paths prescribed by the centrifugal morality and the centripetal morality at the same time, even though, as I was often told, parents seem oblivious to this reality. Consequently, Chu Zhenghong, Wu Jian, Pan Hui and many other children from rural China must each negotiate their own paths between the countryside and the city as they attempt to satisfy the conflicting expectations of their parents as well as achieve their own ambitions for the future. This is the context in which countless decisions are made, including those about where to study, what work to do, where to live, whom to marry and when to return home. Such decisions are often reached only after much personal reflection, discussions with friends and arguments with parents. And when such decisions are reached, they are usually only ever partial and temporary resolutions to the ethical dilemma presented by the conflicting moral expectation on children. Parents and children are rarely simultaneously content, and for most the journey continues back and forth.

The moral dilemma faced by young adults from Anhui when contemplating migration should not be understood as an entirely new phenomenon or as unique to Anhui. For centuries, migration has been an option for those from rural areas, whether it was in search of prosperity or access to the higher levels of the imperial bureaucracy. Generations of migrants, especially from south-eastern China, have resulted in a global Chinese diaspora. These migrants would have faced similar moral dilemmas to those discussed earlier as expectations of bettering oneself and one's descendants were balanced with a duty to attend to parents and ancestors. In her chapter in this volume, Bell describes how some migrants to Scotland from Hong Kong left not only their parents but also their young children behind, and in doing so they had to contend with the kinship morality of both the Chinese community and the Scottish host community.

While centrifugal and centripetal kinship moralities were issues for Chinese migrants of previous generations, there are important differences in the contemporary situation. In general, for those earlier generations of migrants, leaving one's native place in the countryside was a means to success but was not desirable in its own right, because with sufficient means one could return to live well in rural areas. As Fei Xiaotong (1953: 132–3) described, the differences between the countryside and the cities, at least until the later years of the Qing dynasty, were not extreme, and a small, wealthy minority of the rural population were able to pursue desirable and highly cultured lifestyles. There was no sense that a rural life was necessarily inferior, and the native places that migrants left continued to be venerated and their origins celebrated. Undertaking a type of migration that Skinner (1976: 335, 1977: 545–6) labels 'sojourning', such people saw themselves as temporary migrants, and the intention to return to their native place was always retained, perhaps even passed down through the generations, even if not actually realized.

The current exodus of young adults from rural Anhui in search of better opportunities and prosperity is but one example of a contemporary pattern of migration in China that brings people from the countryside to the cities and from inland provinces to the coast. In contrast to earlier generations, for these migrants, leaving the countryside is itself highly desirable because it provides them with an opportunity to experience the very different lifestyle found in the cities. Disparities in income between urban and rural areas of China have been growing since the onset of industrialization, but these have accelerated rapidly since the economic reforms of the 1980s. Urban life is associated with better opportunities for work, education and health care, while increasing prosperity is matched by new practices of consumption. Rural residents are doubly excluded from all of these because they are both too remote and too poor to partake. However, rural residents are not ignorant of these differences: they are exposed to them through television and other media. Urban lifestyles are considered highly desirable, while urban styles of consumption have become symbolic of success and personal quality. In contrast, the countryside has taken on a negative moral evaluation, with rural residents seen by many urbanites as backwards, unsophisticated and falling further behind.[1] The positive moral value attached to working the land associated with Maoist philosophy has rapidly been undermined, with agricultural labour now seen as bitterly hard work and tied to grinding poverty.

Older generations, having grown up and lived in the countryside, are not considered to be a source of knowledge useful for gaining access to the modern, urban world. Indeed, this is a view often shared by parents themselves, and thus they stress the importance of schooling as a means by which their children can learn what is required to become successful urban residents. By urging children to make use of the new opportunities for migration, which have opened up since the 1980s with improvements in the education system and the easing of restrictions on movement for temporary migrant labourers, parents are actively encouraging children to leave for the cities.

Several recent studies[2] provide accounts of the difficulties labour migrants encounter in the cities as they discover how their rural dialects, clothing and customs are perceived as signs of backwardness and inferiority. Some may escape the stigma attached to migrant labourers and make a successful transition to become permanent urban residents. More often, the failure to become wealthy, the experience of discrimination and the difficulty of becoming a permanent urban resident result in disillusionment with the life of a migrant, and a decision is made to return home. However, this does not overturn the sense that a prosperous, urban lifestyle, even if unobtainable, is more desirable than anything available back home. Fang's chapter in this volume provides an account of young women migrants to Shenzhen who are dealing with similar issues. For these women, decisions about potential spouses are part of their own mobility strategies as they attempt to realize their ambitions, whether those be to remain in Shenzhen or return to their rural homes.

The wider economic and cultural context in which contemporary Chinese migration takes place has tipped the balance between the centrifugal and centripetal moralities. To simplify, migrants have, in certain respects, gone from venerating their rural places of origin to denigrating them. While children retain the centripetal morality associated with a sense of duty to attend to parents in the countryside, they now strive to be *something* very different from them, and this necessarily means being *somewhere* different from them—somewhere more urban with better opportunities to partake in consumer society and, one hopes, in time, to pass on these opportunities to their own children.

In the remainder of this chapter, I will continue to explore the ethical dilemma associated with migration by focusing on the particular situation of children growing up in the village of Nishui. While the wider context is important, my aim is to explore how such macroscopic influences become meaningful to these children at a local level. To this end, I will first examine children's experiences of the New Year festival, arguing that even at this time when the unity of the family is most emphasized, the celebration of this unity is dependent on the centrifugal morality which threatens it. In subsequent sections, I examine the place of movement in the conflicting moralities of parent–child relations. The descriptions of following paths and negotiating journeys described in this chapter are not just metaphorical, nor does movement only become an issue with the long-distance migration of adults. On the contrary, movement to and from home is an essential part of childhood in Nishui from a young age. By examining the patterns of movement of children and adults in Nishui, I hope to demonstrate, firstly, that movement through the landscape is a crucial means by which children actively learn the different valuations attached to places within the village and beyond, and hence what directions of movement are deemed morally desirable, and secondly, that actions made on the landscape by both children and adults may represent the materialization of ethical decisions which then impact upon those who share that landscape. Finally, taking stock of these ideas, I return to examine some of the ways in which adult children seek to resolve the ethical dilemma they face between leaving and returning.

NEW YEAR AND THE SEED OF THE APOCALYPSE

As Chinese family members gather together for the New Year, they are celebrating their unity and the ongoing continuity of the family. According to Feuchtwang (2001), the New Year is a celebration of the family's survival of the potential 'apocalypse' which is threatened by the 'demonic cosmos' envisioned in the popular heterodoxy. Stafford (2000) suggests an alternative reading of the New Year celebrations to Feuchtwang, in which this survival of the family makes possible the reunion and completion of the family, which he argues is a 'fleeting solution to the separation constraint: a suspended moment during which work is halted, divisions and death overcome, the pace of visits intensified, and meals and games prolonged as if people could produce, through sheer collective will, a state of permanent, celebratory reunion' (31).

To some extent, the ethnography from Nishui confirms the importance of family unity and survival to the celebration of the New Year. The students in their final year of junior-middle school in Nishui treasure their memories of past New Year celebrations, and as the winter holiday approaches again, they look forward to forthcoming celebrations. Those who board at school return home where, as the New Year approaches, they will be joined by swelling numbers of older brothers, sisters or cousins returning from other schools and universities or work in the cities. Most of those parents who work outside the village will also return for perhaps the only time in the year. It is only at New Year, when the absent generation of young adults returns to Nishui, that the village seems busy. The pace of social life quickens with rounds of arrivals, visits, gift-giving, gambling, banqueting and finally departures.

When asked what made New Year so enjoyable, the students stressed the unity of the family, symbolized by their descriptions of the whole family sitting around the table eating on New Year's Eve. The children cherished the social opportunities brought by this unity of the family, which allowed a temporary escape from the pressures and strictures of school life. They highlighted the importance of time spent with parents, visits to relatives, opportunities to play with cousins or children from neighbouring families and their fascination with stories told about life in the cities by people who had returned to the village.

Survival, unity and togetherness are celebrated at the New Year. As such, it would appear to be a manifestation of the centripetal morality of family togetherness. However, the ethnography points to a more complex interpretation, for it seems there is little to celebrate at New Year without the prospect of departure brought about by the centrifugal morality. From the perspective of the students in Nishui, the extent to which New Year would be a joyous occasion for the family was highly dependent on their performance in education. Of particular concern was the great obstacle that stood between them and the New Year: the end-of-term exams. Returning home for the holidays and presenting a poor mark sheet to parents whom they might not have seen all year could ruin the holiday. A promising child would be lauded and spoiled, boasted about and praised by relatives as a hard-working and dutiful child. Poor results would lead to a child being castigated and chided to work harder.

These children would have failed to pay their parents back for all the sacrifices made on their behalf. Hopes of university and future prosperity for the family would be dashed. So, for the students, the happiness associated with New Year depended on doing well in school. As one female student explained,

> At the moment my aim is very simple: I just want to get a satisfactory mark in the end of term exams, because immediately after the exams it is the New Year and all the relatives will get together and discuss many things and this will certainly include the children's school work. Therefore, I can only be happy and have an enjoyable New Year if I do well in the exams.

Education does not just affect the individual student's experience of New Year; it affects the mood of the whole family. A male student explained how his family's New Year celebrations would be affected by his young nephew's performance in school:

> He has just entered kindergarten. He is the happiness of our family. He is the focus of our conversations. In the first half of the year, he didn't learn anything and for two of his exams he got zero, but in the exams at the end of the second half of the year he got two 100 per cent scores. I think that because of this, our New Year's Eve will be even happier than usual.

A joyous New Year requires both family unity and educational success. Indeed, from the perspective of the children of Nishui, it is educational success which permits the exuberant celebration of family unity at New Year; this is despite the fact that it heralds the forthcoming rupture of family unity, because to be successful a child must eventually leave the family home. It appears then that the contradictory centripetal and centrifugal moralities that I have described are both required for the celebration of the New Year. While Stafford (2000) has written persuasively of the importance of separation and reunion to the ideological concerns of the New Year festival, the evidence from Nishui suggests that he may have overstated the extent to which these festivities rely on a willed suppression of the inevitability of separation that gives rise to 'a state of permanent, celebratory reunion' (31). Instead, what I am suggesting is that the promise of future, morally prescribed separation is, for many families, precisely what makes the New Year worth celebrating. Far from being denied or survived, the centrifugal morality is essential to the festivities of the New Year. For families with young children, the celebrations are dependent on the prospect of their future escape from the village. For families with adult children, if no one had any reason to depart the village after the New Year, the family's situation would be pitiable. In this way, the New Year can be understood as a celebration of unity that contains within it the seed of an impending apocalypse which risks tearing the family apart.

LEARNING TO LEAVE AND THE ETHICS OF ORDINARY MOVEMENTS

The conflicting moralities that characterize parent–child relations in Nishui are, as I have argued, inherently about movement. The centrifugal and centripetal moralities instruct children to move in opposing directions, and children face an ethical dilemma as they search for a path that balances these competing demands. To understand how this situation arises, it is necessary to step back from the longer migrations of adult children and instead consider how, from a very young age, the small and ordinary movements of children in Nishui become imbued with moral values. In this section, I attempt to show how the moral judgements associated with movements in particular directions are learned by children as they grow up and move around Nishui and how, in turn, these moralities give a geographic structure to the children's own ambitions.

Life in Nishui is always in motion. Long before any young adult migrates to the city for education or work, they experience the 'perpetual migrations'[3] of life in the village. From birth, a child moves back and forth among home, hospital, the houses of relatives and neighbours, schools, shops and occasionally local market towns or cities. Children are also witnesses to the departures and returns of others. Before turning to concentrate on the movements of the children themselves, I wish to discuss in particular how the return at the New Year of two categories of migrant usually absent from the village might have a significant impact on how the children learn about the morality of movement. The smaller of these two categories is made up of those people from the village—almost always young adults—who have secured permanent employment in cities. With good jobs and urban residences, these migrants return to the village as exemplary elder brothers, sisters and cousins. With fashionable clothes and hair and accessories such as camera phones or even cars, they give off an air of urbane confidence. Business cards are handed out to friends and relatives, recording their achievements for all to see. They have not just moved to the city; they made the permanent transition to become cultured urban residents. This is the future to which schoolchildren are encouraged to aspire.

The other, far larger category is made up of temporary labour migrants, who work in factories or building sites or make a living working for themselves but without the security or status of permanent urban residents. Younger adults in this category may still hope to secure their position in the city through advancing in their careers or, particularly for women, through marriage. Older adults in this category, and this includes many of the parents of Nishui's school-age children, have no expectation of remaining in the cities. They will return to Nishui when they grow too old for labour migration. Children are urged to work hard at school to avoid such a future for themselves.

Interesting questions are raised by the absence of so many parents from the village. It is intriguing to consider how the morality of attachment to one's parents and correspondingly one's desire to escape from life in the village might be affected by a childhood experience of incomplete or only very occasional reunion. With so many young and middle-aged adults living outside of Nishui, many children live with just one parent or with their grandparents or an uncle or aunt. As a result, it is common for children in Nishui to see one or both parents only once a year or sometimes even less. While this is relatively normal for the village, it is understood by the children concerned to be abnormal, and they frequently describe their family circumstances as undesirable and lacking in love. Children in this position compared themselves unfavourably with classmates who did see their parents regularly and, even though they understood that their parents were working for the benefit of the family and to pay for their own education, they often felt anger towards their parents. In this, it is possible to see the inversion of parental attitudes towards adult children who have left the village in pursuit of success in work or education. The fact that it may be necessary or desirable to leave does not negate the sadness of not being united in the village.

Like the adults, the children of Nishui, from the baby carried by its mother to the senior-middle school student travelling by bus to the local town, are constantly moving around the village. As they get older, they spend less and less time at home. By the age of twelve, when they enter junior-middle school, no child lives permanently at home. Some children will have already been boarding for a couple of years before that. In their final year of junior-middle school, all the children in the village will spend six and a half days a week at school, returning home only on Sunday afternoons to wash and change clothes before returning to school on Monday morning. After the age of fifteen or so, almost no child remains permanently in the village, having left the village either to study at a senior-middle school or a private college or to work as a migrant labourer.

As they move, the children are exposed to the way in which life in Nishui takes place both literally and figuratively on a gradient that structures many aspects of local life. Children in Nishui are growing up in an environment in which age, status and wealth are correlated with the geographical terrain. Visiting grandparents is usually a journey up-hill to an old and not infrequently crumbling house. Their grandparents are likely still to work the family land. Their accent, habits, clothes and physical appearance are 'earthy' (*tu*) and betray their poverty and low education. Travelling downhill, however, takes a child past new, large houses towards the school and the main street, where the biggest shops and enterprises in the village are located. Here the children can see adults wearing suits doing business, or if, as usual, business is slow, they will be playing mah-jong excitedly and noisily with large quantities of cash passing from one to another. The contrast between life uphill and downhill, agriculture and commerce, wealth and poverty could not be clearer. Furthermore, as a child travels farther downhill this pattern continues. Trips to the local town, county town or city expose the child to a greater variety of shops and offices plus restaurants, bars and Internet cafes—all evidence of the opportunities and attractions of urban life.

As would be expected from this gradient, the journey of a young child travelling from home to school is usually a journey downhill from an old mud-brick house, where the child lives with parents or grandparents, who have little education, to a school considered to be a repository of valued knowledge, the acquisition of which is essential for a prosperous future. For the children of Nishui, growing up and progressing through the education system is experienced as a process of moving farther from home and from parents and family. As the children get older, they pass through a succession of schools each farther downhill than the last. Those children who live in the highest and most remote parts of the Nishui will have attended four schools by the time they are twelve years old, each new school being considered of higher quality than the last, marked by bigger buildings, better facilities and more highly educated teachers.

Up to and including junior-middle school, children attend the closest school to their home that provides education for their year-group. However, which senior-middle school a child attends, if any, depends on his or her performance in the entrance exam (*zhongkao*), and there is tremendous pressure on children to do well in school not just so that they can remain in education but also so that they can attend the most desirable schools in the county. As might be predicted, the most desirable schools are not the closest and most convenient but the farthest away, located 'out of the mountains' by the county town. It is a pattern that continues for those able to continue in education and attend college or university, with distant universities in cities such as Nanjing, Shanghai or Beijing favoured over local colleges or universities.

As they travel around the village, the young people of Nishui develop a sense of place in which very different values are attributed to different parts of the village largely according to their relative altitude. By using what they hear in the stories of those who return from the cities and what they learn at school and from the television and other media, this sense of place is extended so that the village children are able to locate their home within the larger territory of the nation state even if they have never travelled beyond the closest town.

There is no doubt that the status of Nishui within the nation state is to a great extent determined by the wider political and economic situation as has been discussed. However, for my purposes here, these macroscopic influences are most usefully understood in terms of the impact they have on children growing up in the village. My aim therefore is to use the insights of ethnographic fieldwork to consider how macroscopic influences come to materially influence the young people of Nishui, shaping their desires and prompting their movements. To help achieve this, I use the term 'moral geography'[4] to indicate the interpenetration of the moral and the physical environment together with the wider political and economic environment, recognizing how these may influence each other without giving precedence to any single variable. The moral geography of an area is thus the historical product of the combination of the objective and the subjective factors which shape individuals' experiences of their environment. By considering children's movement through the village as an encounter with this moral geography, it is possible to propose a mechanism through which macroscopic economic and political influences come to be experienced personally and valued morally by individuals and families. In Nishui, we see just such an example in the way that the great economic and physical divide between China's coastal fringe and its mountainous interior becomes experienced in the daily life of the children in Nishui as a gradient that is simultaneously physical, economic and moral. Economic disadvantage and physical remoteness are experienced by the village children foremost as a moral imperative to move downhill, escape from the village and travel out of the mountains.

It is with reference to this moral geography that decisions are made about the appropriateness of movement in particular directions at particular times. The moral significance of the family home as a centre to which the family must return is important, and during certain festivals, this is the morality that dominates. However, for schoolchildren, these festivals are the exception, and for most of the year the moral importance of leaving the village seems to drive the schoolchildren and is emphasized by their parents. As illustrated by the following quotes, there is an almost universal desire amongst the village children to succeed in education, for they perceive this to be the only route by which they can leave the mountains and settle in the cities. It seems that by growing up in Nishui, moving through the landscape and assimilating the moral geography that characterizes life in the village, children are learning that they should leave.

Many students know that for village children like us, with little experience or knowledge, if we don't enter senior-middle school, there is nothing we can do. We are not like children in the city, who have many paths available to them [*keyi zuo hen duo tiao lu*]. Our only path out of the village is to study; it's only by studying hard that our lives will be great. (Wang Shenxiang, 15-year-old female student)

Compared to the children in the cities, children like us living in villages are 'retards' [*rouzhi*]. In comparison with those big cities, Nishui is simply a 'thatched hut': so damaged that it couldn't get any worse and as old as can be. As a result, in the first month of every New Year, the people from here all leave for other places for work. (Cao Yinghan, 15-year-old male student)

CONCLUSION: THE ETHICS OF ORDINARY MOVEMENT

As they grow up, progress through education and later find work, each child must attempt to resolve the dilemma that results from the conflicting obligations required of a good child. In finding their path, they are searching for a solution to an ethical quandary, attempting to balance the centrifugal morality taking them away from their parents and the centripetal morality bringing them back. Theirs is an ethics of ordinary movement.

Perhaps the only people who do not have to constantly move about in search of a resolution are those very few who fail at the earliest stages in education and do not pursue labour migration. For them the solution presents itself, as they will remain in the village to work the fields. Yet while adult children who remain in the village doing manual work are able to attend to their parents closely and take on their labour responsibilities (though of course they may not do so in practice), they are more likely to be criticized as useless and a disappointment for their failure to succeed in education and escape the bitterness of agricultural labour than to be praised for fulfilling their filial obligations.

For the rest, attempts at resolutions almost inevitably require carefully considered movement. Through negotiation between the generations, temporary solutions may be found, but they are mostly partial and unsatisfactory. They likely will include patterns of visiting and other types of physical and symbolic movement between the city and the countryside. When possible or necessary, children will visit their parents. When not, gifts may be sent or phone calls made during which possibilities of future return are discussed and children express concern for their parents' well-being, urging them to keep warm and eat more. In this way, absent children are able to maintain a sense of caring for parents and the prospect of a future return is always kept alive, even if circumstances require that it is endlessly deferred.

In the previous section, I considered how the idea of moral geography facilitates an understanding of how the material landscape may be interpenetrated by morality, politics and economics I described how the moral geography of Nishui shapes the ambitions of children, encouraging them to escape the village. Here, I wish to consider the opposite: how ethical decisions relating to the balancing of the centrifugal and centripetal moralities may take material form and sediment into the moral geography of Nishui. By altering the moral geography in this way, the moral evaluations made about parts of the village take on material form as economic polarization increases and the moral gradient attached to it steepens.

Thus the decision of adult children to reject the agriculture practised by their parents in favour of conducting business down by the main road results in disused fields becoming overgrown. Older houses are left to collapse, while new houses are built downhill by the roads. The purchase of a motorbike allows for more rapid and easier visits to parents in the mountains, but it also enables adult children to move farther away and return for only brief visits. Because women rarely ride the motorbikes themselves, travelling only as passengers, the impacts of these technologies on the motilities of men and women are different. Men are able to depart and return more easily and thereby are able to pursue success in the town while maintaining regular contact with parents and other relatives. Through the accretion of the numerous decisions taken by children about how best to resolve the centrifugal and centripetal moralities, the moral geography is reinforced. The higher parts of the village become depleted of young people, who leave the mountains in pursuit of the success. The village is increasingly associated with the elderly, the ill-educated and immobile women. Civilization is retreating from the mountains, and the need for young people to leave seems ever greater.

Even when living in the cities, wealthy children are able to make a material impact on the moral geography of Nishui. Building a new home in Nishui sustains a link with the village even if one lives far away and the house itself is left unoccupied. The increasing construction of large and prominent tombs in the hills around the village is a consequence of adult children wishing to fulfil the responsibilities to parents or grandparents whom they may not have always been able to attend to in life. The tombs and houses built by adult children give these absent villagers a physical presence in the village and suggest the possibility of a future return. For the audience that remains in the village, the building of these structures affirms the sense in which the parental home remains a centre to which one's life is oriented (cf. Feuchtwang 2004). In this way, the centripetal morality of attachment to parents and the village is writ large on the landscape, to be read by future generations that pass by on their own journeys through the village.

Movement and the morality of parent–child relations are inseparable in Nishui. Decisions about how one should move—when to move, in which direction and towards what destination—are ethical decisions requiring one to consider and choose a course through the complex moral terrain in which one exists. Attempting to fulfil one's obligations as a good child requires one to select a course through the moral geography of the village and beyond in the hope of escaping the village while continuing to satisfy one's parents. In seeking to find resolutions to the dilemma produced by conflicting filial paths, the children of Nishui can be understood to be conducting an ordinary ethics of movement. The ethical decisions they make and hence the paths they take leave their mark on the moral geography of the village, and in doing so they may shape the paths of those that follow.

NOTES

1. The Chinese term *suzhi* (quality) is frequently used to describe these kinds of differences between urban and rural populations. For discussions of the precise meaning and importance of this term, see Anagnost (2004), Jacka (2009) and Kipnis (2006).

2. For examples, see Gaetano and Jacka (2004), Pun (1999), Sun (2009) and Yan (2003, 2008).

3. I take this term from Stafford's (1999: 318, 326) discussion of Myers's (1986) ethnography of the Pintupi.

4. The term 'moral geography' has previously been used by Liu Xin (2000: xi, 6) and Lawrence Taylor (2007). I share with these authors a concern with

how certain places are morally evaluated, but my particular approach and theoretical framework as elaborated here are distinct.

REFERENCES

Anagnost, A. (2004), 'The Corporeal Politics of Quality (Suzhi)', *Public Culture*, 16: 189–208.

Fei, X. (1953), *China's Gentry: Essays on Rural-Urban Relations,* ed. M. P. Redfield, Chicago: University of Chicago Press.

Feuchtwang, S. (2001), *Popular Religion in China: The Imperial Metaphor*, Richmond, UK: Curzon.

Feuchtwang, S. (2004), 'Theorising Place', in S. Feuchtwang (ed.), *Making Place: State Projects, Globalisation and Local Responses in China*, London: UCL.

Gaetano, A. M., and Jacka, T. (2004), *On the Move: Women and Rural-to-Urban Migration in Contemporary China*, New York: Columbia University Press.

Jacka, T. (2009), 'Cultivating Citizens: Suzhi (Quality) Discourse in the PRC', *positions: east asia cultures critique*, 17: 523–35.

Kipnis, A. (2006), 'Suzhi: A Keyword Approach', *The China Quarterly*, 186: 295–313.

Liu, X. (2000), *In One's Own Shadow: An Ethnographic Account of the Condition of Post-Reform Rural China*, Berkeley: University of California Press.

Myers, F. R. (1986), *Pintupi Country, Pintupi Self: Sentiment, Place, and Politics among Western Desert Aborigines*, Berkeley: University of California Press.

Pun, N. (1999), 'Becoming Dagongmei (Working Girls): The Politics of Identity and Difference in Reform China', *The China Journal*, 42: 1–18.

Skinner, G. W. (1976), 'Mobility Strategies in Late Imperial China: A Regional-Systems Analysis', vol. 1, 'Economic Systems', in C. A. Smith (ed.), *Regional Analysis*, New York: Academic Press.

Skinner, G. W. (1977), 'Introduction: Urban Social Structure in Ch'ing China', in G. W. Skinner (ed.), *The City in Late Imperial China*, Stanford, CA: Stanford University Press.

Stafford, C. (1999), 'Separation, Reunion and the Chinese Attachment to Place', in F. N. Pieke and H. Mallee (eds), *Internal and International Migration: Chinese Perspectives*, Richmond, UK: Curzon Press.

Stafford, C. (2000), *Separation and Reunion in Modern China*, Cambridge: Cambridge University Press.

Stafford, C. (ed.) (2003), *Living with Separation in China: Anthropological Accounts*, New York: RoutledgeCurzon.

Sun, W. (2009), 'Suzhi on the Move: Body, Place, and Power', *positions: east asia cultures critique*, 17: 617–42.

Taylor, L. J. (2007), 'Centre and Edge: Pilgrimage and the Moral Geography of the US/Mexico Border', *Mobilities*, 2: 383–93.

Yan, H. (2003), 'Spectralization of the Rural: Reinterpreting the Labor Mobility of Rural Young Women in Post-Mao China', *American Ethnologist*, 30: 578–96.

Yan, H. (2008), *New Masters, New Servants: Migration, Development, and Women Workers in China*, Durham, NC: Duke University Press.

CHAPTER 4

THE GIRLS WHO ARE KEEN TO GET MARRIED

I-chieh Fang

This study draws on my research into the attitudes towards marriage of Chinese *dagongmei* (female migrant labourers) in order to reflect on the relationship between ethics and the ability of women to 'act on their own' and 'be independent' (*zizhu*). For many of the *dagongmei* I met during fieldwork, it seems the most attractive aspect of migration is the opportunity it gives them to meet young men and subsequently marry a person of their own choosing. It is well known that Chinese parents no longer automatically play the leading role in their daughters' marriage planning. This means that many young women have the power and free-dom to make their own marriage decisions. But it also means that they have the *responsibility* to arrange marriages by themselves—something they must navigate while still meeting a range of moral obligations to their parents and others.

Under the old system of arranged marriages, the availability of a husband to a woman was determined largely by the attributes of her parents and especially their socio-economic standing. But now that ar-ranged marriages are no longer the norm, it is believed that a woman's own qualities have a great bearing on the choice of husbands available to her. By extension, the man a woman marries tends to reflect back on her, allowing people to judge her accordingly. As I will discuss in this chapter, this includes judging her 'femininity'. Meanwhile, if a *dagong-mei* does not 'marry out' (*chujia*) by a certain age, she herself has to take responsibility for the consequences of this. She is likely to be at least implicitly punished by those around her, who are likely to say, 'You are not desired because you wouldn't make a "good" wife'. This attribution, which clearly has moral and ethical ramifications, makes girls and young women imagine and gradually learn what kinds of wife are 'good' and then try to fit themselves into that image.

To put this differently: in order to secure a marriage, these young women must, in fact, give up their agency (or at least part of it) and obey the socially constructed standard of what a desirable wife should be. Those surrounding them may punish any behaviour deemed inappropriate by warning them 'you won't be able to marry if you carry on in this way'. And although Chinese people will not judge a woman as immoral when she chooses her own spouse and/or when she marries a man her parents do not like and/or even when she has premarital sex (Yan 2003), they *will* condemn her for failing to marry. The 'freedom' to choose one's own spouse therefore makes at least some young Chinese women sink into a kind of moral panic, I suggest, one in which they are arguably controlled more than ever by traditional gender ideologies.

FEMALE MIGRANT WORKERS ARE KEEN TO MARRY OUT

The young women I met at THS, a Taiwanese-owned electronics factory in Shenzhen, were generally in their late teens and early twenties. They spent much of their leisure time talking to their friends on their mobile telephones. The most popular topic of conversation was how to 'find a good match' (*zhaoge haoduixiang*) and their progress in doing so. For example, one Sunday afternoon I listened as the worker Fond String, a twenty-three-year-old from Jiangxi province whose desk was next to mine, talked to her friends over the Internet from 3.00 p.m. until 8.00 p.m. She talked about what kind of *duixiang* ('object wooed, pursued or looked for', here meaning 'love interest') she would like, while also updating them on her current *duixiang* situation.

For *dagongmei*, trying to 'find a good match' is something distinct from flirting. It is also distinct from falling in love or being romantic or having a casual relationship. Precisely speaking, a *duixiang* is someone a young woman can really plan to marry. When a decision about this is taken, workers will hand out candies, known as 'relationship sweets', to everyone in the factory. They may invite some close friends from both sides to eat in restaurants too. This ritual-like start to a relationship reflects the fact that both sides take it seriously. To *wanwan eryi* ('just fool around' or 'just have a casual relationship') is, by contrast, generally considered taboo for these young women—even if they sometimes engage in it. For example, Fond String said again and again on the telephone, 'I don't regard relationships as a game. I am serious about them. How is it possible that I am not serious about finding a match?' She also told one prospective *duixiang*, 'I hope that you don't just want to flirt and fool around with me if we both agree to start a relationship.' Why is having relationships 'only for fun' taboo for young women migrants? In Fond String's words, 'You [young men] can afford to have a relationship only for fun, but I can't [*wanbuqi*].'

A number of researchers have commented on the prevalence inside Chinese factories of talk about relationships and romance. Pun (2005), for example, describes the jokes and laughter surrounding the topics of love and sex. Citing Paul Willis, she argues that this helps workers cope with the difficulties and tedium of factory life—'having a laff [laugh]' is a way to defeat boredom and fear. Therefore, Pun interprets this love-related talk as a 'weapon of [the] weak' in their battle against alienation (Pun 2005: 154–7). However, my interpretation is the opposite of Pun's. Gossip and romance are much more important to female workers, in my experience, than the development of their own careers (for a fascinating comparative example of this in the United States, see Holland and Eisenhart 1992). Meanwhile, gossip and romance do not, it seems, provide much release to these young women. On the contrary, they seem to feel quite anxious, uneasy and stressed about decisions related to marriage. They hold the belief that they can fail in work but they must not fail in marriage. As they themselves put it, 'Marriage is a woman's biggest enterprise' (*hunyin shi nuren zuida de shiye*).

THE 'UNTRUSTWORTHY' ENVIRONMENT IN WHICH LIFE DECISIONS ARE MADE

So how is this enterprise pursued? Here I need to explain a bit more about life in the factory. One striking thing is that physical relations between workers of the same sex can be very intimate. When I arrived at THS, the room I shared with three *dagongmei* had two pairs of bunk beds. The first night I was there, however, Silk invited me to sleep with her in the same bed. I gradually learned that intimate bodily contact of this kind is not unusual. The workers walk hand in hand, sit on each other's laps, and hold each other to show they are good friends. It is common to see four or five young women walking together hand in hand or holding each other's waists (they almost occupy half of the road) at 6.00 p.m. on the streets around the factories in the Special Economic Zone. Young men also sleep together. Even though their beds are large, they huddle tightly together—'to keep warm', I was told. I got the impression that they rarely seek to avoid contact with others of the same sex. In addition, they seem to feel little need for privacy. They say such things as, 'I prefer hustle and bustle [*renao*]. The more people that gather together, the more hustle and bustle there will be. I don't like sleeping alone, it's too cold and cheerless [*leng qing*].' But they also admit it is because they are afraid. During the weekend, if their roommates all leave, they will move to a friend's room to sleep in order not to be alone.

But what does all this physical closeness imply for the ethics of friendship in this setting? When Silk informed me that her coworker Delicate was definitely 'not my friend', I was surprised and confused. Not only did these two young women work together, they also gossiped about others and went together on shopping expeditions. They slept in the same room. But Delicate also distanced herself from Silk, telling me, 'I don't ask Silk anything about her family or her boyfriend. I am not anyone for her. Why should I bother to ask?' In my experience, migrant workers typically maintain a fine, but firm, boundary between themselves and others in both their public and private lives. If neither of two people intends to build up the friendship between them beyond a kind of 'managed relationship', they may treat each other with incredible indifference: as though they did not exist, like air. This seemed strange to me, especially given that their living space was mostly overlapping. In fact, migrant workers tend to build up their substantive social networks starting with relationships they have *before* moving to the factory. For example, they start with their *laoxiang* (people from the same town/ province), their cousins, their aunts/uncles, their classmates, and so on. Then they extend these social networks, for example, making new acquaintances through introductions. Generally speaking, they don't trust people who come to them without some kind of reference or connection.

One reason workers may not trust each other is that many, if not most, of them have used fake CVs and documents to apply for jobs. Several times I sat in on recruitment interviews at the factory. When the leaders become suspicious, they ask newcomers to recite their ID numbers and hometown addresses. If they cannot, it is assumed they are using a fake ID—they probably borrowed their cousin's or neighbour's card in order to apply for a job (e.g. because they are too young). Clerical workers and managers also routinely lie on their CVs. Gold, for example, claimed to have a university degree, but his colleague State-Union told me that he only had a junior high school diploma. The two of them used to work together on the assembly line in another factory, where Gold was promoted to a leadership post because his uncle held power there.

Living in an environment surrounded by people with vague and hard-to-trace pasts, it is easy for migrant workers to conclude that others are not trustworthy. In addition, migrant workers are vulnerable to deception in other ways. They may be tricked into buying fake goods and fake foods. They may get robbed on their way home. Young men (who, in fact, look similar to the young men working alongside them in the factories) sometimes wait in the street and then steal their wallets and mobile phones. Even those who have not experienced serious problems themselves hear stories about people who have been murdered or raped in nearby streets and workplaces. The prevailing view among these young people is that 'to trust others is a kind of naïve behaviour and only children do it'. They expect that other people will, if possible, take advantage of their goodwill or sympathy in order to put them in an unfavourable position that will harm their prospects. Even a person who still believes in acting humanely—for example, helping somebody in trouble—is taught by her peers that she is too naive and had better be careful (see the discussion of this phenomenon in Yan's chapter in this volume). They exchange stories about scams and fraud, warning each other of the horrible consequence of trusting others. Gradually, they lose not only some of their money but also some of their trust in humanity. In the end, they learn 'not to trust people', especially the ones whose backgrounds cannot be verified.

As a consequence, migrant workers often behave in what might be called an aloof, cold or indifferent way. *Dagongmei* often said to me, 'I'm just concerned with my own business' (*zuohao woziji jiuhaole*). They live in a relatively compact space with limited personal privacy, and they must learn to deal with the untrustworthy social environment around them. They stay close to the people they believe they can trust, in order to reinforce their connections with them, while avoiding others, including some they actually live and work with every day. They also long for new friendships and, I would suggest, for close bodily contact. Therefore, wishing to find a 'boyfriend' to keep them company and then to marry them—so as to form a new family and a new protective environment—is arguably a reasonable strategy for them to pursue.

SEXUAL RELATIONSHIPS AND VIRGINITY

When *dagongmei* start seeing a particular boy, this tends to lead to sexual relationships and pregnancy. Some couples rent a room outside and live together, and then everyone assumes they are having a sexual relationship. Usually, *dagongmei* quit their jobs once they become pregnant. They don't feel any shame about this. On the contrary, a girl's colleagues will normally congratulate her on this outcome. For example, when Jade quit her job because of her pregnancy and went around to say goodbye to each section, the leader of the factory asked her, 'Jade, why are you quitting?' She smiled and answered, 'I got promoted.' Delicate said, 'She has been promoted to be a mother.' Pregnancy before marriage can be a joyous occasion because people tend to assume the pregnant *dagongmei* will soon marry the man who made her pregnant. And it implies a young woman has 'upgraded' her status to wife and mother. Here, the hierarchy of female status in factory workers' minds is clearly demonstrated. But if a young woman gets pregnant and her boyfriend does not want to marry her (this kind of case is rare), the pregnancy will be treated as a secret. Young women in this position will typically quit their jobs and keep everything low profile.

In short, marriage is the ultimate reason to start a relationship. Therefore, a young woman's only serious boyfriend will become her husband if everything goes smoothly. Losing one's virginity before marriage is no longer considered immoral (Yan 2003; Pun 2005: 156). However, virginity is still a concern. Young women certainly do not, in my experience, normally want to give theirs up for a young man who will not marry them.

BEING BEAUTIFUL AND DESIRABLE

Meanwhile, *dagongmei* are very much aware of their looks. In the factory, the employees all wear a uniform: a blue shirt in summer and a blue jacket in winter. However, before going to the shop floor, the young women usually crowd into the toilet to look at themselves in the only two big mirrors in the THS factory. They style their hair by hand and then put on their hats. They adjust their hats to a particular angle and then check their image carefully. Indeed, *dagongmei* seem to really enjoy trying to be beautiful in the service of 'finding a good match'. If they spend money on dressing up, their parents (who know the purpose of this) will not generally accuse them of wasting money. In addition, they seem to enjoy receiving the care and attention of young men. The experience is relatively new for them. Many of these girls grew up as 'children left behind' (*liushou ertong*) in the countryside, that is, with one or both parents migrating outside for work, with the result that they did not receive much care and attention during childhood (at least this is what they say). The relationship between them and their parents is, in many cases, distant and cool. Children left behind are typically taken care of by their grandparents or elder siblings. However, grandparents, I was told, took care of so many grandchildren at the same time that they were often overloaded. The 'children left behind' just learned how to take care of themselves.

Silk, for example, is considered to be a beautiful young woman—therefore, many young men were interested in her at the time of my fieldwork. But she told me she couldn't make up her mind which one to choose. She told me this is because she grew up as a 'child left behind' and therefore actually enjoys being the focus of young men's attention and care. She said, 'When I was in the village, my parents all left home and my grandmother was old; no one really cared about me. Now I finally know what it feels like to be taken care of.' In the Special Economic Zone, *dagongmei* gradually realize that beauty and youth can be exchanged for attention, for money and even for a 'good life'. This provokes some young women to be ambitious. In the hope of securing a better future, young women are effectively gambling their beauty on a man.

Silk first realized beauty is kind of capital for a young woman when she was fifteen years old and was working in a factory in suburban Shanghai. One day, she told me, a male supervisor of the Quality Control section came to the shop floor. He asked all the female workers to stand in a row. Then, he looked them up and down carefully one by one. He picked out a few young women and told them they will work in the Quality Control section with him from then on. Silk was one of them, but her friend was not. Silk asked, 'Do you know why these young women are picked up by this male supervisor?' I waited for her answer. She told me shyly, 'Because these young women were more beautiful than the others'. Silk also found that after she changed to the new section, her workload was lighter and her salary was higher than before.

In her hometown, she told me, the neighbouring family had two daughters. One year when Silk came home, the younger of the two sisters in the neighbouring family told Silk that her elder sister had married a Taiwanese man and moved to Taiwan. Her parents were apparently very happy about this. They believed their daughter would surely have a better life in Taiwan. Silk told me, 'A marriage can change a young woman's life.' That is what she learnt from these stories. I was told several times that migrant workers went to knock on the door of the Taiwanese leader's room at night, wearing nothing, offering their bodies. What they want in return is not only some privileges but also a chance to be intimate and then get married to these leaders.

Although *dagongmei* must eventually 'leave' their natal families through marriage (a consequence of the patrilineal system), at least some of them do not find this sad. Silk, Fond String and Delicate told me they do not envy their brothers who are able to stay at home after marriage. Unlike their brothers, *dagongmei* have choices, they said. No matter whether they are keen to leave their hometown for the big city or other provinces or want to stay in their hometown, they can achieve this through their marriage decisions. They also imagine that life after marriage will be better, as in the stories they hear from their friends, neighbours and relatives. They somehow remain optimistic about this, in spite of the anxiety it provokes. Silk smiled and pointed out, 'Who knows what will happen tomorrow. Right?'

THE VIRTUES OF BEING MARRIED

During a party for the mid-autumn festival in 2008, Peace, a 22-year-old man, proposed that all of us should take turns to talk about our criteria for potential marriage partners. Everyone was excited about this topic. However, Art, a 26-year-old woman, blushed and couldn't say anything. She avoided answering the question by smiling. After a short silence, Delicate urged Art to give us an answer: 'You have to tell us', she said, 'and then we can help you find a man to marry. How old do you want him to be?' Art blushed again. She still couldn't say anything. Her behaviour was very different from what I was familiar with after seeing her working on the shop floor, where she was confident and her subordinates were afraid of her because she yelled at them loudly and never feared their resentment. Sky, a twenty-four-year-old married woman, asked Art, 'Do you want to find a sophisticated and prudent [chengshou wenzhong] man, one with ambitions for his career development [you shiyexin]?' Art nodded repeatedly. She asked Sky, 'How come you understand me so well?' It appeared that Sky had anticipated exactly what Art wanted to say. Sky smiled and said, 'Young women are all the same. Generally speaking, what young women want for their marriage prospects is very similar.' Sky enquired where Art's hometown was located; after Art told her, Sky turned to her husband, Virtue-Bright, and asked, 'Do you have any classmates from there?' Virtue-Bright replied with a young man's name, adding, 'He is tall, good at playing basketball and has a good job.' People laughed again and said, 'Look how fast she acts. Sky, you are really an expert and you should be our marriage consultant!'

People tend to give married women, such as Sky, the authority to speak out on questions related to other people's private lives. That is, married women are seldom challenged by others when they express their opinions on family, children, birth or relationships. For example, Needle and Jasmine, two married women, gossiped about the breast size of each young woman in the factory, about some sex scandals involving drivers and *dagongmei* and also about the relationship choices of their colleagues. As she listened to this, Zhangsan, a twenty-one-year-old unmarried young woman smiled with embarrassment and asked, 'How can you talk about these topics?' They replied loudly, 'It's no big deal [yousheme guanxi], both of us are already married!' Married women also like to lecture unmarried young women, often ending by saying, 'Later on you'll see how it is' (ni yihou jiu zhidaole). Even when unmarried women, such as Silk, do not agree with what they hear, they tend to avoid arguing about it.

As time passes, a single female eventually finds herself in an awkward situation: she cannot successfully transfer her status from the category of 'young girl' (nuhai) to that of 'woman' (funu). She is obviously excluded from the former category because of her age but, by virtue of being unmarried, she also cannot be fully integrated into society as an adult woman. Consequently, her moral status is vague. Her rights, obligations and social relations are not very well defined in the cultural scheme. As Yang notes, these 'women without a man' also tend to be neglected and invisible in the 'state feminism discourse' found in China (Yang 1999). Whilst married women are able to claim their rights, express their 'bitterness' or renegotiate their gender roles by using the discourse of gender inequality, women who remain single struggle to do likewise. In any case, most *dagongmei* would rather suffer from gender inequality within the patriarchal society than remain single. In short, they prefer to remain part of the majority.

THE DISCOURSE AND ETHICS OF FEMININITY

To get married in China is not only about finding a life partner. For some young women in the factory, at least, the point is 'avoiding having to work hard' and 'being provided for in life by a man'. They often told me that career success is not their ultimate life goal. It is not only because they think a career will distract them from their family (actually they made this point implicitly), but also because a career can actually damage their 'femininity'. To quote them, 'Women don't need to be that hard working. They of course deserve a man to take care of them.' Delicate told me, 'If my husband can earn enough money, I will be willing to let him pay for everything for me. Why shouldn't I enjoy his offer? Why bother to work that hard? [*Wo name xinku ganma*?]' A woman's ideal life (*haoming*) should include a husband who is able, and also willing, to provide for her and make her life comfortable. In this environment her 'femininity' can flourish.

But what is femininity? The Chinese term *jiao* means 'delicate' and 'pampered' and can mean 'to act in a spoiled, pettishly charming manner'—something generally considered a good thing in a young woman. Therefore, even though *dagongmei* are capable of being tough and independent, they do not usually want to act in this manner because it will be detrimental to their reputation. For example, in Pun's ethnography, she describes how female supervisors were often 'taken as men' because of their actions (Pun 2005: 145). Thus, *dagongmei* learn to disguise their sharpness, power, ambition and toughness as obedience and weakness in a way that suggests they need help. To do otherwise is to risk being judged as man-like, that is, as lacking in femininity, *jiao*.

One particularly interesting point is that the judgement made about a woman's femininity may partly be a response to the husband to whom she attaches herself. Married women 'compete' with each other over the degree of their femininity using their husbands as a measure. That is, the degree of femininity of the wives is indicated by criteria such as the jobs, titles, salaries, family backgrounds and appearances of their husbands as well as the extent to which the husbands indulge their wives. Here, people judge a woman's femininity by her husband's social status. Finding a rich husband who is willing to be an indulgent husband would be a woman's biggest 'success'. A woman who remains single cannot participate in this femininity competition and, to put it bluntly, she is destined to be a loser.

Before marriage, young women are under the threat of moral judgement, as I have explained. Their parents and other adults caution them that if they do *x*—basically, anything they feel a good girl should not do—these young women are at risk of staying single; that is, no man will want to marry them. (In Chinese: *ni name . . . yihou jiabuchuqu*.) In Pun's ethnography, she describes how the female workers are often reminded of their femaleness. 'As a girl in the process of becoming a woman, one should behave as the culture require[s]: submissive, obedient, industrious, tender, and so on.' Otherwise, the risk is that 'you can't marry yourself out' (Pun 2005: 143–4). Under this pressure, unmarried single women do not in fact stand in a good position to negotiate within the patriarchal structure. However, after getting married, they become wives and then mothers. They are no longer afraid of being *jiabuchuqu* (unable to find a man to marry), and they are now able to negotiate within the patriarchal structure even through the use of radical feminist discourse. (I found that unmarried factory workers were often more conservative and more willing to stick to traditional notions than those who are married.) While in the past the radical action women adopted to subvert male domination may have been the act of resisting marriage (Topley 1975; Stockard 1989; Watson 1994), today the most effective way for *dagong-mei* to undermine male domination may, in fact, be to embrace marriage.

CONCLUSION

Time is limited for female migrant workers, they say. This results from two facts. First, their marriageable age range is limited. Second, the period they will stay in the big city is also limited. Fond String is only twenty-three years old but she told me, 'I am old. I feel I am really old.' This is primarily because her age, twenty-three, is at the edge of what many people consider a marriageable age. Meanwhile, Art, the 26-year-old woman I mentioned earlier, is regarded as *daling* ('old-aged'). She was told by her male subordinate Peace, 'At our age, we have time to pick and choose a perfect match. At your age, anyone should be OK to marry.' However, while a twenty-six-year-old woman is too old in the marriage market, a seventeen-year-old girl is felt to be too young to have a relationship. One month after Admiring decided to be together with Navigate, she was asked to return home immediately because her relatives and parents felt it was inappropriate at her age. However, Fly had had a girlfriend since he was seventeen, when he left home for the factory. He said no one told him this kind of thing was inappropriate. On the contrary, people teased him that he looked more mature after having a girlfriend. In brief: compared to young men, young women's marriageable age comes later and ends earlier.

Meanwhile, the city in which these young people *dagong* (work as migrant labourers) is likely to be a stopping point rather than a destination. They are there only temporarily. 'I will go home in two or three years,' Fond String said. They want to see the world, to learn 'how to be a proper person' (*zuoren*) and to earn some money during their stay in the city. Eventually, they will go back to their hometown. Fond String said, 'Before I go back home, I really want to find a boyfriend as I originally planned' (*wobenlai xiangzhaoge nanyou zai hui jia*). They are fully aware that the period they stay in the city is the best time to meet men from different backgrounds and see interesting things from all over the world. If they are lucky enough, they can change their life overnight by getting married.

Even though they have 'the right to control their own marriages' (*hunyin zizhuquan*), it is not such an easy thing for these young women 'to find a good match'. Their parents (typically living in distant provinces) cannot give them support even if they want to, so young women face the situation more or less alone. They feel pressurized, scared and anxious. Fond String said on the phone, 'I am very afraid to find a match outside my hometown. Sometimes I feel lost and confused.' However, no matter how many troubles are brought by marriage, no matter how difficult *zhaoge haoduixiang* is in reality and no matter how brave a young woman has to be to face the risks and consequences alone in this process, she almost never, in my experience, simply refuses to get married. Giving up marriage means giving up adulthood, 'femininity' and a big chance to achieve what they want.

Today, *dagongmei* are not the victims of their marriages as were women in previous generations. However, the more they understand what a marriage can do for their life, the less motivation they have, it seems, to resist pre-existing gender roles or even stay single. After Chinese women gained 'the right to control their own marriages' (*hunyin zizhuquan*), it is arguably harder for them to form collectives to resist patriarchy (as some traditional 'marriage resisters' did in the past). If anything, women in this situation tend to turn against each other. Staying single is judged by others as an immature act, one that indicates a lack of femininity. Unless they marry, *dagongmei* will never transfer their social status to that of a wife and adult woman, nor will they fit into the corresponding moral role. Meanwhile, a single woman's claim to the status of a woman is also weakened. In short, on the one hand the marriage of a *dagongmei* will greatly determine her rights, responsibilities and identity for the rest of her life. On the other hand, the 'quality' of her husband will determine how her own femininity is judged. Even though the new courtship and marriage practices allow women to renegotiate their gender identities (Lee 1998: 130), thus arguably making them increasingly powerful (Yan 2003), the bargaining power of young women, at least, is inevitably reduced by their urgent need to gain adulthood and femininity and a promising future through a man.

REFERENCES

Barlow, T. (2004), *The Question of Women in Chinese Feminism*, Durham, NC: Duke University Press.

Bray, F. (1997), *Technology and Gender: Fabrics of Power in Late Imperial China*, Berkeley: University of California Press.

Burawoy, M. (1979), *Manufacturing Consent: Changes in the Labor Process under Monopoly Capitalism*, Chicago, London: University of Chicago Press.

Fei, H. (1992), *From the Soil, the Foundations of Chinese Society: A Translation of Fei Xiaotong's Xiangtu Zhongguo*, Berkeley: University of California Press.

Holland, D. C., and Eisenhart, M. A. (1992), *Educated in Romance: Women, Achievement and College Culture*, Chicago: University of Chicago Press.

Lee, C.-K. (1998), *Gender and the South China Miracle: Two Worlds of Factory Women*, Berkeley: University of California Press.

Markus, H., and Kitayama, S. (1991), 'Culture and the Self: Implications for Cognition, Emotion, and Motivation', *Psychological Review*, 98/2: 224–53.

Ong, A. (2007), *Neoliberalism as Exception: Mutations in Citizenship and Sovereignty*, Durham, NC: Duke University Press.

Pun, N. (2005), *Made in China: Women Factory Workers in a Global Workplace*, Durham, NC: Duke University Press.

Stafford, C. (2000), 'Chinese Patriliny and the Cycles of Yang and Laiwang', in J. Carsten (ed.), *Cultures of Relatedness: New Approaches to the Study of Kinship*, Cambridge: Cambridge University Press.

Stockard, J. E. (1989), *Daughters of the Canton Delta: Marriage Patterns and Economics Strategies in South China, 1860–1930*, Stanford, CA: Stanford University Press.

Topley, M. (1975), 'Marriage Resistance in Rural Kwangtung', in M. Wolf and R. Witke (eds), *Women in Chinese Society*, Stanford, CA: Stanford University Press.

Watson, R. (1994), 'Girls' Houses and Working Women: Expressive Culture in the Pearl River Delta, 1900–41', in M. Jaschok and S. Miers (eds), *Women and Chinese Patriarchy: Submission, Servitude and Escape*, London: Zed Books.

Wolf, M. (1972), *Women and the Family in Rural Taiwan*, Stanford, CA: Stanford University Press.

Yan, Y. (2003). *Private Life under Socialism: Love, Intimacy, and Family Change in a Chinese Village, 1949–1999*, Stanford, CA: Stanford University Press.

Yang, M. M.-h. (1999), 'From Gender Erasure to Gender Difference: State Feminism, Consumer Sexuality and Women's Public Sphere in China', in M. M.-h. Yang (ed.), *Spaces of Their Own: Women's Public Sphere in Transnational China*, Minneapolis: University of Minnesota Press.

CHAPTER 5

ETHICAL DILEMMAS FOR HONG KONG CHINESE PARENTS BRINGING UP CHILDREN IN SCOTLAND

Eona Bell

The image of the domineering and ambitious Chinese 'tiger mother' has recently entered the public arena, both through media debate of individual cases such as the American Chinese mother Amy Chua, author of *Battle Hymn of the Tiger Mother* (Chua 2011) and, in the United Kingdom, in policy documents (Daothong 2010; Modood 2004) which hold up Asian parents in general as models of successful parenting. There has been a good deal of recent attention to Chinese parenting styles more generally, both in the academic literature and in the popular press. Scholars have observed how parents seek to guide or control their children's behaviour, as a way to cast light on cultural ideas about the nature of the person and the relation of the individual to the family and the community. For example, Chao and Sue (1996) build on work by Baumrind (1967), who identified parenting styles that might be predictive of school success. They suggest that of three possible parenting styles (authoritarian, authoritative and permissive), authoritative parenting—characterized by high parental control combined with warmth—usually produces academically successful children in Western societies. However, American studies have generally found Chinese parents to be not authoritative but authoritarian, demanding obedience and showing little support.

This chapter draws on ethnographic fieldwork carried out over fifteen months from 2006 to 2007 in Chinese family homes in Edinburgh to discuss some of the ethical questions which arise for Hong Kong Chinese parents bringing up their children in the West. In a context where the definitions of 'good' and 'bad' parents are regularly debated both in public and in private, migrant parents can find that popular discourse on the morality of parenting styles conflicts with their own (remembered) childhood experience and values. For example, parents and teachers in Britain today are encouraged to nurture children's self-esteem through praise for positive behaviour. This contrasts with the way some Hong Kong Chinese parents have sought to discipline their children by drawing attention to faults and failings.

Specific patterns of migration and working practices have shaped the choices which Chinese migrant parents can make concerning childcare in particular. At a more abstract level, migrant parents must manage the tension between allowing their children the freedom to make their own choices in their social, academic and professional lives and protecting them from the threats and prejudice which the parents perceive in the world around them. Meanwhile, the balance of power within the family is shifting as children are often more able, because of differences of language and education, to interact with people and agencies outside the family. As Wickberg (2007: 178) has argued with reference to the Chinese community in Vancouver, immigrant parents are faced with the difficult task of balancing their wish to maintain cultural tradition, by drawing on the best aspects of their own upbringing, with the desire to explore new ways of relating to their children.

Like other parents in Britain, British Chinese mothers in particular devote considerable thought and energy every day to juggling their responsibilities at home and in the workplace, which often includes making decisions about who should take care of the children. This question has an ethical aspect since carers of children not only look after their physical and material needs but also take care of their moral and social development.

Decisions about childcare are obviously constrained in practice by economic and other circumstances, but as with all ethical codes there may be an ideal to be aspired to, a model of the 'good parent' who provides the best possible environment for the child's growth. This is an issue where the younger generations of British Chinese say they differ from their parents and grandparents. It is also an area which British Chinese people say they approached differently from white British people and also from people still living in Hong Kong.

Yunxiang Yan, among others, has written about the marked difference in the ethical codes of different generations in rural China and of the
misery of elderly parents betrayed by their children's failure to conform
to their moral code (Yan 2003, 2009). Elsewhere in this volume, I-chieh
Fang (Chapter 4) has shown that the experience of internal (rural–urban)
migration in China is changing the ways in which young Chinese women
think of their duty to their parents and their own identities as daughters
and as wives-to-be as they come to exert greater independence in their
choice of husbands. Describing a slightly younger age group of children, Johnston (Chapter 3) discusses the ethical dilemma of rural Anhui
schoolchildren who feel torn between their duty to stay at home and care
for their parents and the expectation that they go away to pursue further
education in the towns and cities.

Chinese families in Scotland are also confronted with opposing views
of the proper relationship between parents and children. The issue is
contested not only between different generations within British Chinese
families, but also between Chinese parents and the agencies of the British
state—especially schools—which have a role in the lives of their children
(Ran 2001; Francis and Archer 2005). In this chapter I approach the issue
from the perspective of parents. I relate this to Vanessa Fong's (2004,
2007a,b) work on parent–child relationships in one-child families in
urban China. Fong has shown how parents' mental models of the 'ideal'
parent and the desired behaviour of children can conflict with what they
observe and accept as the right way to act in a rapidly changing society.
Fong's study is based on the lives of only children in families in Dalian,
mainland China, a generation which she describes as 'born and bred to
become part of the first world, [but] frustrated by their parents' low incomes and the scarcity of educational and professional opportunities that
could enable them to obtain First World lifestyles' (Fong 2004: 179).

The difficulties for Fong's informants arise for a variety of reasons:
for one thing, their parents are trying to instil in them moral values and
behaviours that were appropriate in a previous generation but are incompatible with the interpersonal style required to succeed in the new, re-
formed Chinese economy. As an example of their contradictory values,
Dalian parents hope that their children will take care of them in their old
age (and thereby show obedience), as dutiful Chinese children have been
supposed to do for centuries, but independence, not submissiveness, is
the quality needed for a 'modern' young Chinese.

Moreover, in relation to the case of China, while the parents Fong studied are disorientated by the rapid changes in Chinese society and their assumptions unsettled about how to prepare a child for adult life, at least they are assured that what will emerge is a new kind of Chinese morality for Chinese youth. The parents I write about have an even greater shift to make because their children are influenced by the quite alien moral culture of their Scottish friends and teachers. Their parents cannot assume that they will grow up in any way Chinese. A great deal is at stake, in terms of identity and the continuity of culture, for immigrant parents in the West.

CHINESE FAMILIES IN SCOTLAND

There are estimated to be between 3,000 and 10,000 Chinese residents in the City of Edinburgh, out of a total population of approximately 450,000 (City of Edinburgh Council 2001). (The lesser figure of 3,532 drawn from the 2001 national census is regarded by community organizations as a considerable underestimate, caused by language difficulties and the reluctance of some Chinese people to respond to official surveys.) Demographically, Edinburgh's Chinese community provides an approximate sample of the Chinese population in Britain as a whole, being highly diverse in their reasons for migration and their country of origin (Maan and Millan 1992; Neoh 2005; Pieke 2005).

While there are clusters of Chinese living in particular districts of Edinburgh and a handful of community organizations, there is no physical centre of the community, unlike in other British and North American cities that have Chinatowns where large numbers of Chinese businesses and cultural centres are concentrated. In Edinburgh, Chinese families are dispersed throughout the city, so children will frequently attend primary and secondary schools where there are very few, if any, other Chinese pupils.

The families I write about in this chapter are all Cantonese or Hakka speakers with family ties to Hong Kong and the New Territories. Most of them work in the catering trade. They first settled in Scotland in the late 1960s or 1970s, when the original male migrants, who had previously worked in restaurants in England, brought their wives and children to join then in the United Kingdom. Families scattered across the country in search of new business opportunities, opening small takeaway shops and restaurants in towns and villages throughout the British Isles (Benton and Gomez 2008).

Because these families have now been in Scotland for three or four decades, they provide an interesting case of a community with several generations living nearby, established community associations and a relatively long history of involvement in the British education system. Indeed, as is the case for immigrant Chinese children throughout the world, ethnic Chinese children perform exceptionally well in Scottish schools, achieving some of the best exam results of any ethnic group (Scottish Executive 2006).

My Scottish Chinese informants recognized the stereotypes of their children as academically successful and their parents as strict and controlling but generally did not consider that they themselves—or indeed anyone they knew personally—behaved as 'tiger mothers'. One Edinburgh Chinese mother wrote to me in an email (personal correspondence 2011):

> The UK version of Amy Chua would be Vanessa Mae's mother, the famous violinist. She was on a TV programme, telling about her tyrant mother and her childhood. I suppose it all depends on individual mother—how much does she want their child to be successful and famous. For me, the most important is: the children will be able to get a decent job and that they are happy with it.

While most of the people I met denied that they—or their own parents—would push their children to extraordinary success, many of the British-born generation spoke about forms of discipline at home which they considered 'old-fashioned Chinese' and contrasted with Western treatment of children. Often they would mention grandparents in particular punishing disobedient children by hitting them with a feather duster or a stick. I will return to the issue of discipline in the second part of the chapter, after describing the larger picture of family decision-making in connection with childcare and education.

LIFE STORIES: THREE GENERATIONS BRINGING UP CHILDREN IN THE WEST

This section presents the stories of three families, arriving in Scotland from Hong Kong at different times, who took different decisions concerning the care of their children. As I discuss the choices made by individual families with regard to childcare and schooling, I also consider the various factors which affect these choices: the particular constraints of parents working long hours in catering; the geographical separation of many households from their extended families; their hopes and aspirations for the children's formal education; and the parents' willingness to trust other people to care for their children. Clearly Chinese immigrant families are not alone in facing these dilemmas, and there is a growing body of work by anthropologists who draw attention to the implications of migration for parent–child relationships (see, for example, Greenfield and Cocking 1994; Hondagneu-Sotelo and Avila 1997; Schmalzbauer 2005). Here I argue that the ethical choices made concerning childcare relate to people's sense of security and belonging in British society: often parents would express negative emotions such as fear over their children's physical safety as well as the harmful influence of British values on their moral development. They also anticipated condemnation of their parenting choices by non-Chinese neighbours, demonstrating a view of 'British' and 'Chinese' practices and values as contrasting and often conflicting.

1970s: GRANDPARENT SOCIALIZATION

Mrs Shek[1] moved to Scotland from Hong Kong as a young bride in the 1960s: her husband and his five siblings all came and opened small takeaway shops in Edinburgh and the surrounding area. Everybody was needed to work the long hours to establish the family business, so when Mrs Shek's babies were born, she took them back to Hong Kong to be cared for by her parents until they reached school age. James Watson (1975) described this as the usual practice for childcare when he started his fieldwork in an emigrant village in the New Territories in the late 1960s. He refers to a 'crisis of discipline' among children left in the village, where grandparents would overindulge them, to the despair of the village schoolteachers (Watson 1975: 192–5).

From another point of view, British educationalists in the 1970s condemned Chinese immigrant parents for sending their children away (Garvey and Jackson 1975). At that time children of Chinese origin were seen to struggle and underachieve in British schools, and British teachers put much of this down to what they saw as the traumatic experience of having been separated from their parents during the early years, then brought to the United Kingdom at the age of five or six to live with parents whom they barely remembered. From a Western perspective, it seemed harmful for a child to be separated from his parents, and this reflects the established norm of the nuclear family. From a Chinese point of view, perhaps, these children were not experiencing a huge disruption because they were still being cared for by members of the extended family.

Mrs Shek justifies her own decision to send the children away not simply as an economic necessity, but also a rational and purposeful strategy to keep the family together. She says that other Chinese families in Britain in the 1960s chose British private foster carers to look after their children for up to six days a week, including overnight. This practice was not dissimilar to childcare arrangements in Hong Kong (Martin 1997), where it was common for female factory workers to pay other women to care for the children twenty-four hours a day. According to Diana Martin's analysis, the need of parents, and especially mothers, to pursue a career took precedence over any belief that a small child should remain with its mother as principal carer. When Chinese children were fostered in Scotland, their parents would see them once a week, but this was not enough to prevent the children from rapidly becoming more fluent in English than Cantonese and over time forming stronger emotional attachments to the foster carers than to their own parents. There was one case in Edinburgh which I heard about indirectly from three or four different people, where the courts had to intervene to decide custody arrangements for a Chinese child who no longer wanted to return to his parents' home because he felt more secure with his white Scottish foster carers. All of the Chinese parents who told me about that case thought it was shameful that the child's parents should have allowed the situation to reach that point. It was to avoid that extreme scenario of family breakdown that Mrs Shek decided her children should be brought up by their grandparents in Hong Kong.

When her children reached school age, Mrs Shek brought them to live with her in Scotland. Since she and her husband were still very busy at work, and spoke poor English, they realized that they could not help their children with their schoolwork. In common with many of their contemporaries, they decided to send their children to private schools, assuming that the teachers would have the time and resources to give the children the direction they required. An Edinburgh-born Chinese man describes this ironically as a 'typically Cantonese approach: if you have a problem, just throw money at it'. The cost could represent a significant financial sacrifice for the parents, as Mrs Shek told me: 'For years we lived in a tiny flat, and I drove a very old and ordinary car. All our money went on my son's school fees.' She also boasts that although she was working in a takeaway and had very little time to spend with her son, she used their time together for the maximum benefit: as she drove him to school every morning, she would question him about his lessons and ask whether he had any problems or difficulties understanding the teacher.

1980s: CHILDREN 'UNDER THE COOKER'

By the 1980s, more Chinese parents were choosing to keep their children with them in Scotland. Tommy, the father of two young sons, had no option in the matter as his own parents had also moved to Britain and they were busy running their own restaurant in another city. His wife's parents lived in mainland China and could not take care of the grandchildren. Tommy describes how his wife would carry her sons on her back as she worked at the hot wok in their takeaway shop, constantly aware of the physical danger of the working environment but having no other option but to keep them there. When the boys were older, they spent evenings playing among the sacks of rice in a storeroom at the back of the shop. It would have been more interesting for them to watch TV by the counter, but their parents knew that the customers might not like to see children there. They were afraid of being reported to the authorities for child cruelty.

Similarly, Lily, who was born in Glasgow in the 1970s, recalled as a young teenager being left alone at home with her brother while their parents went to work, after leaving strict instructions not to open the curtains in case the neighbours saw. In fact, the children would often sneak out of the house to meet their Chinese friends, whose parents were also out working in their restaurants until late in the evening. Brothers and sisters would collude with each other to answer the phone when their parents called to check that everyone was safe at home.

Although it seems to be less common now, my informants told me that there are still British Chinese families, especially young couples running their own takeaway shops with no outside help, who keep their small children 'under the cooker', as Tommy put it, and leave their teenagers unsupervised rather than pay a stranger to take care of them. Many have no option because it would be hard to find a childcare provider who would look after children during the evening or overnight, and the cost would be prohibitive.

If we are to ask how children learn about ethics and good behaviour, then these examples may show how the children of immigrants first acquire a sense of stigma and moral condemnation surrounding their parents' choices and daily practices. Intertwined with the family's sense of their own difference, and derived from their distinctive work in the ethnic catering industry, is the knowledge that their family life is considered abnormal and even pathological by wider society: my informants were constantly aware of their parents' fear of condemnation by neighbours or customers who might accuse them of neglecting their children. British Chinese people themselves, including Mrs Shek, who cited the case of a boy taken from his parents by law, take the view that the consequence of all this is broken trust between the generations and children's loss of respect for their parents.

2000s: CHILD-CENTRED FAMILIES

Lily, who has unhappy memories of a lonely childhood with her parents usually absent from the family home, decided when she got married that she would not have children until she and her husband could take care of them themselves (i.e. without the help of grandparents or anyone else). In fact, her husband earns a good income from his restaurant, so it has been possible for Lily to stay at home with their two children. She spends much of her time driving her son and daughter to swimming lessons, karate club and children's birthday parties, as well as to learn Mandarin at Chinese school on Saturdays. Her children's busy lives, which are barely distinguishable from those of their white Scottish classmates, differ enormously from Lily's own experience of isolation and boredom as a child in Glasgow twenty years ago.

This change in circumstances is also associated with British Chinese people choosing to leave the catering industry and seek other kinds of work. Tommy, who previously ran a takeaway shop with his wife, keeping their small boys hidden from the customers, sold the business when their first son started high school. Tommy took a job as a postman, which he describes to me as the best decision of his life. Meanwhile, his wife became a care assistant. He gives two reasons for the move: first, it allowed them to support the boys' education by being at home in the evenings, but second, it made it possible for the parents to take days off and take annual holidays, something they could never do when they were running their own business.

Parents such as Lily and Tommy contrast their lives favourably with those of relatives still living in Hong Kong. They speak of the huge pressure on their Chinese nieces and nephews to perform well at school and of the physical harm done to children by reading too much and carrying very heavy book bags to school each day. In contrast, they were proud that in Scotland it was possible for their sons and daughters to enjoy a more leisured childhood, and because they had all grown accustomed to a gentler and less competitive pace of life, neither the first-generation migrants nor the British-born children I spoke to were keen to move to Hong Kong or China to live. This preference for a more relaxed lifestyle was interesting, considering the prevailing stereotype in Britain of all Chinese parents as driven and determined for their children to work extremely hard.

THE MORAL DUTY OF PARENTS

Diana, the 18-year-old daughter of restaurant workers, claims, perhaps rather surprisingly, that she is very unusual among Scottish Chinese teenagers in working hard at school and aspiring to go to university. She credits this to her parents, who decided that her mother should remain at home with her while she was small. In an email to me, she wrote:

> I think having an adult 'idol' or in general, someone to 'look up on' is important for any child growing up because we tend to imitate the people around us. And for me, I had my parents looking after me, to tell me what's right and what's wrong and to actually have the time to nurture me and to teach me. Whereas with a lot of [Chinese] teenagers here, their parents have been working in takeaways ever since they were born, they have just grown up with parents too busy to look after them and to teach them.

One day I asked Vicky, Diana's Hong Kong Chinese mother, what a good parent should do to prepare her child for the future. She answered,

'I have to teach her how to make the right choices, how to be a proper person [Cantonese *jouh yahn*, Mandarin *zuo ren*]. The teachers at school can tell her things I don't know, but I have to teach her how to be a good person.' This statement in part reflects the great difference in the experience of schooling between Vicky, who had completed only a few years of primary education in Hong Kong before her family's poverty obliged her to leave school to start work in a factory at the age of eleven, and her now 18-year-old daughter. They had immigrated to Scotland when Diana was seven years old, and she had quickly become more fluent in English than Cantonese. At the time of my fieldwork, Diana was preparing to take her final-year school exams and planning to study law at university.

Vicky's self-defined role as moral guide to her daughter was brought to the fore when Diana came home from high school weeping one day because she had discovered that her boyfriend, also a British-born Chinese teenager, had been seeing another girl. For days Diana appeared anxious and miserable and barely spoke to either of her parents. One day Vicky accidentally discovered a long letter Diana had written to the boy in which she told him she was so low, she had thought of suicide. The fact that the letter was in English, which Vicky struggled to read, only compounded her distress at the knowledge that her daughter was so deeply unhappy but unable to communicate this to her mother. Confronting her daughter in Cantonese, she begged her to talk about her worries. Diana merely told her not to worry and assured her that she was dealing with the situation in her own way. Vicky remained deeply concerned that the emotional upset would unbalance Diana, especially as she approached her exams and needed to be as calm as possible.

Vicky clearly saw it as her responsibility as Diana's mother to help her navigate the emotionally stormy sea of her love affair. Vicky longed to guide her daughter to a resolution of the problem, to help her to react in a dignified and mature way, but was frustrated by the linguistic barrier between them, which added to a teenager's reluctance to share her inner life with her parents.

PARENTAL CONTROL OVER CHILDREN

Although they may lack the knowledge and linguistic skills needed to help their children with academic work, many parents see their role as teaching them discipline and protecting them from possible harm. This can extend to behaviour which the children can perceive as overprotective, in comparison with the relative lenience of white Scottish parents. It has recently been argued that one reason for the educational success of British Asian (including Chinese) children is that their parents strive to protect them from some of the negative influences of Western youth culture (Modood 2004).

Chris, the 16-year-old, British-born son of Tommy the postman, told me about his family's 'house rules' which he feels are extremely strict in comparison with those of his non-Chinese friends. He is never allowed to sleep over at the home of a school friend: his father always objects that he would not get enough sleep and would be too tired for school the next day. Likewise, he has never been allowed to bring a friend home. His parents say they have so much stuff lying around, they would be unable to see if anything had been stolen, indicating a fundamental lack of trust in other people's children. The only one of Chris's friends whom his parents trust is another Scottish Chinese boy whose aunt used to work with them.

Chris says, 'My parents always know where I am.' He is allowed to go into the city centre to hang out with friends by day, but his father always comes to collect him in the car, while Chris's friends may travel independently by bus. The one time his father became furious and grounded both his sons was after Chris's older brother Paul was half an hour late in coming out of a concert.

Another absolute rule is no drinking, smoking or drugs. Tommy and his wife do not object to people having the occasional drink for a special occasion but hate the British habit of binge drinking. 'Good people lose control of themselves when they're drunk,' Tommy points out. He tells me he often fears for the boys' safety when they go out with friends: a drunk person might attack them because they are 'foreigners'. If they themselves drink too much, they might take unnecessary risks.

Chris is learning judo. He sees it as a good way to get fit, but for his father it is a valuable skill for self-defence. He quotes the story of a Chinese man who was punched at random by a stranger while waiting at a bus stop in Edinburgh's main shopping street, and he is exasperated by the way that his sons apparently underestimate the threat to them as members of a visible ethnic minority.

Tommy's anxieties, and his strategies for controlling them by setting strict limits for his teenage sons, arose from their inevitable exposure to Scottish norms of behaviour for young people. As the boys grew older, he and his wife were no longer able to shelter them from these harmful influences, as they had done when the boys were tiny and had stayed under the watch of both parents in the takeaway kitchen. Western parents also may be mistaken to believe that they have the greatest influence over their children's development: peers and siblings are equally and sometimes more influential (Harris 1999). However, for immigrant parents the sense of powerlessness can be all the harder to accept.

In many ways, contemporary British culture supports a shift in power from adults to children, and this can cause great anxiety for some Chinese parents of British-born children. One Hong Kong–born mother who teaches at a Chinese community-language school complained to me that her students regularly fail to do homework and answer back if she shouts at them, telling her that she is not 'respecting their rights'. Her friend, also the mother of teenagers, agreed that it was almost impossible to discipline her own children and said that her daughter had once threatened to phone the telephone helpline ChildLine if her mother scolded her. In response to my question about Amy Chua's 'tiger mother' approach to parenting overseas-born Chinese children, this mother said, in an email:

I believe Chua's experience is familiar to every Chinese mother and we won't be surprised. My family turned into a war zone a few years ago and I had pulled a white flag. Sometimes I wonder [if] the rebellion genes in children is common which always target the 'mother'. It seems to happen to all children regardless of their nationalities.

However, when Chua thought that she was right by copying her own childhood life to her daughters, she failed to consider the two different cultural environments of where she and her daughters [were] brought up from. I assume her parents are both Chinese so she didn't have other choice while her daughters are Eurasians and they have choices to go for East &/or West culture. Chua also neglected the education system here which tells children their human rights on the first day of school while she probably did not know her rights until she got her PhD.

While these two Hong Kong–born mothers smiled wryly as they told these stories, they expressed frustration as adults forced to reconsider their own roles and positions in relation to the younger generation.

They could not fall back on the model of adult behaviour which they had observed from their own parents and teachers in deciding how to discipline their own children.

CHILDREN'S CARE FOR THEIR PARENTS: HIERARCHIES REVERSED

While Scottish Chinese parents try hard to guide their children and protect them from harm, on many occasions it is the children who must take responsibility for their parents' well-being. The phenomenon of children becoming 'linguistic brokers' for their immigrant parents is well documented (e.g. Suárez-Orozco and Suárez-Orozco 2001). Because they speak fluent English, the children of immigrants frequently take on responsibility for household matters which would normally not be their responsibility, such as dealing with government agencies, handling tax matters and accompanying their parents to medical appointments, a situation which can be embarrassing for all concerned. In an anonymous blog, one young Scottish Chinese student expressed her frustration at her parents' dependence on her for both practical and financial support:

> I have to wake up at 6am tomorrow to do another past paper and wait until the council people opens so i can phone them up. damn the government, i think my parents would be better off if they were in hong kong but they refuse to go back and sometimes i get angry with them because them wanting to stay here troubles me a lot too— but i cant tel them that because they will just go back unhappily.
>
> Sometimes i think what they expect from me is a little overboard— for example occasionally they ask (politely) if i could just give them as much as i can from my bank account, or if its for holiday, to tell them when i can save up £1000. Or they ask me to phone the council, to help them print stuff, copy stuff, fix stuff . . . sometimes i think its a bit to much to ask from me, from a daughter of a family who is supposed to be the one being helped with all the things shes helping them to do. However, i guess my family is different and there is no one there to help them. That is why i am so vulnerable, i have no one to turn to because honestly, i dont look at my parents as someone who can help me or protect me because they really cant, i dont look up to them or see them as a good example. I know it is sad but it is the truth.

ORDINARY ETHICS AND ETHNICITY

Chinese families have made their homes in Scotland for many years, occupy the same spaces and use many of the same services as other residents, and yet the prevailing discourse on ethnic minorities and multiculturalism continues to highlight the differences between them and white Scots. In multicultural Britain, distinctive moral/ethical codes are often cited as examples of the differences between minority and majority ethnic groups. At the heart of multiculturalism is respect for, even deference to, minority values. Anthropologists such as Unni Wikan (2002) have argued that this principle can in fact do more harm than good to individual immigrants and their children, not least by stereotyping and making simplistic assumptions about the ethical behaviour of individuals based on generalizations about 'cultural norms'.

British Chinese are often considered a 'model ethnic minority' because of their stereotypical moral values—the positive virtues of hard work, self-reliance and strong loyalty to the family. When asked to reflect self-consciously on their own identity, in contrast to the white Scottish majority, British Chinese people will themselves refer to these stereotypical ethical principles. Attempting to explain this to me one day, a British-born Chinese woman in her thirties remarked casually that 'here you just leave your old people in homes, but we wouldn't do that; we really respect old people'. Other value-based definitions of ethnicity revolved around the behaviour of white Scottish young people, as my Chinese informants frequently expressed their concern about the corrupting influence on their children of white Scottish friends who drank alcohol, smoked and generally displayed lazy attitudes toward work and study, in implicit contrast to the more abstemious and hard-working habits of many Chinese migrant adults.

Ordinary ethics can become a marker of group identity. On the other hand, ethnographic observation suggests that in practice ethical issues, like the boundaries of so-called ethnicity, are not clearly defined, and I would argue that in tussling with ethical problems of family life, people are also questioning their identities in relation to culture and place of origin.

A conference of British Chinese community leaders convened in 2007 by the Chinese in Britain Forum discussed the theme of 'Success for Our Children: Missed Opportunities for Our Community?' This seems to encapsulate the ambiguous position of the Chinese population of Britain, which is both admired from outside and proudly self-aware of the moral values of hard work, self-reliance and respect that are stereotypically associated with Chinese people in Britain as elsewhere in the world. At the same time, many within the community now acknowledge that the economic and educational success of Chinese people has been won at the expense of less measurable achievements, such as trust and intimacy within families, and, more generally, social and political engagement with mainstream British society. Success in business has also masked individual stories of loneliness and isolation, broken relationships, frustration and disappointment. These same moral values can motivate people but can also cut them off from others in damaging ways.

This chapter has considered some of the ways in which these tensions are manifested in the everyday decisions which parents must make concerning the care of children. One theme which emerges from the stories of Scottish Chinese families is the apparent need for families to choose between two ways of being 'good parents': establishing emotional intimacy and spending time together, or providing well for children in material ways. Tommy and his wife chose the former but paid the price of a lower income from paid employment when compared with the money which can be made in catering. Vicky was painfully aware of her household's relative poverty and wished they could move to a bigger house, but she knew they could never afford it if she did not go out to work. Both Tommy and Vicky justified their choices by comparing their children favourably with those of parents who were wealthier but spent less time at home: the offspring of those families, they would say, became lazy and acquired bad habits such as drinking and taking drugs. Only a few households, such as Jenny's, are rich enough to achieve something of a balance between earning money and paying attention to the children.

There is a sad irony in the way that some British Chinese parents are ultimately condemned by their own children and their peers as 'bad parents' because they did not spend enough time with their offspring. These people worked hard in the demanding catering trade, at great personal cost, with the highly moral goal—as they would see it—of achieving economic security and a better future for their children. It is precisely because of the schooling their parents have made possible for them that the children have learned English and become part of British society. This in turn gives them power to undermine and challenge parental authority, specifically because their parents remain socially and linguistically isolated by the very nature of their work.

NOTE

1. All names used in this chapter are pseudonyms. Most of my informants use Western given names in everyday life.

REFERENCES

Baumrind, D. (1967), 'Child Care Practices Anteceding Three Patterns of Pre-school Behavior', *Genetic Psychology Monographs*, 75: 43–88.

Benton, G., and Gomez, E.T. (2008), *The Chinese in Britain, 1800–Present: Economy, Transnationalism, Identity*, Basingstoke, UK: Palgrave Macmillan.

Chao, R. K., and Sue, S. (1996), 'Chinese Parental Influence and Their Children's School Success: A Paradox in the Literature on Parenting Styles', in L. Sing (ed.), *Growing up the Chinese Way: Chinese Child and Adolescent Development*, Hong Kong: Chinese University Press.

Christiansen, F. (2003), *Chinatown, Europe: An Exploration of Overseas Chinese Identity in the 1990s*, London: RoutledgeCurzon.

Chua, A. (2011), *Battle Hymn of the Tiger Mother*, London: Bloomsbury.

City of Edinburgh Council (2001), *Edinburgh's Census 2001: Ward Factsheet*, Edinburgh: The Council.

Daothong, J. (2010), *What More Can We Takeaway from the Chinese Community? British Chinese Community and Educational Achievement*, London: Black Training and Enterprise Group.

Fong, V.L. (2004), *Only Hope: Coming of Age under China's One-child Policy*, Stanford, CA: Stanford University Press.

Fong, V.L. (2007a), 'Parent-child Communication Problems and the Perceived Inadequacies of Chinese Only Children', *Ethos*, 35: 85–127.

Fong, V.L. (2007b), 'Morality, Cosmopolitanism, or Academic Attainment? Discourses on "Quality" and Urban Chinese-only-children's Claims to Ideal Personhood', *City and Society*, 19: 86–113.

Francis, B., and Archer, L. (2005), 'British-Chinese Pupils' and Parents' Constructions of the Value of Education', *British Educational Research Journal*, 31: 89–108.

Garvey, A., and Jackson, B. (1975), *Chinese Children*, Cambridge: National Education Research and Development Trust.

Greenfield, P.M., and Cocking, R.R. (1994), *Cross-cultural Roots of Minority Child Development*, Hillsdale, NJ: Erlbaum.

Harris, J.R. (1999), *The Nurture Assumption: Why Children Turn out the Way They Do*, London: Bloomsbury.

Hondagneu-Sotelo, P., and Avila, E. (1997), '"I'm Here, but I'm There": The Meanings of Latina Transnational Motherhood', *Gender and Society*, 11: 548–71.

Maan, B., and Millan, B. (1992), *The New Scots: The Story of Asians in Scotland*, Edinburgh: John Donald Publishers Ltd.

Martin, D. (1997), 'Motherhood in Hong Kong: The Working Mother and Child-care in the Parent-centred Hong Kong Family', in G. Evans and M. Tam (eds), *Hong Kong: The Anthropology of a Chinese Metropolis*, Honolulu: University of Hawaii Press.

Modood, T. (2004), 'Capitals, Ethnic Identity and Educational Qualifications', *Cultural Trends*, 13: 87–105.

Neoh, D. (2005), 'The Chinese Community in Scotland', in J. Beech (ed.), *Scottish Life and Society*, vol. ix, *The Individual and Community Life*, Edinburgh: John Donald.

Pharaoh, R., et al. (2009), *Migration, Integration, Cohesion: New Chinese Migrants to London*, London: Chinese in Britain Forum. Available online: http://www.chinesemigration.org.uk/download/MigrationReport.pdf.

Pieke, F. (2005), *Community and Identity in the New Chinese Migration Order*, Oxford: Centre on Migration, Policy and Society.

Ran A. (2001), 'Travelling on Parallel Tracks: Chinese Parents and English Teachers', *Educational Research*, 43: 311–28.

Schmalzbauer, L. (2005), *Striving and Surviving: A Daily Life Analysis of Honduran Transnational Families*, London: Routledge.

Schofield, K. (2005), 'Number of Chinese Pupils in Scotland Doubles in 4 Years', *The Scotsman* (26 April).

Scottish Executive (2006), *SQA Attainment and School Leaver Qualifications in Scotland: 2004/05*, Edinburgh: Scottish Executive.

Shang, A. (1984), *The Chinese in Britain*, London: Batsford Academic and Educational.

Suárez-Orozco, C., and Suárez-Orozco, M. M. (2001). *Children of Immigration*, Cambridge, MA: Harvard University Press.

Watson, J. L. (1975), *Emigration and the Chinese Lineage: The Mans in Hong Kong and London*, Berkeley: University of California Press.

Wickberg, E. (2007), 'Global Chinese Migrants and Performing Chineseness', *Journal of Chinese Overseas*, 3: 177–93.

Wikan, U. (2002), *Generous Betrayal: Politics of Culture in the New Europe*, Chicago: University of Chicago Press.

Yan, Y. (2003), *Private Life under Socialism: Love, Intimacy, and Family Change in a Chinese Village, 1949–1999*, Stanford, CA: Stanford University Press.

Yan, Y. (2009), *The Individualization of Chinese Society*, Oxford: Berg.

PART II

ETHICAL ACTION AND MORAL EVALUATION IN RURAL COMMUNITIES

CHAPTER 6

SOME GOOD AND BAD PEOPLE IN THE COUNTRYSIDE

Charles Stafford

This chapter focuses on what might be called the ethics of moral judgement. The ethnographic material I draw on comes from research in a farming village in north-east China. However, I want to start by mentioning something I observed in the Taiwanese fishing community of Angang back in the 1980s.

When I was living in Angang, I often watched people watching television. Almost every home and shop had at least one television set, and in the evenings these were almost always on. The most popular programmes were dramatic serials; these were basically 'soap operas' based in either the imperial or modern eras. Due to the nature of social interactions in Angang, however, these programmes were often half-watched or even completely upstaged by everything else that was happening. In the evenings, a steady flow of people walked between and through local houses, creating sequences of (often very lively) exchanges as they did so: fights, card games, divination sessions and so forth (Stafford 1995). This was incredibly distracting, of course. But if there was a lull in the conversation as someone walked through a house, the passer-by might stare at the television screen for a moment, narrowing his or her eyes to see what the show was about. Catching some dialogue and singling out a character, such passers-by would routinely ask, 'Is that a good one?' (*chit e ho e?*) or 'Is that a bad one?' (*chit e phai e?*).

Perhaps it isn't surprising that people in Angang should expect the goodness or badness of a character to be made immediately obvious because that is exactly what is done in traditional Chinese opera (a genre they are very familiar with thanks to performances at temple festivals and on television). In opera, the use of facial paint and masks makes explicit—before a word is sung or spoken—what type of character one is dealing with. A white face equals cunning and treachery, a red face equals loyalty and bravery and so on. And while we might think that characters whose moral standing is difficult to grasp, perhaps unknowable, should be much more interesting for viewers than these 'obvious' ones, whether this is true remains an open question. Indeed, one of the enduring attractions of Chinese operas—not to mention televised dramatic serials which are partly inspired by them—might well be the existence in them of characters whose goodness or badness is quickly, sometimes instantly, revealed.

***

The people I've met while conducting fieldwork in China and Taiwan constantly judge those around them, labelling individuals 'good ones' and 'bad ones' in various contexts. My field notes are filled with this phenomenon, even though I was usually not looking to record it. Sometimes the moral evaluations I encountered were blunt, even crude or unfair, while at other times they were strikingly nuanced and complex. One interesting question is why this happens, that is, why it is that in some circumstances we put quite a bit of *effort* into moral evaluation, while in other cases we do not.

It may help clarify this issue to consider two ongoing areas of debate in psychology and philosophy. The first concerns what is sometimes referred to as the 'fundamental attribution error' (also known as the 'correspondence bias').[1] Imagine, for a moment, two ideal types of moral evaluation. On the one hand, in considering the behaviour of another person you might feel that what he does tells you something about what kind of person he is, that is, about his essence—for example, that a man who does something bad has actually shown himself to *be* bad. On the other hand, you might feel that his behaviour tells you more about the situation he finds himself in than it does about his intrinsic goodness or badness. In the psychological literature, the former kind of judgement is known as a 'dispositional attribution' (i.e. an attribution based on the dispositions of the person being judged), whereas the latter is known

SOME GOOD AND BAD PEOPLE IN THE COUNTRYSIDE

as a 'situational attribution' (i.e. one based on the situations which cause this person to act in a particular way). Of course, the two things might be combined to varying degrees. But the much-debated finding in psychology is that we have, on average, a preference for dispositional attributions when it comes to judging others. That is, we tend to judge them—and this is the 'error'—as if what they do automatically tells us something about *them*, ignoring or downplaying situational factors that might in fact provide better explanations for their actions.

It has been argued that we tend to make this error because, among other things, we are usually ignorant of the (often hidden) situational factors affecting others. It therefore takes a good deal of cognitive effort for us to figure such things out, as opposed to drawing inferences from easily observed 'good' or 'bad' actions. Meanwhile, it seems that people tend on average to explain their *own* behaviour with reference to context, that is, situationally: if I do something bad, it's because I was compelled by circumstance to do it, not because I am intrinsically bad. This whole complex is sometimes referred to as the 'actor–observer bias', meaning the tendency to interpret one's own behaviour with reference to context while interpreting the behaviour of others—uncharitably, we might say—with reference to character.

***

Most anthropologists (however sympathetic to psychology) would probably doubt that preferences of these kinds could be universal, and indeed for some time a number of psychologists, notably Richard Nisbett and his colleagues, have been investigating cultural variation with respect to them. In particular, it has been suggested that people from notionally 'individualistic' places are more prone to ignore context when explaining the behaviour of others than are people from notionally 'collectivist' ones, such as China and Japan. When presented with psychological tasks of various kinds, the former (i.e. the individualists) tend to pay attention to focal objects, such as the lead character in a given scenario, whereas the latter, as part of their more generally collectivistic/holistic outlook on life, tend to pay attention to underlying situations, such as the environments in which events unfold and/or the actions of a wider cast of people surrounding a lead character (Nisbett 2003).[2] To put it simply, then, those from collectivist places such as China should be less likely, according to this research, to ignore context and background when judging others; that is, they should be less likely to make the fundamental attribution error.

I find this fascinating, but I think something important could be added by reminding ourselves of an obvious fact: at least in the kinds of communities where anthropologists have typically carried out research, and among rural populations in particular, individuals—irrespective of culture—usually know a good deal, and often a great deal, about the situations affecting the behaviour of most of those they judge. This should, in theory, militate against them making context-free evaluations of the kind associated with the fundamental attribution error. I'll return to this point later.

Meanwhile, it is also worth noting a further 'cultural' point here. Let's assume that Nisbett, among others, is correct in saying that Chinese people apply a holistic view of the world to their understandings of others, which roughly means that 'context' is as important for them as 'action' when it comes to judging what others do (i.e. they don't judge others based simply on their actions). Plus, let's assume that, as I've just been saying, in rural China and Taiwan the 'context' of others' actions is, in any case, typically well known—so it shouldn't be cognitively difficult for people to take it into account. This implies that they should, on the whole, be very sympathetic judges! Against this, however, could be set the traditional Chinese notion that—almost regardless of underlying context—'action' is, in the end, a very significant thing, and in particular *ritual* action. As has often been noted, the Chinese cultural tradition does not neatly divide the form and content of ritual acts; that is, it really does mean something to *do* something, such as offering incense to the ancestors, whatever you may *think* about while doing it (cf. Sutton 2007). Certainly, when it comes to everyday life, people in rural China and Taiwan appear to be very concerned that proper form and etiquette should be followed, regardless of the private thoughts of individuals about the matter at hand. This raises a question, for me, about the extent to which, Chinese collectivism/holism notwithstanding, such people would be prepared to downgrade the significance of action in relation to context when it comes to judging others. It seems likely that in China to *do* something bad is to *be* bad (i.e. the action tells us about your essence). So, in short, while Chinese 'holism/collectivism' might, as Nisbett (2003) suggests, decrease the likelihood that the fundamental attribution error would be made, Chinese 'ritualism' might well actually increase it.

***

The second area of debate I want to mention (briefly, before moving on to some ethnography) is linked to the classic issue of determinism and free will. In at least some philosophical traditions—including the Aristotelian one—it is only considered proper to really blame somebody for what they do when they can be said to act freely, that is, without obvious constraint and with some knowledge of what they are doing. Conversely, it becomes harder, some would say impossible, to blame them if their actions are known to be 'determined' in some way. Among other possibilities, *theological determinism* (versions of which vary hugely, of course) suggests that a divine/spiritual force of some kind determines what happens, including what people do. *Scientific determinism* suggests that processes of natural causation (e.g. the laws of physics) determine what happens, including what people do. And then there is the rather different notion we could label *sociological determinism*. This suggests that human actions are determined not by gods or nature but rather by a combination of the social/historical/existential circumstances in which people find themselves—for example, by their low social standing, by the cruelty of their parents, by their ignorance (which results from the kind of education they did or did not receive), and so on. Note that a belief in a strong version of sociological determinism should, at least in theory, militate against us making the fundamental attribution error, because it would dispose us always to look for contextual clues to behaviour. Perhaps more to the point, if we believed in a strong version of *any* of these three determinisms (theological or scientific or sociological), we might find it hard to ever really blame a person for what he did. We would rationally know that his behaviour was determined, in a substantive sense, by factors—determinants— outside his control.

However, the philosopher Peter Strawson (2008 [1974]) has argued that to put the problem of moral judgement and 'holding responsible' in these terms (i.e. as an issue of the degree of determinism) is to over-intellectualize ethics and morality, as if ordinary people thought about the problem of blame in a philosophical way. In an influential essay, he suggests that our moral evaluations derive instead from the (obvious) fact that we, as humans, care a great deal about how other people treat us. We are embedded in interpersonal relationships and we *necessarily* have what he calls 'participant reactive attitudes' towards the actions of those around us. (By the way, Strawson's emotion-focused approach to morality and responsibility is close in certain respects to Edward Westermarck's (1906/1908) anthropological approach.) Moreover, Strawson suggests that, even if we wanted to, we couldn't simply do away with these participant reactive attitudes—for example, on the 'objective' grounds that everything people do is determined by external causes—because to do so would seriously impair our ability to live life as we know it. To put it simply, then, Strawson treats morality less as an intellectual problem and more as an interpersonal and emotional one and moreover as something which is always embedded in particular forms of collective life (Strawson 2008 [1974]; McKenna and Russell 2008; Baker 2010; Stafford 2010).

***

While I was living in north-east China during 1992–3, I made a brief side trip to a relatively isolated village in a mountain region, quite a few hours away by bus, where I stayed for three or four nights, no more. In spite of the fact I have quite limited knowledge of the people I met there, I want to describe a series of encounters I had in that place.

Soon after I arrived, I was walking on a pathway between farmhouses when two very friendly schoolboys came up and started talking to me. They seemed incredibly excited to meet a Chinese-speaking foreigner and kept running in and out of their house to bring me little gifts, first some green onions, then some cornbread, then some hot water, before finally dragging me inside the house to meet their 87-year-old grandmother, who declared that the boys were 'happy to the point of collapse' to see a guest from so far away—*tamen lehuai le!* They proceeded to make me another gift, a little three-dimensional charm put together from a scrap of cardboard and some brightly coloured thread.

The boys' family consisted of their grandmother, her son and his wife (i.e. their father and mother), and the two boys themselves, students in the sixth and eighth grades. They lived in a rickety but rather beautiful wooden house that they said was over 200 years old. They were *nongmin* (poor farmers), but in the post-Mao reform era their circumstances had improved markedly after they started raising chickens in a spare bedroom and selling eggs in the nearest market town (their father went there every morning in the darkness by bicycle). They were planning to build a new house but would keep the old one for the chickens.

The boys' mother and father soon arrived, and the six of us had some polite if rather generic exchanges about Chinese traditions and differences with the West. Among other things, I asked the boys if they planned to *shanyang fumu*, take care of their parents in old age. They replied earnestly that yes, of course, they would, at which point their mother commented drily, 'Children always say this—it doesn't mean they will do it!'

***

It was agreed that I would come back the next day for a meal with the head of the household, the father, and I duly showed up in the late morning. Although it was a school day, the eldest son (the eighth-grader) and a couple of the boy's friends were also there, obviously having skipped classes. The grandmother and her daughter-in-law mostly stayed out of sight except to serve food.

We had barely started eating a rather modest lunch when the boys' teacher walked in—agitated and a bit under the influence of drink, I thought—and began sharply criticizing the boys for running off from school, even under these exceptional circumstances (he clearly knew that a foreign guest was the excuse). The teacher, a fidgety man in his fifties wearing a kind of military-style outfit, was made to sit down and join us for lunch, of course. Even as he began to eat and drink, he continued with a little speech about the boys' performance in school and his feeling that it was his duty to be harsh with them in order to keep them from turning bad. This was especially true of our host's eldest son, who had a lot of potential, the teacher said, and for whom he had very high hopes. He intended to push him especially hard.

As the teacher rambled on, the boy's anxious-looking parents (his mother was serving food and hovering around the table at this point) smiled, nodded and spoke in complete agreement with all that he said, filling his glass with rice wine and to some extent treating him rather than me as the guest of honour. The teacher relaxed a bit and pointed

107

out that in this part of the world you do, after all, have to drink when eating together, because otherwise the occasion will 'not be meaningful enough' (*bu gou yisi*). As for the boys' mother and grandmother not joining us at the table, well, he said, that was the tradition here because women are 'a class below' (*xia yi deng*).

He went on to tell me about his life as a teacher, noting that he earned 200 kuai per month (something like $1 per day). This, he said, would be just about enough for him and his family were it not for the problem of *ganli*, that is, the problem of having to attend and take gifts to the ritual celebrations (weddings, funerals, house-building ceremonies) held by all of his friends, relatives, neighbours and colleagues. In the country-side, all these people want to 'grab your money' (*naqian*) when it comes to such occasions, he said.

As the conversation went on, I was pushed to eat and drink more but kept saying I was full. The grandmother said, 'We feel so happy when you eat!' (*ni chi anmen jiu le!*).

***

After the meal, the boys returned to school with their teacher, their father went off to do some work and I stayed behind to chat with the 87-year-old grandmother and her daughter-in-law. Among other things, they were somewhat critical of the family I was actually staying with dur-ing my brief visit—their nearest non-kin neighbours, as I remember the location of the houses. They pointed out that whereas they themselves were poor *nongmin*, these neighbours (local administrators) had quite a good and secure income because 'they are earning government cash'. They felt it revealed something bad about the head of this household, their neighbour, that he once failed to use his connections to secure a place in a good school for his own relative's son when he was asked to do so. Moreover, they were annoyed that once, when the daughter-in-law was bitten by this neighbour's dog, he had offered them a negligible amount of cash by way of compensation.

We talked about the system of gift-giving in the countryside, that is, about 'the problem of *ganli*' which the boys' teacher had mentioned over lunch. Because they have a large number of relatives in the area, the women said, a good proportion of the family's income is spent on *ganli*. However, the resulting network of relatives, friends and associates does more or less guarantee, as they recognized, a significant level of assistance when it is required, for example, when they need cash in order to build a new house or to marry off their sons.

At one point in our conversation, the daughter-in-law stepped outside to deal with some matter and the old woman immediately turned to me, rather conspiratorially. She said that, basically, things had really gone downhill during her lifetime. She came from what had been a big, prosperous family, but the chaotic history of this part of the world—specifically the era of Japanese rule followed by the civil war and its aftermath—had seriously disrupted all of that. According to her neighbours, this family had indeed been reduced to genuine poverty up until a few years ago. Now things had improved, but the old woman still found various things annoying—for example, the way her son and daughter-in-law were raising their children. They actually hit the boys! And then she, as the grandmother, had to intervene to try to protect (*hu*) them, showing them how to be good, upright people by example. I had the impression from her tone of voice that she was not terribly impressed with her own son and her daughter-in-law, but what can you do? At least the two grandsons were promising.

Later, when I got back to the house where I was staying, my hosts pointed out that although the family I had met was indeed an interesting and admirable one, not least in relation to their recent economic successes, they were not perfect. They found it shameful that an 87-year-old grandmother was still, so far as they understood, being made to work around the house, preparing food and cleaning up in spite of her greatly advanced age.

***

The purpose of my side trip to this village in north-east China was not to study morality and ethics as such. However, my field notes over a few days illustrate the extent to which moral/ethical acts and evaluations in one form or another pervade the everyday life of people there. In quick succession we encounter the ethics of dealing with unknown guests (i.e. with me), the ethics of dealing with *known* guests (the teacher), the ethics of intergenerational support (the boys with their parents, their parents with their grandmother), the ethics of teacher–pupil relationships, the ethics of gift-giving and reciprocity, the ethics of gender, the ethics of neighbourly disputes and probably other forms of ethics that don't immediately occur to me.

While much of the explicitly moral/ethical behaviour and commentary I have cited may seem routine or even stereotypic, one doesn't have to scratch far beneath the surface to find complexities and nuance in it.

For instance, on the question of intergenerational support: the boys formulaically say they will provide care for their parents as they age, but their mother responds drily (even sarcastically) to this claim. Meanwhile, the neighbours observe—without me asking—that the family's treatment of their 87-year-old grandmother is improper. To me, she seems happy enough; however, she spontaneously points out (in the first and last sustained conversation we will ever have) that she dislikes some things about her life with her son and daughter-in-law, at least hinting, or so I felt, that they are beneath her own level. Now, I presume she has quite a subtle theory of *why* they might be beneath her level, if that is what she thinks of them. Could it be put down to their innate character or aptitude, to a lack of proper schooling during their childhoods, to the bad influence of others? Surely she has some ideas. Meanwhile, the neighbours (the people I was living with) presumably know very well factors that might help explain *why* this particular family treats the old woman as they do, making her work. For example, they know that the daughter-in-law has serious health problems which sometimes prevent her from working, even around the house; they know, more generally, that in very poor families everybody has to pitch in; they know that the level of formal schooling of the people in this household (and therefore of their 'culture' and understanding of proper morality, in Chinese terms) is considerably lower than their own, and so forth.

In short, the grandmother (if she wanted to) and the neighbours (if they wanted to) could be generous in judging the actions of her son and his wife. And, perhaps more to the point, if they judge them harshly, it is certainly *not* for lack of information about the context or situation or circumstances in which they live. To relate this back to the debate about the fundamental attribution error: even if Chinese culture inculcates, in individuals, a 'holistic' way of seeing the world (which leads them to look for context and background when explaining the behaviour of others) and even if in rural communities the context of others' behaviours is, in most cases, perfectly well known, it's as if there is something else pushing in the opposite direction. That is, it's as if something is pushing people not to give *too* much weight to context, at least not if doing so would lead to them having to suspend ethical judgement and forgive everything.

***

Having said this, people often forgive a good deal. Consider the situation of the teacher, both as a teacher and as a guest. He arrives, slightly drunk (I think) and berates the students for skipping class, knowing perfectly well, of course, why they have done so. It is a performance. And then he performs what is, in effect, a 'face-giving' move for the parents: praising, in front of a foreign guest, the ability and potential of their eldest son, saying that he, the teacher, is strict with this talented boy simply because he wants to stop him from going bad. The parents, for their part, treat the teacher with respect, plying him with food and drink. They even say that he should by all means hit their son if that's what it takes to discipline him! Ah, he says, that sort of thing regrettably isn't allowed any more.

All of this is fairly standard stuff. One thing that isn't stated out loud, however, is the almost universal view in rural China—one likely shared by the boys' mother and father—that 'local schools' (wherever they are) are never as good as those located farther away and that, more specifically, the level or 'quality' of the teachers in them is not up to scratch (cf. the discussion by Johnston in Chapter 3 of the migration of students away from the Chinese countryside).[3] The teacher in question here was an older man, likely a relic of the Maoist era, badly paid, rather shabbily dressed, someone who might well have been treated with contempt, even by farmers—not least for barging into their house in the middle of the day in a somewhat aggressive manner. Instead, he was treated with some care and even warmth.

Perhaps this was simply pragmatic: they wouldn't want to annoy their son's teacher nor, for that matter, would they seek to cause unnecessary problems with anybody from the local community. There may also be an element of 'ritualism' here, I would guess. To be rude to someone who shows up in this way, in the middle of a meal, would be an aggressive breach of etiquette and would reflect badly on the ethical standing of the hosts, no matter what they really thought about their guest. But I think there may well be an element of generosity in their reactions too, which amounts to an awareness of the context within which someone like this man (and maybe *this* man in particular) becomes a rural schoolteacher, dresses badly, perhaps gains a reputation for drinking and behaves as he does. In other words, the flip side of holding responsible—something we do because to stop doing so would diminish (in the sense intended by Strawson) our collective life—is the process of holding back from holding responsible. People in rural communities are generally very aware of the contexts which cause people to fail, socially and morally, and it therefore isn't difficult for them to be generous, at least part of the time. Just as my field notes are filled with accounts of people judging their relatives, neighbours and friends rather harshly, so too are they filled with accounts of people refraining from saying what could all too easily be said. The tension between these two kinds of reactions to what other people do is surely an important site where ordinary ethics is played out, perhaps especially in rural communities where people live at close quarters with others for decades at a stretch.

***

By way of conclusion, I would like to return briefly to the question of determinism. As I noted, we should, in theory, find it harder to blame somebody for what they do if we believe in a strong version of 'theological', 'scientific' or 'sociological' determinism. Many of the people I've known in rural Taiwan and China accept a version of all three. They certainly invoke social/sociological factors in explaining, sometimes excusing, the behaviour of those around them; in particular, they seem very clear that economic standing can have a lot to do with how people end up behaving. But then they also accept a kind of theological determinism—more specifically, the idea that 'fate' (which, among other things, helps determine your social circumstances, such as your level of wealth or power) is set at birth and only altered with some difficulty. This Chinese theological determinism, moreover, is broadly naturalistic in outlook, and so it shares quite a lot with the sort of scientific determinism a philosopher might invoke. That is, it is a theory of the natural forces and patterns that cause the universe to be as it is at any particular moment, something which sets the general framework within which human fate and human action unfold.

That these three interlinked determinisms are *not* used to excuse everything everybody does is a vindication, perhaps, of Strawson's perspective on morality—which, as I have noted, stresses the 'participant reactive attitudes' that motivate our judgements of those around us and keep us from invoking objective reasons for not blaming these people for anything. Against this background, deciding that the people around us are 'good ones' and 'bad ones' may be not only psychologically satisfying (since it resolves a tension surrounding the generic difficulty of attributing blame, once the context of people's actions is taken into account), but even socially necessary. Equally, however, *not* attributing blame—perhaps a more challenging proposition in psychological terms—can be said to have many social uses, and I would certainly say that it plays a crucial part in ordinary ethics in rural China and Taiwan.

NOTES

1. See Ross (1977), Jones and Harris (1977) and Gilbert and Malone (1995).
2. Interestingly, it seems that people who have been raised in a tradition which, in some respects, is as 'Western' as it is 'Chinese'—e.g. those raised in Hong Kong—can be primed to think in Western or Chinese terms about these things. That is, if they are shown 'Western' images and then asked to make moral judgements, they will on average make use of dispositional (i.e. context-free) attributions, whereas if they are shown 'Chinese' images they will on average make use of situational (i.e. context-led) attributions (Nisbett 2003: 111–35).
3. At the time of my fieldwork in the early 1990s, teaching was held to be an especially bad profession, underpaid and undervalued, with none of the potential for financial success found in other professions during the post-Mao economic reforms. The situation since has changed markedly, with improvements in teachers' salaries and conditions of work. But it still remains the case that schools in remote locations are typically derided.

REFERENCES

Baker, J. (2010), 'Philosophical Comments on Charles Stafford and Francesca Merlan', in M. Lambek (ed.), *Ordinary Ethics: Anthropology, Language and Action*, New York: Fordham University Press.

Gilbert, D. T., and Malone, P. S. (1995), 'The Correspondence Bias', *Psychological Bulletin*, 117/1: 21–38.

Jones, E. E., and Harris, V. (1977), 'The Attribution of Attitudes', *Journal of Experimental Social Psychology*, 3: 1–24.

McKenna, M., and Russell, P. (2008), *Free Will and Reactive Attitudes: Perspectives on P. F. Strawson's 'Freedom & Resentment'*, Farnham, UK: Ashgate.

Nisbett, R. (2003), *The Geography of Thought: How Asians and Westerners Think Differently . . . and Why*, London: Nicholas Brealey.

Ross, L. (1977), 'The Intuitive Psychologist and His Shortcomings: Distortions in the Attribution Process', in L. Berkowitz (ed.), *Advances in Experimental Social Psychology*, vol. x, New York: Academic Press.

Stafford, C. (1995), *The Roads of Chinese Childhood*, Cambridge: Cambridge University Press.

Stafford, C. (2010), 'The Punishment of Ethical Behavior', in M. Lambek (ed.), *Ordinary Ethics: Anthropology, Language and Action*, New York: Fordham University Press.

Strawson, P. (2008 [1974]), *Freedom and Resentment and Other Essays*, London: Routledge.

Sutton, D. L. (2007), 'Ritual, Cultural Standardization, and Orthopraxy in China: Considering James L. Watson's Ideas', *Modern China*, 33/1: 3–21.

Westermarck, E. (1906–8), *The Origin and Development of the Moral Ideas*, 2 vols, London: Macmillan.

CHAPTER 7

THE ETHICS OF ENVY AVOIDANCE IN CONTEMPORARY CHINA

Hui Zhang

Envy, according to Planalp (1999), is, on the whole, seen as an 'immoral emotion' in the Western philosophical tradition because 'it is often malicious—wanting to deprive the other person of something you value rather than acquiring it yourself'. Consequently, 'people with advantages [in society] . . . serve to benefit by demonising envy, whereas people who want a more level playing field serve to benefit from encouraging it' (Planalp 1999: 175–6). On the other hand, institutionalized forms of envy, as Wolf (2001) describes them—such as 'evil eye' attacks among the Amhara (Reminick 1974), black magic practices in Mongolia (High 2008) and the invocation of sorcery and witchcraft among the Zulu (Berglund 1976) or the Desana (Buchillet 2004)—are often described as punishment for the immoral act[1] of those who are envied. Following Planalp, I therefore want to distinguish here between the sin of envying others and the sin of being envied oneself. As a violation of the Ten Commandments and one of the 'seven deadly sins' within the Judaeo-Christian tradition, the sin of envy may be characterized as an un-neighbourly desire for other people's possessions or attributes, the desire to deprive them of these things and (in some cases) the fact of acting on these desires. By contrast, the sin of *being envied*, at least within the Chinese tradition—where institutionalized forms of envy are generally lacking—normally comes from the failure to conceal one's desirable possessions or attributes, thus providing a reminder of other people's inferiority and provoking them to commit dishonourable acts.

A well-known Chinese saying (drawn from classical literature) sets out a persuasive moral lesson: 'If the tree stands out in a forest, the wind will surely wreck it; if sand spreads out from the shore, floods will wash it away; if your behaviour is more worthy than that of others, others will attack it' (*muxiuyulin, fengbicuizhi; duichuyuan, liubituanzhi; xinggaoyuren, zhongbifeizhi*).[2] By highlighting the risks of being (or appearing to be) better than others, this saying warns us of the dangers of standing out. And by drawing irrefutable examples from the natural world, it implies that punishment for the sin of being pre-eminent is inevitable.

This, however, should not be taken to mean that success is not encouraged or that one should not aim to be pre-eminent. Rather, one should be aware of the extra price one might have to pay for success. Lu Xun, one of the most famous Chinese writers and social critics of the early twentieth century, recognized the existence of such an attributed sin (i.e. the sin of provoking envy in others) but denounced it as narrow-minded and regressive. As he wrote sarcastically in one of his articles, 'If something [in China] seems to be slightly eminent, there is someone holding a sword to cut it flat.'[3] Public opinion was deemed to play a critical role in exerting such a form of moral punishment in China. As the saying goes, 'One can die under [the effect of] the tongues of others' (*shetou xiamian neng siren*). In criticizing behaviour that might foster 'malicious envy' (*jidu*),[4] China could be said to possess what Schoeck (1969) calls 'a carefully institutionalized attitude designed to avert envy'. That is, 'anyone setting too high a value on his abilities or his stamina perpetrates the social sin of regarding himself as better than his fellow men' and will be punished for it (Schoeck 1969: 55).

Yu Qiuyu, a well-known contemporary Chinese writer, has also pointed out that although someone might be talented and brave enough to fight thousands of enemies, they (as Chinese) were undoubtedly aware that once they were targeted by 'malicious envy' (*jidu*), everything could quickly turn to ashes. He further stated that the wisdom inherent in life in ancient China had much to do with the avoidance of the envy of others. The hostile actions of envious people were often seen to be socially acceptable, while the objects of their envy were often widely condemned. Even today, Yu says, the *targets* of envy and jealousy may be rebuked as arrogant or ignorant while the people who envy them are said to represent public opinion. The end result of this has been that people who are envied are often made to feel guilty and may be held in public contempt while, by contrast, the people who envy them are entitled to feel self-righteous, supported as they are by the masses.[5]

What is the basis of these attitudes? Helen Siu (1990) reminds us that at the core of traditional Chinese culture is 'a set of rites and mutual obligations within the cardinal social relationships (ruler-ruled, parent-child, husband-wife, older siblings-younger siblings, friend-friend)' (8). Furthermore, 'human fulfilment comes with the realisation of these relationships through moral self-cultivation and social practice. Cultural vitality emerges from this inner force and extends outward to order family, society and universe' (8). The fulfilment of both mutual obligations and self-cultivation is essential, but these two aspects do not necessarily come together without contradictions. For people who are envied, the problem is that one's self interests have breached one's relational responsibilities to/for others, a situation that is not easily dealt with. As Harrell rightly summarized, the ' "Maoist" mentality of class-struggle-based moral absolutism' has both discredited the 'Confucian' morality of graded obligations and provided the background for the phase of post-Mao recovery (Harrell 2001: 143). Therefore, in reform-era China, the difficulty of compromising one's self interest to one's relational responsibilities is apparently manifested in the tension between the desire of individuals to enjoy and celebrate their newly found success and the moral responsibility (for government officials in particular) to maintain socialist ideals of equality. As it might be put, 'We are not meant to be *this* unequal in China, and the widening inequality we see is only supposed to be temporary.'

This chapter is based on ethnographic fieldwork I carried out in Hebei province—where, as in the rest of China, inequality has greatly increased in the post-Mao era. My focus is on the avoidance of envy. I introduce the concepts of good *renyuan* (good 'social relationships') and *suzhi* ('quality', as in the expression 'a person of high quality'), both of which have been prevalent in Chinese moral discourses in recent years. I suggest that, in the local understanding, one should actively cultivate good *renyuan* in order to avoid provoking malicious envy in others. But this theory of good *renyuan* is only felt to work when the potentially envious others are individuals of 'high quality'—that is, when they are knowledgeable, understanding, civilized, and so forth. If this is not the case, they may indeed be envious and malicious actions may follow. My discussion of *renyuan* and *suzhi* will demonstrate, among other things, that local people are very much aware of the moral responsibility they have to avoid provoking envy in others.

GOOD *RENYUAN*, NO 'RED EYE'

In the summer of 2008, as we sat in a Western-style cafe, Xu Shuming, a middle school teacher in her early thirties, seemed genuinely interested in discussing envy and 'red-eye' with me. Red-eye (*yanhong*) is a collo-quial expression for *jidu*, which I translate as 'malicious envy' (by way of contrast with mild envy, which is not normally seen to be dangerous). She told me, 'If you handle [social relationships] in the correct way, there won't be any red-eye.' For her, having good *renyuan* (again, hav-ing good social relationships—in effect, being popular with others) was the key question when it came to both attracting and avoiding red-eye. If you have good *renyuan*, she explained, red-eye will not be directed at you even if you have things that people envy. And in those cases where red-eye *is* provoked, she said, if you know how to 'behave properly' (*hui zuoren*) the situation should be manageable. Otherwise, those with red-eye will 'look for ways to bring you down' (*zhao jihui xiashou*).

Xu Shuming went on to explain: suppose a teacher was privately tu-toring eighty or ninety students during the school break for extra money while other teachers had far fewer students or no students at all. Paid tutoring and organized classes outside of official school education are strictly forbidden by the regulations. Therefore, this teacher might well be denounced to her school. But if she was turned in by someone, this showed two things: first, this teacher was bad at social relationships (*re-nyuan cha*) and, second, as a result he or she had been 'red-eyed' by someone for attracting many students for private tutoring and making more money than the rest. As it happens, Xu Shuming did extracur-ricular tutoring. Her own strategies for cultivating *renyuan* and avoiding red-eye were as follows:

> If I am actually able to earn fifty thousand RMB,[6] I make sure I only make forty thousand RMB. You cannot be unjust to others [*duibu qiren*]. I need to employ other teachers to tutor the students who have come to me since I am only a Chinese teacher and cannot teach all the subjects. I may give out 200 RMB extra to employ teachers over

holidays or festivals. *Renyuan* is a long-term investment. You need to share some of the money you earn with others [to avoid red-eye]. Never forget the presents you are supposed to give and don't say bad things behind other people's backs. [When eating with others], you should place the right dishes in front of the right people [*jianren xia caidie*]. For the people who like chatting, chat with them; for the people who like drinking, invite them for drinks. If you have good human relations, people may envy you [i.e. in a non-malicious way] but they won't normally have red-eye. Red-eye will normally be directed at those who suddenly get rich and who themselves despise other people. If you know how to behave, there won't be any problem with red-eye [*ren zuodehao, bu cunzai yanhong de wenti*]. Be generous to others and then, even though you are raking in lots of money, others won't mind. Otherwise, you are encouraging jealousy and hatred [*jihen*].

Another example given by Xu Shuming of red-eye in the teachers' community involved what are known as 'group appraisals' (*minzhu pingyi*). Large-scale meetings are held in which professional rankings of teachers are determined along with admission to the Communist Party. If one had evidently performed well in terms of teaching and work abilities but received surprisingly few votes at such meetings, she said, this was probably because of bad *renyuan* and red-eye. 'It is important how others think about you, especially when candidates are under equal conditions. If you have good relationships with others you will win in those competitions,' Xu added.

The art of social relationships in China has already been thoroughly examined and analysed by Mayfair Mei-hui Yang (1994) and others. For Yang, '*Guanxixue* [i.e. the explicit art of social relationships] involves the exchange of gifts, favours and banquets; the cultivation of personal relationships and networks of mutual dependence; the manufacturing of obligation and indebtedness' (Yang 1994: 6). These practices and the ideas behind them reveal 'the primacy and binding power [in China] of personal relationships and their importance in meeting the needs and desires of everyday life'. Moreover, when taken together they represent an 'underlying cultural assumption shared by Chinese everywhere, on the mainland before and after the Communist Revolution of 1949' (Yang 1994: 6).

In her analysis, however, Yang has arguably underestimated the importance of good *renyuan*—in effect, an individual's level of popularity or success with others. In my experience, this has a direct connection to the effectiveness of one's *guanxixue* practices. In other words, for Yang, *guanxixue* is about people cultivating human relations by employing certain ethics, tactics and etiquette to actively and consciously get what they need. In this chapter it is argued that if people do not at the same time inspire personal popularity, any of the gains achieved in this manner may yet be sabotaged by red-eye. Therefore, *guanxixue* is not only about actively acquiring but also about passively protecting. As Xu Shuming noted very clearly, 'Red-eye, in essence, is a problem of your relationships with other people [*renyuan wenti*].' In the following sections I will discuss how *renyuan* is practised to fend off red-eye in a 'model village' where, despite rapid growth in the overall prosperity of the community, individual variation in wealth creates tensions and breeds envy.

THE MODEL VILLAGE

Wang Village was the envy of everyone, it seemed. It was not only a 'model village' at the national level but had also been named the foremost village within the county, in which two other villages, Lanying and Xitai, were located. In 2006, the village committee invested 0.13 billion RMB in order to purchase a formerly state-owned iron ore company; the gross annual value of village-owned enterprises subsequently reached 0.3 billion RMB in 2007. By contrast, the assets of Xitai were valued at no more than about 20,000 or 30,000 RMB. The collective assets of Wang Village were worth 0.16 billion RMB in 2007 and the net revenue of the village was already 40 million RMB in 2006, with per capita income of 8,000 RMB.

When I visited Lanying and Xitai during my fieldwork, the villagers told me how they envied the lifestyle of those in Wang Village, where it seemed that the best possible solution for rural dwellers had been achieved—that is, they had a city/modern lifestyle in a non-urban setting. Wang Village was well known in the region mostly because the party secretary, Wang, was a local celebrity accorded hero-like status. He was elected as a representative for the 15th and 16th National People's Congress, which was extremely unusual for an official from the village level. Numerous awards were conferred on Wang in recognition of the exceptional progress he had brought to his community, including 'National Model Worker', 'Excellent Provincial Communist Party Member' and 'Provincial Ten Outstanding Youths', to name just a few. Wang's story is widely known and he is often featured on local television broadcasts.

In the eyes of local people, Lanying and Xitai were lagging far behind Wang Village, and whenever they saw news on TV about Wang Village, they would comment that this was how villages should look in the future. I was told by some of those who had worked in Wang Village or transported iron ore there that their dream was for their own community to be like Wang Village in a few years, so that they could all live in multi-storey buildings, enjoy subsidies for festivals and have pensions for everyone over sixty. The people of Wang Village were aware of their high profile and of how other people envied them. They were proud to live in Wang Village and had a degree of self-confidence rare for rural residents given the general rural–urban hierarchy in China.

But within Wang Village, it was still sometimes a case of *qiongdeqiong, fudefu* ('the poor get poorer, the rich get richer'), as Wang himself later told me. In Wang Village, 400 households out of 480 ran their own businesses while 30 had private cars. Besides the collective enterprises, there were seventeen enterprises owned by individual villagers, ten of which were large-scale, with a gross product value amounting to 0.1 billion RMB in total. For those who owned mine-related businesses, the price of one ton of iron ore was 660 RMB in 2007. About two months later they could easily sell up to 1,000 tons and the profits could be in the tens of thousands. In the meantime, there were around 1,700 migrant workers in Wang Village, this being almost equal to the number of local villagers. In general, those working as wage-labourers were slightly higher paid in Wang Village than in Xitai, wages ranging from 2,000 to 3,000 RMB a month there. Lao Li, a middle-aged man who was staying in his daughter's house,[7] told me,

It is good here, but at the same time you need to spend money on everything. In a normal village, you may only spend 10 or 20 Kuai [RMB] per month on electricity but here it costs at least 100. You have more electronic devices of course, but they all cost money to run. Our refrigerator, for example, isn't even plugged in. I said to my daughter that in winter we certainly don't need to use it but my daughter told me that in summer we don't dare use it either [because of the high cost of electricity].

Newly found wealth meant that the cost of living in Wang Village was much higher than in any of the other nearby villages. This simultaneously meant that for those who were less wealthy, life could be difficult, as the case of Lao Li indicated. The prices of vegetables, food and transportation, so I was told, were all much more expensive. Sometimes prices were even higher than in the nearest city. For example, there were many cars lined up in the main street for private hire; for a ride that in other places would cost 10 RMB, it cost double that in Wang Village. Wang's wife, Aunt Zhao, said to me that people knew Wang Village had money, and hence many just came for the purposes of peddling and raised prices while they were at it.[8]

Despite its overall economic success, Wang Village was the one place where envy was not especially evident to me and where I rarely found anyone who would discuss it. This could in large part have been due to my close connection with Wang—I lived with his family while doing fieldwork in Wang Village.[9] Indeed, I could only talk really freely to strangers in the community by concealing the fact of where I was living. Moreover, since Wang was perhaps the most 'enviable' person in the village and I was closely attached to him, it seemed I was supposed to avoid discussing envy—because this might have invited unexpected malicious envy or hostile actions. Still, this connection also meant that I was able to observe the people who were enjoying most the benefits of the economic success of the village and who therefore most needed, one might predict, to fend off the envy of others.

CULTIVATION OF GOOD RENYUAN

Wang's family had a three-bedroom apartment, fully decorated with a television in each bedroom and a 32-inch television in the living room. It was also packed with jade, green plants, a leather sofa, gold ornaments and various (expensive) boxed beverages. In fact, there were boxes everywhere—boxes of shoes, fruit, alcohol, snacks and cosmetics. At the beginning, I thought this was typical of the abundance of goods one would find in a prosperous village of this kind. Later, however, when

I got the chance to visit a neighbour living downstairs, some relatives of Wang and other people I met in the park, I was surprised to learn that this level of wealth was in fact rare. Despite the fact that Wang Village had a relatively high cost of living, my host arranged for me to eat breakfast, lunch and dinner in various restaurants nearly every day. Usually I accompanied Aunt Zhao when she went out, and we often found ourselves surrounded by some truly wealthy people. They had their own businesses, they could earn tens of thousands in a day, they travelled, they chatted over the Internet, they went out fishing, they were talking about plastic surgery and, most importantly, they spent money 'like running water'(*huaqian ru liushui*), as they themselves put it.

Given the fame and wealth the Wang family had, it was to be expected that they might be secretly or openly envied by many, including close friends. I was having meals with Aunt Zhao and her female friends almost every day; most of these people were quite well off and hardly ever cooked at home. Once, Aunt Zhao and I were eating with Lan and her husband and talking about the price of iron ore when Lan's husband suddenly burst out, 'The money we earn in a year can't equal what you earn in a month, no, twenty days. The money we earn is called "bitter money" [*xinku qian*], "tiresome money" [*shoulei qian*].' Aunt Zhao quickly replied, 'The money we spend in a month is equal to what you spend in a year, why don't you reckon it that way!' Lan and her husband stayed silent for a while and then switched to another topic of conversation. What Aunt Zhao resented about the comment, in my view, was the connotation that the money she earned did not come with its own forms of 'bitterness'. This implied that her wealth was not justified, in some way, and that it could therefore be a target of red-eye. Her reaction to the complaint was not directly to deny the point, however. By saying that they spent much more than the Lans, Aunt Zhao implied that no matter how much or how easily one earns money, in the end we are still all the same. What Aunt Zhao did here was not exactly a case of 'excessive modesty' or 'self-deprecation', as suggested by Schoeck (1969: 55), but it nonetheless shared the same spirit. By exposing how much she spent (a high proportion of it, as Lan and her husband would know, on others), she conveyed the intended message that 'after all, I am not as rich as you imagined, and I have my own worries'.

Another day, there were ten women around the table. One of these women said to Aunt Zhao and two of the others, 'Now, I'm no longer able to go out with you. Look what you eat and what you wear, I can't afford it anymore.' Aunt Zhao responded in a deeply hurt tone, 'If you put it that way, you are wrong. If I have things to eat, I won't let you starve; if I have cars to travel in, I won't let you walk.' Another woman picked up the conversation and said,

> You certainly shouldn't think of Zhao in that way. You know, once I was having dinner with the wife of the head of the county and she was really arrogant. I was thinking: who are you? In our village we are equal [*pingqipingzuo*] to the wife of our party secretary and our party secretary even goes to the National Congress! Where did your sense of being special come from [*you shenmo liaobuqi*]?

Unequal living conditions and political status were clearly singled out in this conversation. What Aunt Zhao was trying to achieve was the playing down of these distinctions and the merging of these differences. She did this by offering to share what she had; what her friend also did was to stress Aunt Zhao's nice gesture of treating everyone equally.

Obviously these are performative occasions; that is, people are saying and doing things that may or may not correspond with their inner feelings. Perhaps some of these people were straightforwardly jealous of the Wang family's wealth and prestige. In my experience, however, Aunt Zhao did seem to have very good *renyuan* in the village and had clearly befriended many people there. She was extremely generous and outgoing—it wasn't just for show. When we had breakfast, if there was someone she knew sitting at the next table, she would pay for them; at a banquet she once said to all her friends that if Wang was elected as the representative for the National People's Congress again, she would treat everyone to dinner. She also once told her friends at lunch that she liked people to call her by her name and that if anyone called her 'the wife of the party secretary', her heart sank as this showed that they were treating her like an outsider (*wairen*) and not with their true hearts (*jiaoxin*). Generosity, treating other people with overt respect and as equals, sometimes pointing out to others the negative side of having money (such as having more obligations to spend it), sharing wealth whenever possible (e.g. in the form of gifts)—these are all ways in which a person such as Aunt Zhao might try to maintain good *renyuan* with others and subsequently avoid the danger of provoking red-eye in them.

LOW-QUALITY (*SUZHI*) PEOPLE AND UNDISGUISED ENVY

By cultivating good *renyuan*, then, malicious envy will hopefully be avoided; but obviously this cannot always be the case. Party Secretary Wang once confessed to me that unpleasant feelings targeted towards him and his family had indeed, from time to time, made him not want to be the party secretary anymore. Meanwhile, in the villages of Lanying and Xitai some overt disputes, arguably motivated by malicious envy, were not avoided through the careful practice of *renyuan* either. Of course, it is one thing for rich people to try get along with others in the ways I have described—by being charming and nice on social occasions—and another thing for government officials to deal with criticisms from the communities they are meant to serve. And yet, in terms of the model of envy I am setting out in this chapter, there are some very clear connections between the two things. Local administrators were concerned, as I found out, that their privileged position would provoke the envy of others, and they actively sought to avert this through handling their social relationships (*renyuan*) well. However, in spite of their attempts to do this, there was an outbreak of disagreements, uncooperative behaviour and overt conflict—arguably motivated by red-eye, by jealousy directed at officials and/or those who had been successful. This outcome was explained to me with reference to the 'low quality' of some of those involved.

It should be noted here that in China the direct involvement of political authorities in the construction of society and its ethics is taken for granted. As Helen Siu (1990) has pointed out,

> The realisation that the vast empire [of China] was held together more by a shared cultural heritage and less by military might or legalistic-political administration led the philosopher Bertrand Russell and the sociologist Robert Park, both visitors to China in the Republican period, to comment that the 'Chinese polity is a cultural phenomenon'. (Siu 1990: 7)

Certainly, this is not to deny that China lacked 'despots who obtain compliance by force', though. The issue here is 'the nature and the bases of that power and the means by which they exercise it' (Siu 1990: 7). Most importantly, the responsibilities of local administrators are not only political but also moral. Wang and other village leaders are not only supposed to abide by the rules of governance, they are also expected to represent high moral ideals.

During my fieldwork, tension between the local government and the villagers was in fact rather intense in all three villages. In Lanying and Xitai, few people seemed to trust or have any faith in the village committee, and it was not difficult to hear people complaining about how corrupt government officials were.[10] To put it simply, the government officials were generally charged with enriching themselves while ignoring the fact that the villagers were sharing none of the benefits from the wealth brought by mining activities (thus showing the officials' poor *renyuan* skills). The cadres, aware of these accusations, constantly defended themselves by justifying their endeavours, listing things they had, in reality, done to serve the villagers' needs and depicting the villagers' requests as never ending and nonsensical. For instance, the cadres would argue that the villagers' requests for money from mining companies that had nothing whatever to do with Xitai village were illogical. Such requests, they said, were motivated by red-eye for those who had been successful and who, as the cadres saw it, had been proper in their dealings with others. Moreover, the root cause of the envious attitudes and actions of the villagers was the 'low quality' (*di suzhi*) of the villagers themselves. Note here that the moral discourse has shifted from focusing on *renyuan* (a responsibility of the potentially envied, i.e. the cadres and wealthy in this case) to focusing on *suzhi* (an attribute of the potentially envious, i.e. the ordinary villagers in this case).

So what exactly is *suzhi*? As Anne Anagnost (2004) has explained, the term *suzhi*, which roughly means 'quality' in English,

is hardly a neologism but it acquired new discursive power when it became conjoined with the idea of population (*renkou*) in the economic reforms that began in 1976. The discourse of population quality (*renkou suzhi*) may have first appeared in the 1980s, in state documents investigating rural poverty that attributed China's failure to modernise to the 'low quality' (*suzhi di*) of its population, especially in rural areas. By the early 1990s, population quality had become a key term in the party-state's policy statements and directives to cadres, even as it began to circulate more broadly as a general explanation for everything that held the Chinese nation back from achieving its rightful place in the world. (Anagnost 2004: 190)

Kipnis's (2006) work has further shown that

[r]eference to *suzhi* justifies social and political hierarchies of all sorts, with those of 'high' quality gaining more income, power and status than the 'low'. In rural contexts, cadres justify their right to rule in terms of having a higher quality than the 'peasants' around them. (Kipnis 2006: 295)

As I've been explaining, the term *suzhi* is sometimes used to account for situations related to malicious envy and red-eye. Indeed, I encountered this form of attributing *suzhi* on the first day of my stay in Xitai. During a semiformal meeting with the party secretary of the township, other county officials and the village head of Xitai, the village head said:

Compared to other regions, the *suzhi* [quality] of people in Xitai is pretty low. What they do is like swindling money [*eqian*]. For example, their income based on planting sweet corn on their land would be just two to three thousand RMB but now when there are people who want to rent some parts of their planting land for five hundred or six hundred RMB per year, they don't agree. Think about it, six hundred RMB for doing nothing, what is there to be unsatisfied about? Our prime minister Wen Jiabao's *Qinmin* Policy ['Close to the Peasants' Policy][11] has spoiled peasants too much and now no one dares to manage them properly [*meiren ganguan*].

He was complaining specifically about his problems managing local people, something that might negatively affect the pace of mining investment. There were constant conflicts and disagreements between peasants, who he felt were greedy and short-sighted, and the businesspeople and entrepreneurs[12] who were supposed to bring prosperity to the region. The recent policy coming from central government gives greater support to the peasants through measures such as abandoning the agriculture tax, raising the prices of agricultural produce and ensuring greater protection of peasants' interests. Peasants' rights have also been strengthened by, for example, new regulations and limitations on leasing agricultural land (which have been used tactically to negotiate with mining companies) and by the introduction of informed consent into family planning policy, meaning that abortion and other coercive actions could no longer be imposed. These policies, from the local government's perspective and from the perspective of the village head in particular, gave rise to extra difficulties when it came to the overriding pursuit of economic development. What's more, these policies also made it difficult to control 'trouble-making' activities, which were allegedly motivated by red-eye.

In the meantime, there were unproven suspicions and rumours concerning the current village head of Xitai too; everyone was gossiping that he was a millionaire and that he was possibly embezzling money that different mines gave to the village. This village head used to be a manager in a mine company and was able to earn several thousand RMB a year; in 2003 this figure was in the tens of thousands. He left that job, however, because there was a fatal accident for which he was held responsible and thus fired. That was when he started to campaign in the election. Cadres at the township level supported him, applying the underlying logic that 'We should have the rich as village heads, and then at least they won't embezzle village money. If you find a poor one, he will only take advantage and embezzle money from the collectives.'

The accusation that village cadres are corrupt is of course not uncommon. A village head from an adjacent community defended himself against such allegations in a more blunt way than the village head of Xitai:

I don't want to be head of the village any more. The peasants are now so eager [to get rich] that they become red-eyed. Everyone wants to get 0.2 million RMB or 0.3 million RMB and move away [i.e. to vacate their current homes for the setting up of mines]. You know, the salary earned by working as a village head is even less than what I earned from my own business. My own mine site could sell for up to several million RMB. They just see me building a two-storey building, driving a crappy car and start calculating how much money I've embezzled. I heard that they have employed an accountant to look into the village account, saying that there was 0.5 million RMB allocated from the upper level and only 290 thousand RMB in the account. It was fortunate that we had those meeting minutes and they eventually gave up with no evidence at all. The rumours are just everywhere. I don't want this job, my family doesn't want me to do it but those who supported me don't want me to quit.

It was clear that when opportunities and money were coming into the villages, there were more conflicts and disputes as well. Everyone understandably wanted to benefit from the economic development, and the local government had the responsibility to make that happen. The local government also undertook the significant task of maintaining social order: that is, reducing the incidence of conflicts and disputes or at least solving them peacefully. The tension between the local authority and the villagers was acute. Certainly not all actions were motivated by envy or jealousy though, only the demands that were unreasonable, such as what the village head called allegations of 'swindling money' or behaviours referred to as 'spreading unfounded rumours' or purely 'making trouble'.

According to those who have laid the blame, those actions were seen as the result of the low quality of the villagers who were incapable of achieving satisfaction for themselves and who were unable to disguise their envy. Low quality can therefore be variously interpreted as illiterate, irrational, impulsive and ignorant of laws and regulations. Moreover, the type of actions engaged in by low-quality people were seen as damaging to others but at the same time did not seem to be advantageous for the person taking the action either, thus making it difficult to find a solution to the general problem within the system of laws or regulations. 'Low quality' was therefore a convenient way of explaining why these claims were being made; it was convenient, too, in that it allowed the cadres to avoid moral responsibility for provoking the misconduct and their failure to prevent it.

CONCLUSION

In the Judaeo-Christian tradition, envy—when people desire something that is not theirs—is generally thought to be unattractive and dishonourable, something that should be avoided. But in China, at least, the responsibility for this lies with both sides. It may be considered shameful to reveal malicious envy or 'red-eye' in public, to expose one's bad intentions towards others and to engage in overt acts provoked by envy.

But it is also wrong to do certain things, such as conspicuously celebrating one's advantages, that may provoke feelings of envy in others.

As I said at the outset, the moral responsibility associated with envy weighs most heavily, in China, on those people who may be objects of envy. In Xu Shuming's view, as I pointed out, the damage caused by malicious envy is mostly due to the inconsiderate behaviour of the envied people. If they were careful about applying certain strategies in order to cultivate good social relationships, the evil-minded envier and their subsequent vindictive actions could be largely avoided. People who act on their envy take risks—both of failure and of incurring public contempt. Therefore, when people *do* act on malicious envy, it is generally the case that the people whom they envy have done something very wrong to provoke them. Envy is generally believed to be normal and controllable, but it can quickly turn to hatred when the people who are envied are thought to have not deserved their success and yet still behave in such a way as to demonstrate that they clearly feel good about this anyway. This is what drives the envious to want to inflict hurt on those whom they envy.

In the context of the villages of Lanying and Xitai, however, things were less black and white than this summary may suggest. The large amount of money pouring forth from mining activities in recent years had made virtually everyone envious in some way. Certainly, though, not all cases of envy were malicious, and even fewer involved people actually acting on their envy. Most of those who had been categorized by local officials as 'troublemakers' had been denounced as 'red-eyes'. The reasoning of the officials invariably went like this: the troublemakers were red-eyed about people getting rich but had no means of making money themselves (for instance, no skills, no connections, no knowledge) and therefore tried to get money through making trouble. The risk of being thought of as 'bad people' was not of much concern to the troublemakers because they were not good people in the first place and so did not have much to lose.

It can be seen that the rich and the government officials who were the target of the troublemaking gangs (as they saw it) not only bore the moral responsibilities of having made the 'troublemakers' red-eyed but also feared the possibility of losing public approval. Therefore, the wealthy and powerful seemed to be in a very difficult position and when possible condemned the troublemakers, invoking the well-established *suzhi* discourse to rebuke and stigmatize them. The logic behind this behaviour of those government officials was therefore that envy-avoiding strategies involving cultivating *renyuan* only worked when one was dealing with grateful and well-behaved recipients, that is, with 'good-quality' people. The sin of being envied is therefore lessened, in effect. That is, if the envious nonetheless still act on their envy despite the attempt of the envied to maintain good social relationships, then it is *they*, the envious, who should bear the moral responsibility for this.

NOTES

1. Often this immoral act is described as non-traditional behaviour, for instance, in Reminick's case, the threat of an equal situation; in High's case, earning 'polluted' money; or unwelcome success in the Zulu and Desana.
2. Li Kang (196–265), *Three Kingdoms Wei: Yun Ming Lun* (*Theory on Luck and Fate*).
3. In Yu (2000: 153–76).
4. Many theorists have tried to distinguish different types of envy, and the distinction I am using here is between non-malicious envy and malicious envy, as Parrott (1991) has called it. As defined by Parrott, the focus of non-malicious envy is 'I wish I had what you have' while the focus of malicious envy is the removal or destruction of the envied object or quality (Parrott 1991: 9–10). In Chinese terms, as I am arguing here, *xianmu* could be translated as non-malicious envy and *jidu* as malicious envy.
5. Yu (2000). Unless otherwise indicated, all the Chinese texts are presented using my translation.
6. 1RMB (renminbi) was approximately equal to 0.067 GBP at the time of this research.
7. His daughter had married into Wang Village. He and his wife had come to help with taking care of a newborn baby, and he was temporarily working as a security guard at an explosives storage site.
8. The locals are reluctant to run small businesses such as growing or peddling food. Some products therefore rely on external supply, which inevitably means higher prices.
9. Wang is a friend of my family. A close member of my family got to know Wang in the early 1990s during a business trip. I was, therefore, closely attached to this family, and many thought I must be a relative of Wang to explain why I was living with them.
10. Given the overall success of Wang Village and the admirable status Wang held, the accusations here were not overtly the case in Wang Village.

11. The *Qinmin* policy literally refers to being 'close to people'. It was the guiding principle under the current leadership (2004–), and in rural areas *'min'* was directly interpreted to mean the peasants (*nongmin*).
12. Some of the cadres tried to conceal the conflicts by saying there weren't any, but others said it was 'alright for her to know' and that there was 'no need to hide from her'.

REFERENCES

Anagnost, A. (2004), 'The Corporeal Politics of Quality (Suzhi)', *Public Culture*, 16/2: 189–208.

Berglund, A. I. (1976), *Zulu Thought-Patterns and Symbolism*, London: Hurst & Company.

Buchillet, D. (2004), 'Sorcery Beliefs, Transmission of Shamanic Knowledge, and Therapeutic Practice among the Desana of the Upper Rio Negro Region, Brazil', in N. L. Whitehead and R. Wright (eds), *In Darkness and Secrecy: The Anthropology of Assault Sorcery and Witchcraft in Amazonia*, Durham, NC: Duke University Press.

Harrell, S. (2001), 'The Anthropology of Reform and the Reform of Anthropology: Anthropological Narratives of Recovery and Progress in China', *Annual Review of Anthropology*, 30: 139–61.

High, M. M. (2008), 'Wealth and Envy in the Mongolian Gold Mines', *Cambridge Anthropology*, 27/3: 1–18.

Kipnis, A. B. (2006), 'Suzhi: A Key Word Approach', *The China Quarterly*, 186: 295–313.

Parrott, W. G. (1991), 'The emotional experiences of Envy and Jealousy', in P. Salovey (ed.), *The Psychology of Jealousy and Envy*, New York: Guilford Press.

Planalp, S. (1999), *Communicating Emotion: Social, Moral, and Cultural Processes*, Cambridge: Cambridge University Press.

Reminick, R. A. (1974), 'The Evil Eye Belief among the Amhara of Ethiopia', *Ethnology*, 13/3: 279–91.

Schoeck, H. (1969), *Envy: a Theory of Social Behaviour*, London: Secker & Warburg.

Siu, H. F. (1990), *Furrows, Peasants, Intellectuals, and the State: Stories and Histories from Modern China*, Stanford, CA: Stanford University Press.

Wolf, E. R. (2001), *Pathways of Power: Building an Anthropology of the Modern World*, Berkeley: University of California Press.

Yang, M. M.-hui (1994), *Gifts, Favors, and Banquets: The Art of Social Relationships in China*, Ithaca, NY: Cornell University Press.

Yu, Q. (2000), 'Lun Jidu (About Jealousy)', in *Shuang Leng Chang He (Frosty River)*, Writers Press.

CHAPTER 8

THE ETHICS OF IRONY: WORK, FAMILY AND FATHERLAND IN RURAL CHINA

Hans Steinmüller

Most of the data I gathered in my PhD research in Bashan, Hubei, could be classified under the headings of work, family and the state in rural China (Steinmüller 2009). If I were to write a book about this in French, it could be titled *Travail, Famille et Patrie dans la Chine rurale*. This might sound innocent to the English reader but perhaps quite unsavoury to the French one. *Travail, famille, patrie* was the motto with which Marshal Pétain replaced the republican *liberté, égalité, fraternité*. The new slogan stood for the conservative ideals of the Vichy regime under Pétain during the Second World War. In France, it is cited frequently as the epitome of authoritarian and reactionary government and of right-wing ideals in general. Condemning these ideals as *pétainisme* has a special clout: it refers to their dishonesty. After all, this regime that had *patrie* in its motto collaborated with the enemy. The leaders of the Vichy regime were probably not very receptive to such ironies—it seems that a high degree of literalism is a general characteristic of authoritarianism. But there seem to have been many cases in which ordinary people didn't take the slogan quite as literally. The poet Léon-Paul Fargue, for instance, famously said it should read '*tracas, famine, patrouille*' (hassle, famine, patrols) instead.

China has a form of government that has been often described as authoritarian. In public, the same values of work, family and fatherland[1] are continuously extolled. Still, there are many cases that do not quite live up to these ideals. What I want to draw your attention to in this chapter are the ironies that arise from the mismatch between ideals and realities. There are specific tensions between the expected and the experienced, the categorical and the contingent, the official and the vernacular, and it is these that I will emphasize in what follows. Confronted with such tensions, people often resort to ironic strategies. Certainly there were moments when the people I met were explicitly ironic or sarcastic. But there are other senses of irony that go beyond the merely rhetorical. Irony is sometimes 'situational' as well—that is, it may be interpreted and/or found in a situation, rather than being referred to explicitly.[2]

In what follows, I will refer to irony in both of these senses, that is, the rhetorical and situational. I do not assume that the first is emic and the second etic—which might imply that ordinary people use irony only rhetorically and that the recognition of situational irony is the privilege of intellectual observers. Instead I will try to show that when people use rhetorical irony and when they face (potentially) ironic situations, they become observers of their own moral actions. In this chapter I will follow the definitions of morality and ethics, according to which morality is any discourse or action which implies value judgements and ethics is the reflection or observation of morality (Luhmann 1991: 84–5). As such, I will argue, irony is fundamentally ethical.

The discussion which follows is framed around three cases: first, how people in Bashan make sense of success and failure in terms of family and work; second, the ways in which people relate to the state, its officials and its ideologies; and third, issues arising from my own outsider–insider position during fieldwork.

FAMILY AND WORK

The ideal of a family, and the work which maintains it, is certainly one of the most serious issues for people in Bashan.[3] Bashan is the place where I did fieldwork for one and a half years in 2006 and 2007, a remote township in the Wuling Mountains in eastern Hubei province. Whilst much has changed in the last two decades, the region is still predominantly agricultural. In recent years, many farmers have switched from staple crops (rice, corn, potatoes) to cash crops (tobacco, tea, vegetables). Yet most of the cash income for many families comes from outside remittances. Most families have at least one member labouring outside the village. Generally young people leave the countryside as teenagers and come back to marry several years later. The choice of a spouse and the way someone works to build and maintain a family are decisive criteria determining how people are judged and esteemed in local communities. This is a serious issue: those who do not find a marriage partner live the most horrible lives, according to local views. The coldness and dampness of the bachelor's home stands in opposition to the 'fire-red' (*honghuo*) and 'noisy-hot' (E. *naore*)[4] home of a family with many children.[5] Similarly, the judgement within the local face-to-face community is quite harsh against those who do not manage to offer their family some prosperity or who squander the family's resources.

Wealth, sons and long life are the three most important measures against which the 'happiness' of oneself and others is judged. Wang Mingming (1998) demonstrates how people in villages in Southern Fujian see happiness in exactly these terms. He further elaborates how people rationalize achievement and failure based on two elements: a person's capability (*nengli*) on the one side and his or her 'fate' (*ming*) on the other. Wang delineates the opposition of 'capability' and 'fate' as a 'local social ontology', structurally similar to the opposition of 'structure' and 'agency' in the social sciences. The metaphorical relationship between 'capability' and 'fate' is paralleled in life histories and in particular in the ways people present the successes and failures in achieving family prosperity by working hard or by other means. When asked about their life stories, and specifically the reasons for success or failure in their lives, many people in Bashan would end either by stressing their capabilities (*nengli* or *benshi*) or by bluntly relating life outcomes to their good 'fate' (*ming*). Every time I insisted on this point, trying to force a decision, people would admit that it is in fact both elements and the relationship between them can never be finally determined.

Whilst it may be impossible to know exactly whether it was someone's *ming* or someone's *nengli* that explains his or her success, it is plain to see what someone is doing: farming the land, doing business, working as a migrant labourer or serving as a government official. These are the most common occupations in the region. For most families, agricultural work has increasingly become less significant as a source of income. It is clear that even with the added income from cash-crop production, agriculture cannot provide the income necessary to pay for motorbikes, televisions, new houses or the education of children. Young people who have left the countryside for many years often find it very difficult to move back and start farming again.

Related to this is the fact that the valuation of work has changed. Until recently, hard work was highly valued, in particular farm labour. But nowadays agricultural work is generally only done by the older generation. Many young people, especially those who have some higher education or those who have lived in the city for extended periods, have low opinions of agricultural work: it is 'damned peasant work' (*si nonghuo*) that will never get you anywhere. Meanwhile, old people sometimes complain about the moral decline of the young, as did Mr Tan, an old farmer:

> In the past people had scrolls like 'maintain the household with hard work and thrift' [*qin jian chi jia*] on their door frames. When I see the young people now, it makes me think they should write 'eating, drinking, and revelries' [*chi he wan le*] instead.

Whilst such crude condemnations are rather rare, most people agree that what counts more than hard physical work today is having 'brains' (*tounao*) and 'intelligence' (*congming*). Mr Song, a teacher at the primary school of Bashan, explained this to me quite clearly. We had been talking about the fate of landlord families, who had lost all their property during the land reform in 1951 and had to start toiling just like the lowest labourers before. I wanted to enquire about the moral intricacies of such cases (whether it was just what had happened to them, whether they bore grudges, etc.). Characteristically, Mr Song didn't give any direct answer to these questions. Instead he said that everyone can do 'bitter labour' (*xia kuli*), and so did the former landlords then. But those who were 'intelligent' (*congming*) and had 'capability' (*nengli*) could later improve their life. Others, however, who lack any further abilities, will just continue doing hard physical work all their life and are incapable of doing anything about it. It is their 'fate' (*ming*) to be a poor labourer.

Obviously, 'capability' or 'brains' are not good in themselves: they can be put to various aims. Farmers, businessmen, officials and criminals can all have 'capabilities'. So let me give an example of someone whose capabilities are morally dubious.

KANG II

Kang 'the Second' (*lao'er*) was one of the first people I got to know on the market street of Bashan. He usually sits there next to the stand where his wife is frying oil sticks (*youtiao*) and flat cakes (*shaobing*) and sometimes helps her to sell the fried snacks. Bald, wearing a white vest with fat spots and a pair of shorts, he looks like many other middle-aged men on the street. On this first day he called me over and asked me to sit down for a chat. Coming closer, I realized that he had several tattoos on his arms and no little finger on his right hand. We had a quick conversation, and he asked me what I was doing in Bashan. He gave me a sceptical look when I said I wanted to learn about local custom. Then he said he could get things done and that he could organize whatever I needed, really anything. He had a quick look at my notebook, and when I asked him about his profession, he wrote in crawly characters his phone number and his name into my notebook and next to it his profession: *Kang lao'er liumang* (Kang the second, gangster[6]).

Kang II is, in fact, an ex-convict who has served several prison sentences since the early 1980s for various crimes including assaults, robbery and battery. After spending a total of fifteen years in different prisons and labour camps all over Hubei province, Kang was eventually released in 2002. Instead of moving to another town or province, Kang moved back to Bashan where his family was and resumed an ordinary life there. Having spent most of his adult life 'floating' (*liulang*) and in prison, the first thing Kang did after his release was to find a wife and settle down in order to build a family. Relatives introduced him to his current partner, and in the same year he built a house on the market street. For the purchase of the plot, for the necessary government permits and for construction material, he allegedly used former contacts and took advantage of the awe and fear that most people have of him. According to local gossip, neither the township government nor the local police dare to interfere with him. Many people in their forties or older remember the stories of Kang II and the feats of him and his gang. But nowadays Kang goes around the town unnoticed most of the time. One contemporary of Kang claimed that in the 1980s when they were only in their early twenties they didn't know better, but then Kang II and his cohort matured and became ordinary citizens:

> There was no clear line back then to distinguish what was right from what was wrong, we didn't have a sense of the law [*meiyou falü de gainian*]. Now he's just a man like everyone else, he has a family and works hard to earn his living.

Kang has gone some way to prove that he can lead the life of an ordinary and conventional person. He lives with his wife and two children in their house on the market street, helps his wife sell snacks and engages in occasional jobs in the construction business. His network of relatives, friends and acquaintances is very wide, of which the number and amounts of gifts for family celebrations such as weddings, funerals and birthdays are the most obvious sign in local society. In these ways, he receives recognition in the local face-to-face community, including from many people who would have avoided him in former times.

After the day I first met Kang and he had written his name and profession into my notebook, I remained quite fascinated by him. I met him several times on the market street and at weddings and birthdays in the villages; but I never had the opportunity to have a longer conversation with him. (I was also somewhat over-cautious about the image I would be giving to others, and partly I was just too shy to talk with him.) But when I was with other people in Bashan, we often ended up talking about Kang II. Whilst many people condemned his past, others also emphasized that because of his experiences as a gang member, he was a particularly 'loyal' person (*jiang yiqi*). Especially amongst young men, who had lived in cities for some time, there was a certain element of admiration when he was mentioned. One of them said:

> In the past Old Kang was a tremendous and tough guy [*xiong*].[7] But nowadays no one is afraid of him anymore. Actually I have a friend in Enshi who is much tougher and much more powerful than he is.

Expressions such as 'loyalty' (*yiqi*) and 'toughness' (*xiong*) may remind Chinese listeners of the attributes of life lived along the 'rivers and lakes' (*jianghu*). This latter expression is used to refer to a life outside the community, where people are 'floating' (*liulang*) from one place to the other and relying on friends and brothers. Novels of 'rivers and lakes' are a traditional genre of Chinese literature, dealing with knights errant and their ethics of brotherhood. In contemporary Chinese, *jianghu* is also often used to refer to the 'black society' (*heishehui*) of gangs and mafia-like organizations.[8]

Old Kang has left the *jianghu* and settled down. Yet how people talk about him, and how he still demands respect, is clearly influenced by his past. In the ways he presented himself to me and in the stories others told me about him, he was always in between the contradictory characterization of a criminal and an upright member of the community. The last time I met him I openly confronted him about his past for the first time. It was my last week in Bashan, and after attending a long departure meal with much Chinese liquor, I thought I should meet Old Kang one last time. I called him on the mobile number he had written in my notebook and asked him to come down to the market street to have 'night snacks' (*xiaoye*) and drink beer. He answered that he couldn't leave and I should come to his house. We sat down, his wife offered tea and we started a conversation. After a polite introduction, I asked him about his past and whether he still could mobilize his people and get things done. I now spoke a passable Enshi dialect, he had known me for more than a year and had often seen me with government officials. He assured me that he was now a hard-working family man and that he wanted to provide his daughters with a good education. The past was the past, and now he lived the life of an ordinary man in Bashan, he said, quite literally.

In the past, Kang obviously lived in contradiction to what is expected from everyone in terms of family and work. Even though he has settled down now, his air still reminds people of the *jianghu*. Now let me introduce another man, who lives not too far from Kang on the same street. This man has lived a much more 'ordinary' life, in which the coordinates were family and work throughout. But he also relates to his own achievements and failures in rather ambiguous ways.

WEN YUNFU

Wen Yunfu is a respected man in the township of Bashan. In his seventies now, he spends his days playing cards with friends, chatting with visitors, taking care of his flowers and doing odd jobs. The humble wooden house he lives in wouldn't tell the visitor immediately how wealthy his family is. His children provide him with good food and relatively expensive cigarettes. Old Wen and his family are generally seen as an example of achievement and prosperity: he has four sons and one daughter, and the family has a wide network of relatives and friends. For every family celebration, many relatives and members of the extended family come over to his house. All together, the house of Old Wen represents precisely the three elements of the 'good life' mentioned before: wealth, sons and long life.

Over time, I became a frequent visitor at Old Wen's house. He very much enjoyed talking about times past, about the intricacies of local custom and about the many stories of his family and the people of Bashan. Most important for me, he was very patient when I didn't immediately grasp the meaning of an idiom or the gist of a matter, as happened often.

Many of the stories he told me were about the past of his own family. The vagaries of destiny by far overwhelmed the diligence and hard work with which he and his ancestors had tried to build their lives. Several times Old Wen told me the life stories of his father and his uncle. Wen's father had been a relatively wealthy tea merchant, but he spent most of his money on opium. So when Old Wen started to go to school in the late 1930s, his father couldn't even pay the fees. His uncle Wen Yaohua owned a rice and corn mill and was much better off. The uncle happily sent him to school and paid for it. Wen Yaohua was respected in the local community and was a leading member of a brotherhood (at the time, so-called *hanliu* brotherhoods controlled the tea and opium trade and shaped public life as authoritative nongovernmental organizations). Until 1949, he was one of the most powerful and wealthy men in Bashan. But the Communist revolution was disastrous for him. All of a sudden he became a 'class enemy' and 'landlord'. During the initial confusion, he thought he could still mobilize powerful friends to protect him, but he was soon disappointed. When retaliation began in 1951 against 'rightists and landlords', Wen Yaohua went into hiding and ran towards Enshi city to seek refuge in the house of relatives. But on the road he met a battalion of soldiers. They didn't hesitate long; they killed him and left his corpse there. Old Wen's father, however, had spent much of his wealth on opium, and when the Communists arrived, he was quite poor. Hence he was not classified as a 'class enemy', and his son could later even become a small official—which was impossible for his cousins, the children of Wen Yaohua, who were 'class enemies' and 'sons of a landlord'.

After the Communist revolution, Old Wen's family had become 'peasants' (*nongmin*), even though before they had been a family of merchants. Old Wen often recounted stories of the private school he had visited before the 1940s: after 1949, the private schools were closed, and he had to start working the land. He repeated several times, 'I had the capability to study, but not the fate to study' (*you dushu de nengli, mei you dushu de ming*).

Still, being a 'poor peasant', Old Wen had the opportunity to become a minor official (only the 'good classes' were accepted for these positions). He could establish good relationships with many people in the market town, and so he and his family did quite well throughout the Maoist era. He could offer his children a relatively good education and supported them in their first jobs. Of his five children, one owns a restaurant on the market street, and two of them are successful bosses in the construction business in the city of Enshi. His only daughter is now a teacher in a higher-middle school in Enshi. Old Wen could talk for hours about the difficulties of getting his daughter a permit to study at higher-middle school, or how he was helping one of his sons to get the first contract for a construction project. He talked about mobilizing his network of relationships (*guanxi wang*) and his exploits in turning a situation to their favour.

Through our countless conversations, Old Wen and I had become good friends. When my departure from Bashan was imminent, he asked me several times to take a picture of us together. And every time he said it he would add, with a smile, that I should write on the picture that this is 'a Chinese peasant and a German scholar' (*zhongguo nongmin he deguo xuezhe*). I always refused humbly and said that neither could I count as a scholar nor was he a real peasant.

In these ways, Old Wen's stories are far from claiming literally that he was a 'peasant' who was 'working hard' for his family. With time, I learned to understand the subtexts of what he was telling me. And surely I still have missed many of the connotations of his stories, which were always full of allegories and idioms. Yet it is apparent that he almost never referred to his success (and failures) in a literal way. Whilst the inalterable forces of the state and of 'fate/life' (*ming*) had their own logic, sometimes they could be manipulated in the right direction. And surely his stories might have been much less riveting without his humour and irony.

My third example is of someone who is far from the secured 'happiness' that Old Wen has achieved. The following is a narrative of suffering and struggle.

LIU DAWEI

Liu Dawei is the youngest of three brothers. As his seniors, the first two brothers 'divided the family property' (*fenjia*) first. That is, they got their part of the family property, built their own houses next to the parents' house, married and established families. Liu Dawei, as the youngest brother, stayed in the house with the parents, even after he got married. This is quite common in the region: the youngest stays at home and will inherit the house after the death of the parents. Liu Dawei, however, was very hard-working and ambitious and wanted to build his own new house. He chose a place right next to the primary school and village administration of Shuanke. Normally calculating the *fengshui* of a place is indispensable before choosing the place and situating the fundaments of a house. *Fengshui* is the traditional Chinese practice of geomancy, a popular cosmology that connects astrological signs and cosmological elements with the shape of the lived landscape. Interpreting the particular *fengshui* of a place is done to take advantage of its positive 'energy' and to adjust to it. But Liu Dawei chose a place on the downward-slope side of the road, which arguably didn't have very good *fengshui*.[9] Nonetheless, he accepted this disadvantage, given that this was the only place available next to the school and Liu Dawei and his wife planned to open a small shop to sell groceries and foodstuff to the students. The house was finished in 1990, and until recently the family was doing relatively well. However, in 2003 Liu Dawei started feeling ill more and more often; he was sleepy all day, and later he couldn't move at all. Even the easiest movements consumed all his strength, and for the last four years he has been barely able to do any work. The many doctors he visited couldn't help him, and finally doctors in the prefecture hospital in Enshi diagnosed him with a 'chronic osteomalacia', that is, rheumatism. As a result he had to spend a good part of his meagre income on hospital bills, operations and medicine.

In 2007, things went from bad to worse, and his 65-year-old father was diagnosed with throat cancer. Because both men in the family are now barely able to work, Liu Dawei had to borrow a lot of money from the local bank and more still from relatives and friends. In this situation, he became more and more convinced that this house was bringing him only bad luck and that he had to move out with his family somewhere else.

It seemed impossible to most people in the village, but in autumn 2007, he started to build a huge new house right next to his old house. Before building the house, he carefully consulted several *fengshui* experts and selected a suitable place according to their recommendations. He plans to sell the old house and use the money to invest in his new house.

The neighbours first couldn't believe that Liu Dawei would really start building a new house. How could he, if everyone knew that he and his father had been ill for years and that the family carried a heavy load of debts? Liu Dawei had been a prime example of someone who has bad luck (E. *huoqi bu hao*). The only explanation the neighbours had was that his brother-in-law was really financing the new house. The brother-in-law was indeed supporting Liu Dawei, but in this case he was just lending him some money again—as far as I know. But there is some truth in what the neighbours said: Liu Dawei can rely on the good relationships he has with most of his relatives and with many friends. In fact, he often lectured me on the 'art of relationship-making' (*guanxi xue*). When he was planning to build the new house, the village officials initially opposed his plan. He then invited the vice secretary of the township government for several meals at the best restaurant in Bashan and offered him several boxes of expensive cigarettes. Liu Dawei also pointed out to me that he had chosen this secretary because he shares the same surname with him, even though he is not a direct relative. After this treatment, the village government eventually granted him permission to build.

All his efforts notwithstanding, the most pressing issue for Liu Dawei himself was still to change the forces of luck and fate. In several conversations with me, he mentioned his own 'fate/life' (*ming*). When I asked him how he could have been so brave that in his difficult circumstances he still dared to build the new house, he answered that in the past he was very cautious and didn't have courage. But the worse his situation got, he said, the bigger his courage grew (*danzi da*). He said, 'I decided that I had to change my life/fate' (*ming*).

So far I have written about the tension between 'capability' (*nengli*) and 'life/fate' (*ming*) as a local discourse. Yet this local discourse invokes some further levels of meaning (and irony). *Ming* is not quite the same as 'fate' or 'life'. It is also the life of someone as part of wider cosmic forces. In the practice of *fengshui*, the geomancer tries to align the cosmic forces in the landscape with the position of the house and the *ming* of the inhabitants. To this end, he will use the 'eight characters' (*ba zi*) of the year, month, day and hour of the birth of the relevant individuals.[10] These eight characters are the basic information about a person, necessary for any divination and geomancy concerning that person. Diviners and geomancers then put the 'eight characters' into complex relationships with sets of cosmological elements, such as the two cosmic forces yin and yang, the five elements (*wu xing*, which are fire, water, wood, earth and metal), the sixty-four hexagrams of the Book of Changes and a whole plethora of other symbols. These elements themselves stand in relationship to each other and influence each other. Certain combinations of symbols bode well, whereas others prefigure bad luck.

The problem with all these ideas (including the notion of *ming* as the 'fate' of someone decided by cosmic forces) is that they are 'feudal superstitions' according to official discourse. This leads me to the third point in my title, next to work and family.

FATHERLAND

The institutions that represent nation and state in China generally promote a relatively unambiguous official discourse regarding the primary source of success: hard work. In every government campaign, slogans such as 'maintain the household with hard work and thrift' (*qin jian chi jia*) are repeated. The recent campaign entitled 'eight honours and eight shames' (*ba rong ba chi*) explicitly notes that 'to labour industriously is glorious, to be indolent and despise labour is disgraceful' (*yi xinqin laodong wei rong, yi hao yi wulao wei chi*). During my time in Bashan, party members and students had to recite these slogans in study sessions, and the campaign posters covered many walls in government buildings and schools.

From the perspective of this official discourse then, reference to *ming* smacks of fatalism. Let me go back for a moment to the case of Old Wen. As mentioned, four of his children are rather successful in their jobs. Only the youngest son, who lives together with Old Wen in his house in Bashan, has not made it very far: Wen Lihan is still working the little land that Old Wen received as a farmer in the 1980s. Wen Lihan's 24-year-old daughter, however, is already the manager of a private nursery school in Enshi. At a dinner I had at his house together with a minor official from the city government, we came to speak about this daughter. Wen Lihan mentioned that in comparison to himself, his daughter has a 'good fate' (*ta de ming hao*). The government official immediately jumped in: 'That you got fundamentally wrong. It is not her fate, but the fact that she has been working hard.'

Explaining someone's achievements by his/her *ming* runs counter to the official discourse (and the official in this case saw himself compelled to emphasize that). Not only does *ming* contradict the praise of hard work, but it is also associated with the entire field that is categorized as 'feudal superstition' (*fengjian mixin*) in the official discourse. The practices of *fengshui* and divination are obvious examples of this. During the Maoist era, people were persecuted for following such 'feudal superstition'. Even though political control has loosened a good deal, references to *fengshui* and related practices such as astrology and divination are usually not made in public. They will be spoken about in private instead, and almost always with a somewhat ironic undertone.

The denunciation of 'feudal superstition' is only one part of a much wider modernizing discourse. Here 'feudalism' (*fengjian zhuyi*) and 'peasant thinking' (*nongmin sixiang*) are the characteristics of a 'backwards' (*luohou*) 'small peasant economy' (*xiaonong jingji*). The central objects of this modernizing discourse are 'the peasants'. The category of 'the peasant' (*nongmin*)—introduced to China with its modern connotations at the beginning of the twentieth century (Cohen 1993)—carries with it a thorough ambiguity: first of all, the 'peasant' is the negative counter-image of the citizen (*gongmin*); he/she is backwards, trapped in traditional and feudal culture, and has to be 'modernized' to become a full member of the nation. Yet on the other side, 'the peasant' is also seen as representing the 'roots' of China. The peasants who are bound to their soil, and who are 'soiled' (*tu*), are also standing in for China as a whole.[11]

Intellectuals occupied with constructing the modern nation-state and a national identity have grounded much of their efforts on the categorical distinction of the peasant 'Other'. This is certainly true for the nationalist and revolutionary period in China (Cohen 1993; Flower 1997). The attempts to turn 'peasants' into 'citizens' have parallels in European history (Weber 1976) and continue in many facets to the present day. Rural education and the contemporary discourse of 'population quality' (*renkou suzhi*) are primarily aimed at this goal (Murphy 2004).

Raising 'population quality' is frequently declared as one of the main aims of development in official announcements: for instance, in the development programmes promoted as 'Construction of a New Socialist Countryside' (*shehuizhuyi xin nongcun jianshe*). Published in autumn 2006 in party newspapers and announcement boards, one of the aims of the programmes in Bashan read, 'develop education and hygiene, raise the population quality [*tigao renmin sushi*] and living quality [*shenghuo zhiliang*]'. Like any government announcement, this sounds committed and serious.

When the expression came up in everyday conversation, however, it had a different resonance. The first time I heard the word '*suzhi*' in Bashan stands out here. It was in my first week, and I had just boarded the regular bus from Bashan to Enshi. The bus was still stationary—usually the driver waits until the bus is packed to the last seat before taking off. The bus driver started a conversation with me and offered me a cigarette, as is polite custom. I accepted the cigarette and wanted to leave the bus to smoke it outside—we still had some minutes to go. The bus driver laughed out loud and called me back: 'Don't worry, we here are all of low quality [*suzhi di*], we smoke in the bus'—and the entire bus burst out in laughter.

Aside from this remarkable moment of ironic self-recognition, *suzhi* was more often used to criticize others, as in the common claim that local officials had low *suzhi*. The corruption of local officials was a favourite topic for conversation with me, second only to the weather. Taxes and fees levied from private enterprises, several government enterprises and recent land expropriations close to the township where a 'development district' (*kaifa qu*) was built provide high revenue for the local state. Locals frequently alleged that the officials responsible pocketed part of this revenue. In private talk, villagers sometimes compared the local officials to officials they had encountered in other places, especially higher up the governmental hierarchy. Invariably, people complained that the *suzhi* of the local officials was very low. This remark was particularly common for those villagers who had been to the coastal areas and to major cities, such as Beijing, Shanghai and Guangzhou.

The title of this section ('Fatherland') could have implied that I would discuss nation and nationalism. Instead I have focused on state discourses and their local counterparts. But this is also implicitly about nationalism. Even though I might have taken some minor steps towards the perspective of a cultural insider, I could never escape my basic conditioning as an outsider and a foreigner. Time and again I was reminded during my fieldwork that I was not only representing myself, but also 'Germany' and 'the West'; and vice versa, it often appeared that my experiences in Bashan—including my experience of the ironies of life there—would represent 'China' to both myself and the wider world outside China.

THE IRONIC ANTHROPOLOGIST

Irony always cuts two ways, and as such it has an equally unsettling potential for my own person. As an undergraduate student, I chose anthropology to learn more about the 'objects' of development and colonialism. Having myself grown up on a farm in Bavaria, I had a deep interest in the problems of rural development and agricultural politics. After an experience as a volunteer in South America, I wanted to study peasant movements in the Third World. My first research proposal for a PhD was about rural development and peasant identity in China. It was a difficult undertaking to translate that to local officials and ordinary people alike. The exchanges I had with the three people I have written about here—Kang II, Wen Yunfu and Liu Dawei—were all plastered with ironies.

The most felicitous framing, I think, I found with Old Wen. You might remember that he had asked me various times for a picture of the two of us, entitled 'a Chinese peasant and a German scholar' (*zhongguo nongmin he deguo xuezhe*), and that I had refused. Before I left Bashan, we really did take the picture, and with the help of a Chinese friend, I found a much better way of expressing our encounter and the ambiguities of both our personalities. Festive occasions in China are often accompanied by written scrolls (*duilian*), which poetically capture the occasion in a parallel structure. The scroll we commissioned for the picture of Old Wen and me was the following: 'A friendship across ages:

An 80-year-old peasant-merchant happily meets a young German scholar. A 27-year-old descendant of farmers serendipitously encounters an old Chinese sage.'[12]

As recounted earlier, I left on a much more 'literal' note with Kang II. Here as well, our rapport was ensnarled in ironies: in our first memorable encounter he had written his profession (gangster, *liumang*) into my notebook. The last time we met, however, he thoughtfully accentuated his role as a family man and husband. In between these two encounters, the not-quite-reintegrated convict and his allures of lawlessness and brotherhood fascinated me, just like many others.

But my predicament as a foreigner, a 'guest of the people's government', impelled me to use the utmost caution when it came to anything that was politically sensitive, including such diverse things as criminality, corruption, superstition and the workings of the local government. As for this, let me give a last example of the (mis)understandings reached. The following is a newspaper article that appeared in the *Enshi Evening News* in December 2006. By then I had spent half a year in Bashan. A friend from the local university in Enshi had told a reporter from the local newspaper about my presence, and together with the township government, a press team came over to interview me and film me for a day. One result was the following newspaper article, entitled 'A German Lad in Bashan':

In the village of Zhongba, Bashan Township, Enshi City, people can now frequently see a young foreigner who is tall and has blond hair, and walks from house to house in the villages. [. . .] His Chinese name is Shi Han, and originally he is a German from the city of Munich. This 1.82 meter tall PhD student is only 26 years old, and he speaks German, Chinese, English, and Spanish fluently. When this reporter interviewed him on the 3 December, Shi Han pronounced the following phrase in all these four languages: 'The rural reconstruction in Bashan Township and Shuanke village is done very well.'

Aside from the newspaper article, some footage of me was broadcast on local TV. Whilst most peasants do not read newspapers and do not have cable TV, several villagers had seen the news and spoke to me about it afterwards. Some spoke about it in rather high tones, saying that my appearance was 'an honour' for the people of Bashan. But others, in particular people I was very close and familiar with, gave me different comments. Two of them stand out.

One of my neighbours in the village, Liu Wenliang, mentioned the matter once in a conversation on the slopes, when I was working with him and his brother. He first talked a bit about the TV programme and then said to me, 'Didn't you appear last week on Enshi TV? And you said that the rural reconstruction programme is well done? I tell you, look at the houses here, off the street: the government doesn't do anything. This fucking reconstruction programme sucks. They serve themselves, and don't serve the people [*wei geren fuwu, bu shi wei laobaixing fuwu*].'[13]

Liu Dawei, the man who was plagued by rheumatism and then built a new house, also had his opinion on the TV programme and newspaper article. In fact, he praised me for having done it. When we came to speak about the TV programme, he said to me that 'finally you have understood how propaganda works here and what the rural reconstruction programmes are all about'. In short, he told me, they are about building up a 'face' (*mianzi*), a facade that looks nice. We continued the conversation, and I told him of my anxieties about writing a good PhD thesis and finding a job. He answered that all this shouldn't be a problem for me. Now that I had understood how things work, nothing would be easier: 'Just write long praises of rural development, the good side of the things you saw here. Then get your friends in the university and in the government to publish it. I'm sure you'll do well.'

CONCLUSION

There are categorical demands and platitudes about what it means to work, to be a member of a family, to be a peasant or an intellectual, to be Chinese or German. Yet surely the contingent realities of doing all these things never quite fit the categorical demands and platitudes. The trope through which such displacements can be expressed is irony.

In this chapter, I have described several levels of categorical demands that provide coordinates of irony: there is the opposition of, first, 'capability' (*nengli*) and, second, 'fate/life' (*ming*). Both can be realized in different ways and are judged in local moral discourses, which is a third coordinate: for instance, the ways in which Kang II and Wen Yunfu present themselves and the ways in which they are judged by others.

With Liu Dawei, we have seen a fourth coordinate of irony: the wider cosmological order into which humans, with their fate, their capabilities and their moral actions, are placed. In divination and geomancy, people attempt to adjust themselves to this order and manipulate it to their own ends. These four coordinates (capability, fate, moral discourse and cosmological order) are local and vernacular; the next coordinate then is the official discourse (of *suzhi*, peasantness, superstition, development, etc.) which is juxtaposed to the local discourses. The tension between the vernacular and official is finally inflected again in the sixth and last coordinate of irony, which is the one opened up by the presence of the foreigner and participant observer, who is also the author of this chapter. Figure 8.1 is an attempt to visualize these coordinates of irony.

What I have termed 'coordinates of irony' here are also moral frameworks. Actions and events can be explained with reference to one of them (as based on capability, fate, etc.). Yet in reality, they are mostly compared to several of them. These moral frameworks overlap and partly contradict each other. What I have attempted in this chapter is to draw out some of the ironies arising in the fissures between them. This is not to say that irony is ubiquitous. There are moments when irony turns into sarcasm and cynicism (as, for instance, in the

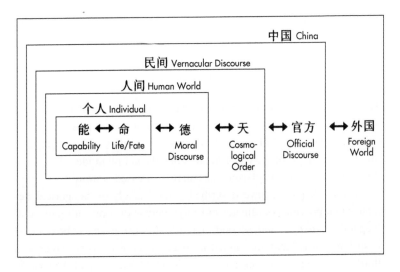

Figure 8.1 The Coordinates of Irony

comment of Liu Wenliang about my appearance on TV). At other points, people attempt to be taken literally (as did Kang II at our last encounter). In such ways, the uses and refusals of irony are examples of everyday ethics.

According to one common—though certainly not universally accepted—definition, ethics is the second-order reflection of morality, 'a kind of reflective and reflexive stepping-away from the embodied moral habitus or moral discourse' (Zigon 2008: 17). If we accept this distinction, then the uses of irony discussed in this chapter can be justifiably called 'ethical': in such ironies, ordinary people are 'stepping away' from moral frameworks, putting them against each other and creatively reflecting on them. Furthermore, in the uses and refusals of irony, people reproduce moral communities, as irony requires that the actors involved share an intimate knowledge of the 'coordinates of irony', that is, the moral frameworks they refer to.

What I have described here are, however, not only explicit and rhetorical uses of irony. The predicaments of Kang II, Wen Yunfu, Liu Dawei and myself are all inherently ironic. As I have described them, they are torn between family values and the *jianghu* (Kang II), between their own efforts and the forces of fate (Wen Yunfu and Liu Dawei), between vernacular practices and official discourse, between participation and observation (me). If one would portray them literally in the terms of one of the respective opposites only, one would miss most of the moral and ethical complexity of these people.

NOTES

1. I use 'fatherland' just for the sake of the pun with Pétain's slogan. In reality, it is a more difficult question whether the Chinese words for nation (*zuguo*, the 'ancestral country') and state (*guojia*, the 'country-family') should be translated as 'fatherland'. The connotation of the 'father' in the English and French words is not present in the Chinese words, which are more obviously related to the family. It seems that most Chinese would translate it into English as 'motherland'.
2. Not aiming at a comprehensive definition, the 'rough distinction' between rhetorical and situational irony nevertheless serves, Lambek suggests, to 'offset the assumption . . . that irony is properly to be consigned to the rhetorical, as an intentional mode of presentation' (2004: 2). Lambek's text is the introduction to the edited volume *Irony and Illness* (Lambek and Antze

2004). Another collection of essays I take major inspiration from is the volume *Irony in Action* (Fernandez and Huber 2001).

3. All names of persons and places below the prefectural level are pseudonyms.

4. Chinese words are written italicized in the standard Pinyin form. Words in the Enshi dialect that markedly differ in pronunciation and meaning from standard Mandarin (*putonghua*) I have marked with an 'E'.

5. Since family planning has been enforced in the 1980s, most families have one or two children only. Adam Chau describes similar discourses of 'red-hot sociality' in rural Shaanxi (cf. Chau 2006, Chapter 8).

6. The word '*liumang*' can be translated as hooligan, thug or rogue. The etymological origin of the word is 'floating people' who don't have a stable profession and who don't have a home. Criminals, beggars, ghosts and foreigners might fall into this category.

7. '*Xiong*' means 'evil, ferocious, inhuman' in standard Chinese. In the Enshi dialect the word is also used as meaning 'capable, tough and tremendous'. Another word often used in similar contexts in standard Chinese would be *lihai*. The character '*li*' means sharp, fierce and dangerous; it can also mean 'evil ghost', as in '*ligui*'. Both words are often used to 'compliment' some extraordinary achievement or attribute, and both connote some moral ambiguity: that which is inhuman (such as ghosts and criminals) can be the source of awe but also fear.

8. The opposite of the *jianghu* would be the *miaotang*, i.e. the life of 'temple' and court, the realms of the official discourses of family and government. From the perspective of the *jianghu*, the *miaotang* is seen as full of compromise, cowardice, submission and moral corruption, whereas in the *jianghu* absolute morals and absolute loyalty reign.

9. One basic rule of *fengshui* is that a grave and a house should have a slope at its back and a free view on the front side.

10. As given in Chinese peasant almanacs, every year, month, day and hour has attached to it two Chinese characters. The 'eight characters' of the birth hour result from the combination of two characters for the year, two for the month, two for the day and two for the hour.

11. The best example here is a classic in the anthropology of China: Fei Xiaotong has immortalized 'China from the Soil' in his book with the same title (*Xiangtu Zhongguo*; Fei 1992 [1948]). It is here where the axioms that 'real' China is rural and that the rural family is really the base and core of Chinese society are expressed most clearly (cf. Liu 2002).

12. *Wang nian zhi jiao: ba xun nonggu xinfeng deguo xuezi san jiu muyi qiaoyu zhonghua laoweng.*

13. The last sentence was echoing Mao Zedong's famous slogan 'to serve the people' (*wei renmin fuwu*).

REFERENCES

Chau, A. Y. (2006), *Miraculous Response: Doing Popular Religion in Contemporary China*, Stanford, CA: Stanford University Press.

Cohen, M. (1993), 'Cultural and Political Inventions in Modern China: The Case of the Chinese "Peasant"', *Daedalus*, 122/2: 151–70.

Fei, X. (1992 [1948]), *From the Soil: The Foundations of Chinese Society, A Translation of Fei Xiaotong's Xiangtu Zhongguo*, with an introduction and epilogue by G. G. Hamilton and W. Zheng, Berkeley: University of California Press.

Fernandez, J., and Huber, M. T. (eds) (2001), *Irony in Action: Anthropology, Practice and the Moral Imagination*, Chicago: University of Chicago Press.

Flower, J. (1997), 'Portraits of Belief: Constructions of Chinese Cultural Identity in the Two Worlds of City and Countryside in Modern Sichuan Province', unpublished PhD dissertation, University of Virginia.

Lambek, M. (2004), 'Introduction: Irony and Illness—Recognition and Refusal', in M. Lambek and P. Antze (eds), *Irony and Illness*, New York: Berghahn.

Lambek, M., and Antze, P. (eds) (2004), *Irony and Illness*, New York: Berghahn.

Luhmann, N. (1991), 'Paradigm Lost: On the Ethical Reflection of Morality: Speech on the Occasion of the Award of the Hegel Prize 1988', trans. D. Roberts, *Thesis Eleven*, 29/1: 82–94.

Liu, X. (2002), 'Urban Anthropology and the Urban Question in China', *Critique of Anthropology*, 22/2: 109–32.

Murphy, R. (2004), 'Turning Peasants into Modern Chinese Citizens: "Population Quality" Discourse, Demographic Transition and Primary Education', *The China Quarterly*, 177: 1–20.

Steinmüller, H. (2009), 'Everyday Moralities: Family, Work, Ritual and the Local State in Rural China', PhD dissertation, Department of Anthropology, London School of Economics.

Wang, M. (1998), 'Xinfu, ziwo quanli yu shehui bentilun: yige zhongguo nongcun zhong "fu" de guan'nian' ('Happiness, Self Empowerment and Social Ontology: The Notion of "Happiness" in a Chinese Village'), *Shehuixue Yanjiu* (Sociological Research), 1: 23–36.

Weber, E. (1976), *Peasants into Frenchmen: The Modernization of Rural France 1870–1914*, Stanford, CA: Stanford University Press.

Zigon, J. (2008), *Morality: An Anthropological Perspective*, Oxford: Berg.

CHAPTER 9

SAME DREAM, DIFFERENT BEDS: FAMILY STRATEGIES IN RURAL ZHEJIANG

Daniel Roberts

One cold February afternoon, I was sitting with 63-year-old Wang Cheng Xiang in his home beside the central crossroads of the small village of Wangcun in eastern Zhejiang province, eating sunflower seeds and discussing families. His was a particularly interesting local example, since he was the eldest of nine brothers, all but one of whom still live in the village and work as farmers. Like most others in Wangcun, Wang Cheng Xiang's family was not wealthy and—during a childhood of considerable hardship—neither he nor his brothers received much by way of formal education. His wife once told me, 'If there is harmony, there is strength in numbers',[1] and she was right: to others in the village today, the Wang family are known primarily as violent gamblers who, after dark, may often be found playing cards and drinking long into the night. Though they are not really criminals, the Wang brothers dominate their production team, and fights between the brothers and other villagers broke out on a number of occasions during my fieldwork. Wang Cheng Xiang was conscious of his family's reputation and that afternoon, with a gruff chuckle, joked that:

> In terms of comparing whose household is good, and who has harmonious relations with their relatives, of course this happens! There's a lot of gossip. Everyone *hopes* to be good!

My primary interest in this chapter is whether and how families in a rural Chinese community achieve this goal and how they are judged by fellow villagers. I hope to demonstrate that, while sharing common moral ideals, families in Wangcun adopt quite different strategies of residence and support in their efforts to survive, to succeed and 'to be good'. Essential to securing the approval of other villagers is the perception that a family has made judgements in household management which have led to harmonious relations among family members and also within the wider community. Taking a longer historical view over a century of profound political change and economic development, evidence from Wangcun reveals considerable continuity in the morality of kinship relations over the past three generations.

***

Although the distinction is subtler than the scope of this chapter allows, Chinese philosophy was historically far more concerned with harmony than truth. In contrast with the European pursuit of abstract, objective universalism, Chinese intellectuals concentrated on the practical establishment and maintenance of harmonious relationships extending to a harmonious society.[2] In ironic reference to A. N. Whitehead's remark that all of Western philosophy is a series of footnotes to Plato, Hall and Ames (1998: 1423) note that 'all of Chinese thinking is a series of commentaries on Confucius', and for Confucius (2003: §I.2)—whose central interest is the cultivation of moral character—'being good as a son and obedient as a young man is, perhaps, the root of a man's character'. Kinship relations, then, are not just another sphere of life in which people make moral choices and judgements. In China, the morality of kinship provides the foundation for one's closest relationships and the basis of engagements with friends, with more distant associates and personal conduct within wider society.

Didier Fassin (2008: 334) has recently argued for a 'moral anthropology' centred on 'the human belief in the possibility of telling right from wrong and in the necessity of acting in favour of the good against the evil', but this seems unable to accommodate individuals who choose to act immorally (or amorally) in their own interests or the various perspectives and consequences resulting from diverse moral priorities. I suggest therefore that we are more concerned with judgements of actions as 'good' or 'bad' (and the shades between) than the moral absolutism of 'right' and 'wrong', which leaves us with the question of how best to locate these moral judgements.

Drawing on the work of Martin Heidegger, Jarrett Zigon (2007, 2008) has proposed an approach which concentrates on moments of 'breakdown' (similar, as he acknowledges, to Foucault's (1991) 'problematisation'), during which moral issues appear before individuals as objects for contemplation. Such moments of 'breakdown' are, I believe, necessary in our consideration of morality, but they are not sufficient. While these 'moments' crystallize the intangible and taken-for-granted principles by which individuals live and interact, they may be unrepresentative of and say little about the long-term, dynamic dispositions which guide judgements in the quotidian drudgery of life.

In focusing on everyday judgements of this kind, I follow Michael Lambek's (2010: 44) call for a study of 'ordinary ethics'—one that accepts, among other things, the 'fundamental givenness of ethics'. As has been noted in the introduction to this book, the use of the term 'ordinary' here 'implies an ethics that is relatively tacit, grounded in agreement rather than rule, in practice rather than knowledge or belief, and happening without calling undue attention to itself' (Lambek 2010: 2). Only by approaching the issue in this way can we understand that: (a) morality is not just about moments of 'breakdown' or dilemma; (b) morality can guide everyday life without necessarily requiring much reflection or even articulation; (c) morality is neither a structural nor attitudinal prescription, and individuals may wish to act 'appropriately' through their own volition as much as to conform with expectation or obligation; and (d) judgements—both of how to act and of the actions of others—are central.

To explore the 'ordinary' morality of Chinese kinship in greater detail, I will now turn to examples from my own work in Wangcun. I will outline key themes in local kinship morality before introducing three families who have adopted different strategies of household management—each held to be admirable, or morally 'virtuous', by fellow villagers—and relate their reflections on how families ought to live. Complementing other contributions to this volume—including Jing Shao and Mary Scoggin's chapter on HIV/AIDS in rural China and Eona Bell's discussion of Hong Kong immigrants in Scotland (Chapters 13 and 5, respectively)—where moral questions are brought daily to the foreground due to informants' problematic or marginal status, I will treat the distinct patterns of kinship organization in Wangcun as longer-term structural answers to implicit, 'everyday' moral questions about family life.

THE 'ORDINARY' MORALITY OF KINSHIP IN WANGCUN

Located on the fertile soil of a river valley in the middle of Zhejiang province, the village of Wangcun (or 'Wang Village') has around 550 registered inhabitants, although the true population is a little lower since many of the younger villagers have moved to the nearby city of Jinhua or farther afield in search of better-paid off-farm employment. Throughout Wangcun's 600-year history, the village has been home to a comparatively poor agricultural community, and surrounding fields were owned by wealthy landlords from neighbouring towns until the Communist victory of 1949 and subsequent land reforms. Before then, villagers were engaged as tenant farmers and paid in kind for their labours. Although residential and social mobility was limited, many of today's elderly villagers left their natal households as youths to work as agricultural or domestic labourers and tradesmen, returning home for marriage or household division.

All evidence suggests that the vast majority of villagers enthusiastically embraced their new government after (what was a very literal) Liberation. In the campaigns of the Cultural Revolution, all households burned their ancestral records and—with the notable exception of the Yang family, discussed later in this chapter—no household in the village today keeps or expresses much interest in a family genealogy (*jiapu*). The village's modest ancestral temples were destroyed or have fallen into disrepair, except one now used to house the Elderly Residents' Association (*laonian xiehui*). Grave sites—traditionally situated on a hillock covered by orange orchards—are today located in a public cemetery. Apart from a few families who have opened their front rooms for card games and make a small supplementary income from selling cigarettes and household sundries, there are no local businesses or industries. Employment options are limited to farming, short-term contract jobs (*xiaogong*) such as road-building, or finding work in the city.

The most significant development in recent years came in 2004, when a large area of village farmland was requisitioned by the local government and sold to a European bus manufacturer which had another factory in Jinhua and hoped to expand local operations. Unfortunately for the foreign concern, their application for planning permission was subsequently denied under legislation designed to protect China's agricultural land. As a result, households were paid substantial windfall payments[3] in compensation for the loss of entitlement to allocations of village land, but they continue as before to farm and derive incomes from their plots. As will be discussed later in this chapter, the windfall payments have reduced financial dependence among kin because each generation is now able to meet daily living expenses and material expectations, leading villagers to report a transition from economic to emotional support within their families.

Discussions of morality—including the morality of kinship relations—arose often in conversation with villagers. In this short chapter, I shall confine my examples to moral judgements of interpersonal conduct (excluding such issues as marriage, funeral practices or raising children) and concentrate on how living relatives interact with one another and are perceived by others. Of course, discussing these matters is not always easy: regarding folk accounts of morality, Charles Stafford has noted that 'anthropologists typically get content-poor answers when they ask informants explicitly moral questions' (2010: 197), which is why I choose to focus on the structural manifestations of those moral decisions in this chapter. That said, few villagers would disagree with retired cadre Li Shuang's views on children:

In my opinion, the most important thing [for a son or daughter] is that he is intelligent, with good morals and of Chinese ethnicity. If he can make money that's also good, but he must have the moral excellence of the Chinese people. He must be good to his parents, and to others; be virtuous and polite; and neither foolhardy nor do anything illegal. He mustn't go down the wrong path.

Another elderly gentleman, Huang Jian Jun, once reflected wistfully on the help he provides by looking after his grandson so his own son can go out to work:

If a child is born, you have to bring up the child. You don't have any choice; it is the duty of being a grandfather. This is the course of history: one generation hands down to the next. My father helped me to grow up, I helped my son to grow up, now I still help to raise my grandson. This is just the tide of history, as one generation passes on to the next.

While these reflections may be expressed in terms of obligations, this need not devalue their importance if realized, as many choose not to honour their responsibilities. Of course, a shared morality in matters of kinship does not mean that these relationships are straightforward or immune from occasional difficulties: there were stories of children squandering their parents' savings through gambling, keeping mistresses in other villages or failing to 'respect the old and cherish the young' (*zunlao aiyou*). Supporting Howell's (1997: 9) view that 'moral principles . . . express simultaneously an inherent dynamic relationship between the "ought" and the "is"', moral values in Wangcun are often revealed as villagers seek to bridge any gap between how things 'are' and how they feel things 'ought to be'.

One such example is Ma Hui, an elderly gentleman who receives almost no support from his three sons after dividing their household. He contrasts his situation with fellow villager Wang Zhan Chao, who has stayed in Wangcun to care for his aged mother while his wife and adult children run a tea shop in Beijing:

> My children and grandchildren are no good. I have lived too long; it is difficult for them to look after me now . . . [Each day], my wife and I each have one yuan [£0.10] to live on—that is all given to us by our three sons—and the country gives us nothing . . . [Wang's] family conduct themselves well, and have a real sense of morality [*you daode*]. My speech is very simple, but people should behave in a moral way.

For many villagers, the changes of the last thirty years have resulted in two main developments in the nature of kinship morality. First, individuals of all ages desire and hope to achieve a greater level of 'freedom', ideally not at the expense of good relations with kin. Second, as agricultural incomes have stabilized and gradually increased—and particularly in the case of Wangcun, where families received large windfall payments after the land requisition but continue to farm their fields—households are better off than ever before. This has led to a change in how villagers meet their felt moral obligations to provide mutual support. Since each generation is generally able to meet its own living expenses and expectations of material comfort, villagers speak of a desire to maintain regular contact through visits and hope one day for kin—geographically separated by economic necessity and, perhaps, the desire for independence and modern lifestyles among younger villagers—to be reunited.

Although fundamental moral ideals of mutual respect, self-sacrifice and family-centrism remain, there has been a gradual shift in emphasis from economic interdependence to emotional support among adults within the same family.

I should like to illustrate these trends with specific reference to three families in Wangcun who are broadly admired as 'virtuous' by villagers, despite adopting very different family structures and strategies. Before doing so, it is worth briefly explaining my terminology. In a small and historically poor community without populous lineages or significant corporate property, the villagers of Wangcun never did exhibit the classical model of Chinese kinship: none could claim membership of even the lowliest 'A' in Freedman's alphabetic lineage continuum (Freedman 1958: 131–7). Instead, within the framework of agnatic descent, families in Wangcun historically aspired to one of three models of kinship relations: (*a*) the 'large' family, where many relatives would live and work together in close cooperation; (*b*) the 'dispersed' family, in which members would encourage one another to venture outside the village and diversify their agricultural and sideline incomes to maximize opportunities; and (*c*) the 'concentrated' family, in which small or nuclear families would use their close kinship ties as the foundation for family-based sidelines or enterprises. As I will discuss later, it is not the structures themselves that are praiseworthy, but the ability of these families to succeed while maintaining 'harmonious' interpersonal relationships, suggesting that everyday moral judgements are more concerned with 'how to act' than 'what to do'.

THE 'LARGE' FAMILY

The first of these families, which I characterize as exemplifying a 'large' family model, is the Yang family, who arrived as immigrants fleeing failed harvests in another part of Zhejiang around eighty years ago. Relative newcomers to the village, the Yang family have since remained a tightly knit group who retain close ties with relatives in their ancestral home of Dongyang, fifty miles from Wangcun. The family is dominated by the six sons of patriarch Yang Zhao, and they are the only family in the village to keep genealogical records (*jiapu*). Local carpenter Ma Wen Jun explained his admiration for the family of one of the sons, Yang Cheng Wen, who grew quite wealthy working as a labour contractor.

His mother and father are still alive and in good health, and although they have divided the family, he has two sons who have given birth to two grandsons. Their family already has four generations under one roof [*si shi tong tang*]![4]

For another of the six sons, Yang Cheng Wu, supporting his aged parents is an important commitment:

Of course we want to support [our parents], and—for example—we six brothers give them their living expenses. Now that the land has been requisitioned, they have their own money. Before that, we brothers shared their medical expenses equally. Now, each of us gives 300 *kuai*[5] for living expenses, and we also each give them 100 *jin* of rice . . . If they should ever fall ill and cannot work, then we will go to help them keep their house clean and things like that. But I think we will take it in turns, from the eldest to the youngest . . . In the village, I would say that our family's level of parental support [*shanyang fumu*] is relatively good, and there are no fights between our parents and us.

The Yang family's successes make it rather difficult for the younger generation to reciprocate the care and support that they have received. Perhaps, as the unemployed 28-year-old Yang Xiao suggests, their opportunity to honour shifting moral obligations will come later:

If I lived outside [Wangcun], I would certainly send money home if my parents needed it, but it would be better to live near to my parents so that I can look after them when they get older. At the moment, they don't really need any care and they have their own money. Before, when everyone was farming, we never had so much money, but now that the land has been sold, every household has got tens of thousands of *kuai*, and everyone has money and houses.

THE 'DISPERSED' FAMILY

The second illustration of family life in Wangcun is the Zhang family, who represent the 'dispersed' model of kinship organization. Like many other families in the village, the younger generation has moved away from Wangcun for marriage, education and employment. Elderly widower Zhang Zhi Hai, now eighty-one years old, lives alone in an unheated, single-storey house and still shuffles to his fields each morning to farm. He described to me the impact of economic changes on intergenerational moral obligations following household division (*fenjia*):

> 'When your sons are grown up, you should always divide the house': after dividing it's better, and there are fewer 'contradictions'. Even with one son, everyone should divide [their household]. Even if your daughter-in-law is good, you will still want to divide. Dividing the household is better and you have more liberty. Old people can't eat hard food, they want to eat soft food, and younger people want to eat harder foods. It's not the same, and we old people will choke if we eat hard food.

Many elderly residents share Zhang Zhi Hai's view that an 'independent' old age is desirable; to borrow his metaphor, there is generally very little appetite for co-residence with married children. His daughter-in-law, Xu Fang, explained that few families now cooperate on tasks such as house-building or harvesting crops, since it deprives relatives of the opportunity to earn money elsewhere:

> Before, in the early days of the individual farms, people would always help each other. Now the economic conditions have improved and people prefer to go out [of Wangcun] and do short-term labour jobs. If I ask you for help, you could have gone out and earned a day's salary. If you help [me] then you won't get any money, and I will feel very sorry.

Although economic prosperity has reduced reliance on kin for assistance and broken the cycles of labour exchange common in earlier decades, her husband, Zhang Tian Xiang, does not believe that this devalues ancestor worship at the appropriate times in the festive calendar:

> Of course it's still important to visit graves and pay respects; it's a virtuous tradition [*chuantong meide*] . . . [to ask for] blessing and

protection and for good health [and honour] my great-grandfather, my father's parents and my own parents.

Their eldest daughter, Zhang Xiao Hua, has now married and moved to live with her husband on the outskirts of Jinhua's suburban industrial zone. She rarely visits her parents and seems to have accepted a place in her husband's family:

> I've already forgotten about [the emotional and financial support from my parents]; how could I remember those things after so many years? So I just give them a few things at festival times. I haven't really thought about looking after my parents, but of course I would like to have a son to continue our family line.[6]

With their second child studying for her doctorate in America, the burden of any responsibility falls upon their youngest—Zhang Ao Xi—to provide for his parents. Like Yang Xiao earlier, he too recognizes the changing nature of moral obligation and hopes to act accordingly when the time comes:

> It wasn't easy for my parents to raise me. If I didn't respect them, would I still be a person? Filial piety [*xiao*] has deep roots in the hearts and minds of Chinese people. If my family's financial situation is not so great, then it's important to give material assistance. Of course, at the moment, things are not that bad, so my mother and father hope that their children will find time to come home and keep them company. After all, when people get older, they become afraid of being alone.

THE 'CONCENTRATED' FAMILY

The third and final form to be considered is the 'concentrated' model of kinship organization, epitomized in Wangcun by the Wu family. The 79-year-old Wu Jia Jie was the first of his family to move to the village, and relations with his children deteriorated rapidly after their mother's death. He subsequently remarried and now lives with his second wife in the shadow of his only son's modern, multi-storey residence on the east side of Wangcun. His son, the industrious Wu Tong Yu, is now head of the wealthiest household in the village, together earning over 300,000 yuan (£30,000) each year. Through diligence and cooperation with his son, the family invested their windfall payments to purchase digging machines and began a vehicle leasing business, the income from which is supplemented by diverse agricultural sidelines. Wu Tong Yu, echoing Xu Fang and many others in Wangcun, notes the impact of rural development in easing the primarily instrumental nature of relationships with friends and family in the past:

> Before, you used to help me, and I used to help you. Now each person works for themselves. In the past, if you wanted to build a house, it was always friends and family that helped, whereas today you can just contract out the work. I think that since the economic situation has improved, you have more connections and actually have more friends and family than before.

Although financial interdependence between family members may have declined as the economy has stabilized and improved, Wu Tong Yu's 24-year-old son Wu Guang Bo remains proudly committed to working with his father. He now earns considerably more than his peers in their urban jobs, who often encounter the same difficulties and prejudices as the Shenzhen migrant workers documented by I-chieh Fang in Chapter 4 of this volume. Wu Guang Bo attributes his family's success to their sense of solidarity:

> Normally, young people all go out [to the cities] because there's nothing to do in the countryside. It's relatively easy to make money in the cities, but my family has a real 'team spirit'! We have a collective strength [*jiti liliang da*], so it's easier to get things done!

His younger sister Wu Ying Lu is unlikely to contribute to the family businesses in the near future but feels similarly devoted to the success of her parents and hopes to support them in other ways:

> If I get married and need to live in Jinhua, then I could come home often if I live nearby. If I'm busy with work and I can't manage to do

so, and by chance they fall ill or something, then I will come back to see them. I think it's unlikely that they won't have enough food and clothing, but they always want us to come home to see them, come back and keep them company. I will try my best to stay together with them, and of course I must love them.

CHOICE, STRUCTURE AND CHOICE OF STRUCTURE

The material from Wangcun leads to two initial observations about the nature of contemporary kinship morality in China: first, that it is not, nor does it need to be, internally consistent (one can both wish to see one's children often while encouraging them to work in faraway cities); and second, very different strategies can be chosen or praised based on competing priorities and circumstances. Perhaps neither should surprise us, but from them we may draw together trends in the 'ordinary' morality of kinship in Wangcun today.

Despite successive political attacks on the ideological foundation of traditional[7] kinship morality in the early years of the People's Republic, the Communist Party has not yet established an adequate infrastructure of social services which would allow the state to supersede the family as the primary apparatus of welfare support in rural China. While this has ensured that the fates of children and aged parents alike are typically dependent on kin, the material from Wangcun suggests that neither the basis nor the remit of kinship morality is exclusively economic.

Elderly residents of Wangcun, despite welcoming their Communist liberators and supporting policies of land reform and class struggle, often recalled their shame at being unable to make ritual offerings during the subsequent famines and deprivation (a theme explored by Stephan Feuchtwang in Chapter 12). Regional and national developments—and, in Wangcun, the considerable impact of windfall payments to households after the land requisition in 2004—have brought a level of financial security and material comfort which would have seemed unimaginable thirty years ago. One might expect a morality of kinship relations founded only on economic dependence to have somehow changed in tandem with these advances.

Instead, I venture, the nature of exchange by which kinship obligations are fulfilled has changed, but the morality of those relations has proven remarkably durable. Yunxiang Yan (2009: 22) is surely right to claim that 'the Chinese moral landscape, like other dimensions of social life, is undergoing a process of multi-layered and multi-dimensional changes instead of a linear development', and for that very reason I would guard against any suggestion that Chinese (kinship) morality is on an evolutionary and inevitable trajectory towards materialistic individualism. Concluding his ethnography of family life in the northern Chinese village of Xiajia, Yan (2003) elsewhere notes:

> Unlike in the traditional family, where an individual was nothing more than the personification of the family line, the contemporary individual is concerned with the well-being of the private family and personal happiness in the present; these new concerns are reflected in the decline of ancestor worship, the crisis of conjugality, and the new status of children. (218)

The evidence that I have outlined in this chapter suggests a rather different picture for kinship morality in Wangcun, both in terms of the 'traditional' family and for villagers today.

First, we must reconsider the nature of 'traditional' kinship morality and practices. If by 'traditional' we mean Chinese lives in pre-Communist times, then—by coincidence—the histories of the three families documented here demonstrate remarkable similarities with the domestic challenges of twenty-first-century China. Leaving their ancestral hometown in search of better farmland and fresh opportunities, Yang Zhao and his household established themselves in a new community and later succeeded as labour contractors in the post-collective period. Due to disagreements with his stepmother after the remarriage of his father, Zhang Zhi Hai left his natal household as a young man to work as a farm labourer, only returning to divide the household with his father and brother. Finally, Wu Jia Jie moved to Wangcun to start a new home with his wife, only for his later remarriage to cause major disagreements with his children. These stories of marital problems, difficulties between parents and their selfish children, awkward household divisions and the movement of youths away from their homes in search of better work would seem normal today (or perhaps even novel, when contrasted with Confucian scriptural 'tradition'), but these stories took place sixty or seventy years ago—often before Liberation and long before the market reforms and rapid social changes witnessed since.

In earlier years, families were forced to live together in cramped, single-storey dwellings due to abject poverty and a shortage of housing, rather than any explicit desire to conform to Confucian ideology. Their life histories appear to reveal considerable continuities of labour migration, family cooperation and interpersonal difficulties as individuals balance personal opportunities with kinship commitments. Elderly villagers now speak positively of household division (*fenjia*) as a morally desirable and liberating experience of achieving freedom (*ziyou*), through which they can complete obligations to their children and enjoy an old age unburdened by parental responsibilities.[8] For parents, it would be fair to say that the moral (and material) foundation of patriarchal authority within many households today is weak, but the historical evidence from Wangcun suggests that it was never particularly strong. Nevertheless, the vast majority of adult children in Wangcun—sons such as Zhang Ao Xi and daughters such as Wu Ying Lu—recognize the sacrifices made by their parents to raise them and provide for their education, but local developments have abrogated the need to repay parental investments with remittances from urban incomes.

Second, we must examine whether and how the morality of these kinship relations is shaping and responding to the opportunities and new challenges presented by contemporary society after the tremendous economic changes of the last thirty years. Wangcun's situation is rather unusual, since the windfall payments made to households have provided substantial financial help without (yet) depriving villagers of their land and its produce. Coupled with the stability and growth of their agricultural and sideline incomes (as well as the abolition of rural taxes and the harmonization of state and market grain prices), most households are now able to meet their own material expectations. However, the kinship strategies outlined in this chapter are reflected in how each of the three families concerned chose to use their windfall payments from the land sales. The 'large' Yang family chose to invest in their corporate estate and are now able to boast of an impressive family compound where fathers and their sons live in close proximity in nicely decorated homes. The more 'dispersed' Zhang family dedicated all of their money to supporting their children through university, which has allowed their youngest daughter to pursue her doctoral studies in America and their son to complete tertiary education and secure stable urban employment. Finally, the 'concentrated' Wu family used their windfall payments as start-up capital to establish their vehicle leasing business, which has grown over recent years to provide their family with a handsome income.

Beyond their economic successes, these various strategies are praised by fellow villagers as conforming to widely held views on the morality of kinship relations, despite resulting in quite different patterns of residence and mutual support. Others may have done well for themselves in recent years, but these particular families have succeeded while maintaining good relations within their households and among the village community, suggesting the importance of moral as well as purely economic considerations in the social recognition of success in contemporary China (an issue addressed by Hui Zhang in Chapter 7). Of course, these strategic choices are not made in a vacuum: factors such as mass internal migration (Murphy 2002), birth-planning policies (Fong 2004; Greenhalgh 1993) and the importance of *guanxi* networks (Kipnis 1997; Yan 1996) reflect the rapidly-changing social landscape within which individuals and their families must act. And yet, like Ellen Oxfeld's Mr Zhou—a Hakka Chinese businessman in Calcutta, who must balance the competing pressures of ambition and responsibility—villagers in Wangcun recognize that 'the instincts of individual competitiveness exist side by side with those of familial devotion, love, and duty' (Oxfeld 1992: 287). Those regarded by fellow residents to be admirable or 'virtuous' are best able to align personal and family interests, fulfilling moral obligations while negotiating success on their own terms in the modern economy. Without any particularly notable acts of filial piety or public service as points of reference, each of the three families presented in this chapter is therefore judged to be praiseworthy in a quite 'ordinary' sense by their fellow villagers.

SAME DREAM, DIFFERENT BEDS

Thanks to the political stability and economic prosperity of recent years supplemented by the local windfall payments, material interdependence among co-resident kin in Wangcun has gradually given way to a growing sense of sentimental emptiness as self-sufficient elderly couples seek amicable relations with their middle-aged sons and daughters-in-law, and those middle-aged parents hope to maintain contact with children, many of whom—with the active encouragement of their mothers and fathers—have left the village to find work elsewhere. Catering to the emotional well-being of parents has therefore become a new site of moral judgement, both of how to act and in assessing the actions of others, as villagers experience the transition in kinship obligations from economic dependence to emotional support. Underlying this new currency of exchange are fundamentally moral ideals of care and self-sacrifice which do not appear to have changed markedly in living memory. Such dispositions rarely express or manifest themselves in the form of isolatable moments of moral 'breakdown'. Rather, they are born of, responsive to and negotiated in the course of everyday family life—evening meals, village gossip and card games over New Year—as ever they have been.

For families in Wangcun, these choices do not lead to a single structural outcome, nor is any particular structure virtuous in its own right. For any of the three models outlined in this paper, there are examples—such as the Wang family that we met in the introduction—who share the structural features but whose behaviour is frowned upon by others for failing to achieve internal harmony and maintain good relations within the community. As such, we may wish to move beyond the assumption, however seductive, that rural families in China shared a single developmental cycle in which five generations under a single roof was seen as 'the ultimate aim of all family growth' (see Baker 1979: 2; Cohen 1976: 65–70 for discussion) and instead examine the enduring diversity of kinship structures as the observable outcomes of 'ordinary' moral priorities and decisions, as successive generations respond to and seek to influence the local circumstances of their time.

With widening disparities in incomes and living standards, an ageing generation of mothers and fathers with vastly higher expectations than their own parents and anxiety about the fragility of China's nascent 'harmonious society', we may be sure of many challenges for rural Chinese families in the years ahead. For now, the evidence presented in this chapter suggests that families in Wangcun continue to make judgements and structural choices based on enduring moral ideals in the pursuit of harmonious relations and that, while sleeping in different beds, they share the same dream.

NOTES

The title of this chapter is a play on the Chinese idiom *tong chuang yi meng*, which means to share the same bed but have different dreams.

1. All quotations presented in this paper are taken from verbatim transcriptions of recorded conversations with villagers. Translations into English, and any errors, are my own. Names of the village and villagers have been changed.
2. The establishment of a 'harmonious society' (*hexie shehui*) remains the goal of the current administration of Hu Jintao (*People's Daily*, 20 February 2005, http://theory.people.com.cn/GB/40551/3188468.html).
3. Payments varied slightly between production teams but were approximately 30,000 yuan or £3,000 per person, which—in a community with a typical per capita income of around 6,000 yuan—represented half a decade's earnings from agriculture.
4. Ma Wen Jun's passing remark suggests that popular veneration of the Confucian ideal for 'five generations under one roof'—however rare historically, or legally and financially difficult today (Wolf 1985; Cohen 1992; Selden 1993)—has not been entirely forgotten in Wangcun.
5. *Kuai* is a common colloquial term for the unit of currency, also known as yuan (renminbi).
6. Zhang Xiao Hua is referring to continuing the family she has established with her husband, not the continuation of her natal family.
7. In this chapter, 'traditional' refers broadly to the late imperial period of Chinese history, incorporating the Ming and Qing dynasties, which ruled from 1368 to the establishment of the Republic of China in 1912. However, it must be noted that kinship ideologies and practices—guided by the Confucian cultural inheritance—never ossified and have always proven responsive to commercial, political and even technological developments (as Francesca Bray demonstrates in Chapter 10 of this volume). Over the centuries, 'traditional' kinship institutions gradually arose and adapted accordingly: the widespread writing of genealogical records began during the Song dynasty (960–1279), and ancestral halls were not numerous until the sixteenth century (Baker 1979; Bol 2004; Ebrey 1984; Ebrey and Watson 1986; Nivison and Wright 1959). As such, recent 'revaluations of values' (Nietzsche 1994 [1895]: §61) in living memory—precipitated first by collectivization and campaigns against 'feudal' practices, and then second by the market reforms of Deng Xiaoping—must be judged within a longer history of dynamic social change in China and not against a monolithic pre-Communist 'tradition'.
8. Evidence presented by Goldstein and Ku (1993) suggests that this desire for freedom among the elderly may not be a recent development.

REFERENCES

Baker, H.D.R. (1979), *Chinese Family and Kinship*, London: Macmillan.

Bol, P. K. (2004), 'Local History and Family in Past and Present', in T.H.C. Lee (ed.), *The New and the Multiple: Sung Senses of the Past*, Hong Kong: The Chinese University Press.

Cohen, M.L. (1976), *House United, House Divided: The Chinese Family in Taiwan*, New York: Columbia University Press.

Cohen, M.L. (1992), 'Family Management and Family Division in Contemporary Rural China', *The China Quarterly*, 130: 357–77.

Confucius (2003), *The Analects*, London: Penguin Classics.

Ebrey, P.B. (1984), 'Conceptions of the Family in the Sung Dynasty', *The Journal of Asian Studies*, 43/2: 219–45.

Ebrey, P.B., and Watson, J.L. (eds). (1986), *Kinship Organization in Late Imperial China, 1000–1940*, Berkeley: University of California Press.

Fassin, D. (2008), 'Beyond Good and Evil? Questioning the Anthropological Discomfort with Morals', *Anthropological Theory*, 8/4: 333–44.

Fong, V.L. (2004), *Only Hope: Coming of Age under China's One-child Policy*, Stanford, CA: Stanford University Press.

Foucault, M. (1991), 'Polemics, Politics and Problematisations: An Interview with Michel Foucault', in P. Rabinow (ed.), *The Foucault Reader*, Harmondsworth, UK: Penguin.

Freedman, M. (1958), *Lineage Organisation in Southeastern China*, London School of Economics Monographs on Social Anthropology, London: Athlone Press.

Goldstein, M.C., and Ku, Y. (1993), 'Income and Family Support Among Rural Elderly in Zhejiang Province, China', *Journal of Cross-Cultural Gerontology*, 8/3: 197–223.

Greenhalgh, S. (1993), 'The Peasantization of the One-Child Policy in Shaanxi', in D. Davis and S. Harrell (eds), *Chinese Families in the Post-Mao Era*, Studies on China, Berkeley: University of California Press.

Hall, D., and Ames, R. (1998), 'Chinese Philosophy', in E. Craig (ed.), *Routledge Encyclopedia of Philosophy*, London: Routledge. Available online: http://www.rep.routledge.com/article/G001

Howell, S. (1997), 'Introduction', in S. Howell (ed.), *The Ethnography of Moralities*, European Association of Social Anthropologists (Series), London: Routledge.

Kipnis, A.B. (1997), *Producing Guanxi: Sentiment, Self, and Subculture in a North China Village*, Durham, NC: Duke University Press.

Lambek, M. (2010), *Ordinary Ethics: Anthropology, Language, and Action*, New York: Fordham University Press.

Murphy, R. (2002), *How Migrant Labor Is Changing Rural China*, Cambridge Modern China Series, Cambridge: Cambridge University Press.

Nietzsche, F. (1994 [1895]), 'The Antichrist', in W. Kaufmann (trans.), *The Portable Nietzsche* (US ed.), New York: Penguin Classics.

Nivison, D. S., and Wright, A. F. (eds) (1959), *Confucianism in Action*, Stanford Studies in the Civilizations of Eastern Asia, Stanford, CA: Stanford University Press.

Oxfeld, E. (1992), 'Individualism, Holism, and the Market Mentality: Notes on the Recollections of a Chinese Entrepreneur', *Cultural Anthropology*, 7/3: 267–300.

Selden, M. (1993), 'Family Strategies and Structures in Rural North China', in D. Davis and S. Harrell (eds), *Chinese Families in the Post-Mao Era*, Studies on China, Berkeley: University of California Press.

Stafford, C. (2010), 'The Punishment of Ethical Behaviour', in M. Lambek (ed.), *Ordinary Ethics*, New York: Fordham University Press.

Wolf, A. P. (1985), 'Chinese Family Size: A Myth Revisited', in J. Hsieh and Y. Chuang (eds), *The Chinese Family and Its Ritual Behavior*, Taipei: Institute of Ethnology, Academia Sinica.

Yan, Y. (1996), *The Flow of Gifts: Reciprocity and Social Networks in a Chinese Village*, Stanford, CA: Stanford University Press.

Yan, Y. (2003), *Private Life Under Socialism: Love, Intimacy, and Family Change in a Chinese Village, 1949–1999*, Stanford, CA: Stanford University Press.

Yan, Y. (2009), 'The Good Samaritan's New Trouble: A Study of the Changing Moral Landscape in Contemporary China', *Social Anthropology*, 17/1: 9–24.

Zigon, J. (2007), 'Moral Breakdown and the Ethical Demand: A Theoretical Framework for an Anthropology of Moralities', *Anthropological Theory*, 7/2: 131–50.

Zigon, J. (2008), *Morality: An Anthropological Perspective*, Oxford: Berg.

PART III

TECHNOLOGY, TECHNIQUES AND THE MATERIALITY OF ETHICS

CHAPTER 10

TOOLS FOR VIRTUOUS ACTION: TECHNOLOGY, SKILLS AND ORDINARY ETHICS

Francesca Bray

Sometimes there are situations where [my husband and I] don't say anything face-to-face, but which we communicate through SMS. Like if it's my birthday, neither of us will mention it face-to-face but later, he'll SMS me. Sometimes we'll argue and he'll apologise to me via SMS. I find this function of mobile phones really useful— what you can't say face-to-face, you can say via SMS. (32-year-old teacher, Shanghai, quoted in Lim 2008: 200)

In the chapter-opening quote we see a technological device, the mobile phone, being used to resolve a dilemma in ordinary ethics. This middle-class couple, like many others in China today, are feeling their way between deeply rooted conventions of reticence and formality and new, more demonstrative ideals of companionate marriage. They use their mobile phones as gadgets not only for facilitating communication between family members but also for exploring new emotional registers without losing face. The Shanghai teacher explains that she and her husband use the SMS function of their phones to push the boundaries of etiquette and the conventions of intimacy. I-chieh Fang's study (in Chapter 4 of this volume), meanwhile, shows us young migrant workers in a Shenzhen factory turning their mobile phones to ethical use in at least two ways. The first is quite straightforward: the young women use their phones to keep in touch with their parents. The second is more complex, involving judgements about their own and others' moral personhood: phoning, texting and online chat rooms allow groups of friends to engage in detailed explorations of what constitutes an ideal husband and whether they themselves are making progress in their search for a 'serious' relationship, the 'perfect match' that will be their life's achievement.

It comes as no great surprise to observe high-tech devices such as mobile phones or the Internet deployed as instruments in emergent moral practices. We are all aware that communications technologies, from television to the personal computer to CCTV, can both create and resolve ethical challenges. Social scientists, anxious parents, corporations and nanny or authoritarian states have variously scrutinized their potential for transforming, maintaining or breaching the boundaries of moral personhood and pondered how to achieve the best balance between control and freedom, protection and autonomy. But as anthropologists, can we postulate a more general role for technology in everyday ethics? Is it only the high-tech innovations of recent decades, such as the Internet or 'assisted reproduction', that deserve our attention, or should simple, mundane technologies such as the light bulb or the *kang* (traditional heated bed) figure more systematically in our studies of how people express values and construct moral personhood?

Engineers, says Bruno Latour, play a role analogous to the novelist in analysing and developing the modern human psyche. Yet while we consciously appreciate how novelists manipulate their characters to explore emotional or moral subtleties, we remain largely oblivious to the skills that engineers deploy as they 'shift out characters in other spaces and other times, devise positions for human and non-human users, break down competences that they then redistribute to many different actants, build complicate narrative programs and sub-programs that are evaluated and judged' (Latour 1992: 232). Why are we so blind to the 'subtle beauties of socio-technical embroglios', asks Latour, and to the hidden—or unnoticed—masses of material artefacts with which we have surrounded ourselves? No doubt, he says, because they involve a shift of expression or of frames of reference, from words to material constructions. Rather than the producers and the users of the technologies being linked through a shared consciousness of what the artefacts are there to do and how they do it, the engineering or 'technical shifting-out' effects a mystification of the non-material dimensions of the problem;

'techniques allow [the human actors] to ignore the delegated actors and to walk away without even feeling their presence' (232). This was as true of medieval house-design in China as it is of nuclear weapons testing (Bray 1997; Gusterson 1996). In a much more recent publication, Latour laments, 'The problem with techniques is that people *love to hate them* and also *hate to love them*, no matter if they are academics or not, so it is extraordinarily difficult to get the right distance with the mass of things with [which] they cohabit' (Latour 2007: 129).

This chapter argues for the analytical value of integrating technology, both high- and low-tech, into the anthropology of ordinary ethics and everyday virtuous (or vicious) practice. As a domain of skilled action which shapes and expresses both mental and material worlds, technology offers a potent analytical framework for tracking embodied practices of virtue and for highlighting the tensions and contradictions that may arise between ethics operating within different spheres (Carrier and Miller 1999; Ingold 2001; Bray 2008b).

Most of the contributions to this book focus primarily on the social and discursive practices of everyday ethics. Yet we should beware of reducing ordinary ethics to discursive practices and conscious judgements: some of our most profound experiences of emotion, and our most potent expressions of opinion, follow a grammar of bodily movements and of the manipulation of material objects—conscious at some levels, tacit at others, sometimes interwoven with speech acts and sometimes mute. Often our technical routines and their ethical implications go unexamined not only because of 'shifting out' but because they appear self-evident. The material worlds we construct about ourselves, and the repertories of action that they support, naturalize values and beliefs and inscribe them in social memory; the messages they convey are all the more powerful for being mute (Bourdieu 1973). In consequence, technological innovations at any scale are likely to trigger 'moments of breakdown' (Roberts, Chapter 9, this volume) and are frequently explicitly perceived as posing moral dilemmas. In sixteenth-century China, intensification of textile production led to men replacing women as weavers, a change seen by moralists as undermining the cosmic order of harmonious complementarity between yin and yang (Bray 1997). In Java in the 1970s, reaping-knives were gradually replaced by sickles in pursuit of speed and efficiency, displacing the troops of landless women who had previously participated in the harvest. The innovation was perceived as threatening the supposedly redistributive ethos of village life (White 2000). More recently, new technologies of assisted reproduction have challenged publics and legislators around the world to ponder what constitutes the 'real' bond between parents and child, reaching an astonishing diversity of conclusions (Edwards 2000; Bray 2008c).

Anthropologists and social and cultural historians (most notably perhaps Marcel Mauss, Norbert Elias and Fernand Braudel) have long recognized the silent moral power of established bodily habits—although within anthropology little serious attention was given to the peculiar systemic potency of technology (Pfaffenberger 1992). More recently, as just suggested, the anthropological gaze has fastened upon a range of painful ethical dilemmas raised by a few technological innovations that have posed highly visible and much debated challenges to conventional social values. Less attention has been devoted within anthropology, however, to a far more characteristic phenomenon, that is, to the much less dramatic, more gradual and often largely uncontentious processes of technological adaptation and selective assimilation that steadily transform our everyday experience. It is largely thanks to the new disciplines of technology studies and STS (science and technology studies)[1] that researchers are becoming methodologically and analytically equipped to explore the ethical dimensions and the trajectories of naturalization of mundane yet transformative technological innovations such as supermarket bar codes, cellphone upgrades or new safety codes for domestic wiring.

In this chapter, I therefore propose some concepts and methods drawn from technology studies or STS, including *sociotechnical systems, operational sequences, technological repertories, domestication* and *user scripts, delegation, communities of practice* and *technological code*, to explore the material grounding of ordinary ethics and the ethical impact of technological shifts. Most of my illustrations are drawn from recent anthropological or STS studies of everyday technologies in China.

Technology studies is an interdisciplinary field; the spectrum runs from philosophy to engineering by way of history, sociology and anthropology. By consensus the focus is not on individual gadgets and their mechanics per se, but on how technical features are embedded in the systems or networks—material, social and symbolic—which support their use. As well as the nuts and bolts one must consider the task that is being performed, the resources it requires, its impact, uses and representations. Different societies may solve the same material or social problem through quite distinct technological choices, while an identical gadget in engineering terms may be deployed completely differently in another cultural context. At the same time, technology studies differs from material culture studies in paying due attention to the material constraints and affordances inherent in technological processes: technologies involve a 'tight coupling of causally related elements' (Nowotny 2006: 17), which means that the systems or assemblages of artefacts, institutions and interpretations that the discipline addresses are treated as contingent (Collier and Ong 2005) but not arbitrary, by no means reducible to semiotics.

The field of STS emerged in response to the challenges of technocracy and technoscience and in consequence has focused principally on high-tech; however, its practitioners are increasingly concerned to develop analyses that apply to all human societies and all levels of technological activity. A common concern is to connect individual action and social or political process. Feminist critiques within the field have been particularly effective in highlighting and theorizing the articulations between macro-processes and everyday technological practice (Bray 2007), echoing (if in a different register) the concern of anthropologists of technology to expose the articulations between material work and community autopoiesis (Pfaffenberger 2001; Flitsch 2004). Thomas P. Hughes first proposed the term *sociotechnical system* in a study of the rise of electrical power systems, noting that good engineering alone was not sufficient to guarantee successful electrification: political, legal, social and economic measures were equally necessary—as were cultural and aesthetic adjustments (Hughes 1983; Gooday 2009). 'Sociotechnical systems are heterogeneous constructs that stem from the successful modification of social and non-social actors so that they work together harmoniously—that is, so that they resist dissociation' (Pfaffenberger 1992: 498). In the terms of actor-network theorists such as Bruno Latour or Madeline Akrich, successful innovation depends on enrolling and mobilizing human and non-human elements (actors or actants) to believe in the project, get it working and carry it forward (Akrich 1993). This systemic or network perspective draws consumers and users (or refusers) into the analysis as active contributors to the process of innovation. In the anthropological vein, it encourages us to focus on linkages between the values inherent in the goals and expectations of individuals; in the design, production and distribution of the technical products or services available to them; and in national or supranational levels of investment, regulation and policy. From an STS perspective, failure is as interesting, and as complex a process, as success.

Spanning and linking the domains of domesticity, business and governance, ranging in sophistication from the wok to the microwave, technological devices, practices and choices constitute a rich field for exploring the multiple levels at which shared values and everyday ethical practices, as well as societal shifts in ethical expectation, emerge and are negotiated (Bray 2008a; Oldenziel and Zachmann 2009). The systemic nature of technological practice or innovation also offers useful insights into how new practices, the changes in skill they necessitate and the values they embody, spread and stabilize. Whether high- or low-tech, the investigation of technological practices offers a privileged field for integrating materialist and interpretive analysis and for linking what Raymond Williams dubbed 'structures of feeling' to political economy (Pfaffenberger 2001; Bray 2007; Santos and Donzelli forthcoming).

Everyday ethical behaviour can be viewed as a form of skilled practice, one that always mobilizes social and symbolic resources and that frequently also deploys material, technical skills and instruments. The French school of anthropology of techniques/technology (the term *techniques* has both meanings in French) has developed a practical and flexible analytical method for linking the material, social and symbolic dimensions of technical or technological practices and skills, regardless of whether they are high- or low-tech. The approach grows out of the French anthropological convention of defining technique to include bodily practices (*techniques du corps*) as well as the use of tools. This dates back to Marcel Mauss, who saw *techniques du corps* as distinctive cultural practices, and to André Leroi-Gourhan, who treated tool, anatomy and speech as inseparable in his analysis of the logic of technical action (a position close to that of most classical Chinese theorists of ritual and ethical action). It begins with the documentation of *chaînes opératoires* or operational sequences, 'the series of operations involved in any transformation of matter (including our own body) by human beings' (Lemonnier 1992: 25). Skills (*savoir faire*), documented through operational sequences, are laid out as an ordered convergence of material, mental, social and cultural resources (d'Onofrio and Joulian 2006). The core observational and analytical methods may be deployed within a variety of overarching theoretical frameworks, including actor-network theory (Latour 1993), modes of production (Guille-Escuret 2003) or anthropology of ritual (Lemonnier 2004). It would seem a very promising method for mapping the materialities of virtuous or immoral action and the interfaces and articulations between political economy and structures of feeling. A recent article by Lu Xiaohe (2008) on business ethics in the PRC uses roughly this approach to track the production and decision-making processes of two or three defective or dangerous Chinese products and to identify the key points at which technological choices translate into ethical or unethical decisions.

The operating sequence approach is generally useful for mapping how technological practices translate values. Let me illustrate with two examples developed by anthropologists of technology. One is a reframing of Malinowski by Bryan Pfaffenberger (2001); the second is a study of Northern Chinese *kang*-culture by Mareile Flitsch (2004, 2008). Bronislaw Malinowski's interest in technology was in how it 'reveals the traditional ways and means by which knowledge and industry solve certain problems presented by a given culture' (Malinowski 1935: I, 240, cited in Pfaffenberger 2001: 80)—in the case of Trobriand society, a redistributive economy and a big man political system. Malinowski's account of the construction of the Trobriand yam-house, *bwayma*, presents it as a template for social action, for building the chief's prestige so he can bid for higher rank. In organizing the construction of the *bwayma*, the chief calls forth his kin and draws them into a careful sequence of activities, thus 'building and activating a well-oiled machine that will produce astonishing numbers of yams' (Pfaffenberger 2001: 81). But a focus on the sequence of rituals accompanying the construction of the *bwayma* highlights another fundamental transformation effected by this group activity. The *bwayma* begins as an empty shell and then is stuffed with yams until it is heavy, full—sated.

Malinowski's informants repeatedly stressed that the experience of building the *bwayma* and participating in its various constituent rituals . . . brought about a crucial transformation in the men and women who participated. They began as greedy, hungry people who would not hesitate to eat yams until their entire culture fell apart. But by the time the *bwayma* is built, they lose their hunger for yams. They become the kind of people Trobrianders must be if they are to achieve the goals that, as a community, they set for themselves. (Pfaffenberger 2001: 82)

The technology of *bwayma* building resolves 'the central problem faced by any redistributive culture, namely, how to appeal to individuals to constrain their consumption in favor of accumulating a surplus' (82).

Pre-industrial technologies such as the *bwayma* or the clay structures of the traditional Northern Chinese *kang* (raised living spaces heated by flues) owe nothing to the professional engineer, characterized by Latour as the unacknowledged moral artist of the contemporary world. Nevertheless, they embody a complex structure of social values. *Kangs* were constructed and maintained by the men of the family as an integral feature of the house, the design taking into account the qualities of local materials and fuels, as well as the size of the house and of the family. Women were trained from girlhood in the skills of lighting and fuelling the *kang*, adjusting the temperature for cooking, heating, working and social occasions, and placing individuals with different needs or expectations of bodily warmth (guests, the elderly, infants or sick people, men and women, duck-eggs or girls with newly bound feet) in appropriate patterns across the differentially heated platforms of the *kang*. A rich body of games, riddles, songs and proverbs shows how closely womanly virtues and the technical skills of *kang* management were interwoven in rural culture until the very recent 'consumer revolution' that has transformed the design and equipment of new housing (Flitsch 2008). Tracing the operating sequence of what she calls the *kang*-axis from the construction of the flues and platforms, to the skills of fuelling and temperature control, to the use of the stove and the social and technical management of the heated spaces, Flitsch demonstrates how the skills of *kang* management were cognate with the virtues of a good wife and wise mother: they embodied caring, thrift, foresight, economic productivity, hospitality and a judicious appreciation of what was due to the hierarchies of generation and gender. Flitsch also reminds us that the *kang*-axis united the functions of heating space and cooking food in a single material device and set of technical skills, whereas in recently built homes which do not incorporate *kangs*, the two activities have been divorced. Yunxiang Yan (2003) has noted how the reconfiguration of domestic space in rural North China underpins new conceptions of family relations, including an emerging commitment to privacy. The abandoning of the *kang* and the adoption of a new inventory of domestic technologies will certainly change how the virtues of a good wife are defined—will her de-skilling as mistress of the *kang* be compensated by respect for a new set of specifically wifely technical skills, one wonders, and if so, which skills would they be? Will those new skills be taught by mothers or grandmothers to little girls, whether through games and songs or practical example? Or will there be a generational reversal, as with many high-tech innovations, where it is the children who have to teach their elders how to use the new gadgets?

This brings me to the issue of *technological repertories*. Social units of all kinds—families, households, schools, shops, bridge clubs, hospitals, political parties and nations—rely on a repertory of technologies to reproduce themselves and to achieve their goals. In many cases one can identify what could be called a core 'set' of characteristic technologies and skills that are necessary to fulfil a social role or institutional function or that symbolize the values associated with them (Bray 1997). The repertory of technical devices typical of mothers of infants, parents of teenagers, grandparents, children of various ages or single people in any specific social context is a fascinating topic in itself. The technological repertory of a good wife and mother in a North Chinese village as described by Flitsch included the *kang*, the well, cooking pots and chopsticks, a sewing machine and so on. Meanwhile, a good middle-class wife and mother in California needs an SUV to ferry her children to their various appointments, a set of mobile phones on a family plan for maintaining contact, email and computer access, a large stove, a microwave, a vast refrigerator, a battery of food mixers, toasters, coffee machines and other kitchen gadgets, a washer and dryer, several bathrooms . . . a huge repertory of specialized machines to keep the family fed, clean and going. Embedded with her spouse and children in a community of practice (see farther on), she cannot dispense with this technological repertory or the social and material networks it enables her to participate in: these devices are not luxuries but necessities (Bray 2008b). Compared to the Chinese village repertory, the Californian repertory bears a high environmental price, 'private virtue, public vice' in Carrier and Miller's (1999) terms. Equally striking in terms of everyday ethics is the contrast between the forms of moral personhood, agency and personal fulfilment—for parents and children, male and female—that the two systems support. It would be particularly interesting to develop studies of shifts in value in village China as the economy develops, like those pioneered by Yunxiang Yan, in the light of detailed technological repertories and the forms of personhood they promote.

If we consider technological repertories in relation to the fulfilment of social roles, this casts further light on what STS scholars have conceptualized as user scripts and domestication. *User script* refers to sociotechnical effects built into the design of technological artefacts and *domestication* to users' appropriation of new technologies, often involving resistance to or subversion of the user script. A classic example is the Sony Walkman. It was initially designed with twin headsets, intended to allow young people to share music wherever they found themselves. It turned out that what young people actually wanted was not togetherness but a personal source of music on the move: very soon Sony phased out the dual jacks. The misuse of a technology may reflect a mismatch between the values and assumptions of designer and user. Thus electric washing machines are now accepted throughout the developed economies as time- and labour-saving devices which allow users, in particular mothers, to maintain high standards of health and cleanliness within the family. The cost of water and power has seldom been a consideration for American mothers conscious of their duty to keep their kids in clean jeans. Some mothers in the Hebei village studied by Wu Xiujie (2008) possessed washing machines, usually purchased by their husbands late into a pregnancy to protect them from the health risks associated locally with doing laundry after giving birth. But since they were acutely aware of the high cost of electricity, the women still did all routine laundry by hand—although they would use the machine for bulky quilts or occasionally for washing vegetables prior to pickling (Wu 2008). For these women, thrift as a womanly virtue outweighed convenience. Successful domestication, however, is a two-way process which supposes that users have the power to intervene in the reshaping of a technology. This is not always the case. To appeal to environmentally and energy-conscious women in Europe or Japan, the designers of washing machines produced machines that saved water, ran faster and used sophisticated programming to tailor the washing cycle to the amount and kind of laundry. It is quite unlikely that manufacturers will redesign washing machines to meet the needs or goals of poor Chinese villagers, institutionally positioned as second-class citizens when it comes to technological choice (see farther on).

Let me now return to some of the more obviously ethical impacts or implications of certain types of technology. In the modern world, says Bruno Latour, we have *delegated* many of the everyday ethical dilemmas or choices that we face to technological artefacts (Latour 1992). Engineers design technical devices that translate social or ethical challenges into material terms, producing artefacts which can stand in for the superego—and which may well be more effective, since they often limit or even suppress material opportunities for deviance. To offer just a few familiar examples of what we might call ethical engineering, speed bumps 'calm' impatient drivers passing through residential areas; cars beep at us till we fasten our seat belts or refuse to start if we drunkenly fumble the key in the ignition. The middle-class mothers in Beijing and Shanghai whom Sun Sun Lim interviewed in 2004 felt that they exerted effective control over their children's Internet use by keeping the computer in the living room and occasionally looking over the child's shoulder (Lim 2008). In 2009, however, the government re-delegated the responsibility and tightened control, requiring all makers of PCs for the Chinese market to pre-load parental-control anti-porn software (Oates 2009).

Traffic lights offer a different level of ethical control through technology: they do not materially force us to stop on red, but we have collectively internalized the rule as a *community of practice* comprising pedestrians, drivers, police, insurance agents and addicts of car-chase movies. The term *community of practice* was proposed by the cognitive anthropologists Jean Lave and Etienne Wenger (1991) to describe informal processes of learning and knowledge-building among groups of people who share an interest or skill. The concept has proven its worth in technology studies, focusing attention on how shared skills develop and shared conventions or meanings emerge when new technologies are adopted; it also highlights how novelties become needs or obligations as networks of use consolidate. I-chieh Fang (Chapter 4, this volume) shows us a community of practice emerging as young women develop shared conventions of phone and Internet use in pursuit of their life goals. Mobile phones and computers are now also vital yet risky tools for schoolchildren, in East Asia as elsewhere: as children and teachers develop ever-denser networks of communication through ICTs (information and communications technologies), and as the technological underpinnings of pedagogy and social organization change in consequence, these ICTs and the associated user-skills become indispensable tools for meeting homework assignments and daily schedules. Yet few parents feel they can responsibly allow their children uncontrolled access to the Internet. At what age does a child enter the category of person considered sufficiently responsible and socially aware to be trusted with a mobile phone or a PC? What new kinds of training and supervision do parents need to provide in order to protect their children from harm, and how can they gauge the challenges when their children's technical skills so far outstrip their own (Lim 2008; Matsuda 2008)? At another level of ethical calculation, mentioned earlier, the Chinese state manifests extreme ambivalence towards the trust it places in its citizens when regulating communications technologies such as the Internet.

Online communities of practice have been the object of particular analytical scrutiny in technology studies (Axel 2006). Choong-Hwan Park provides a useful bibliography of studies of the impact of the Internet and forms of netizen-ship in China (Park 2008; see also Liu 2009). Park's own ethnography describes the emergence of a rather unexpected and paradoxical Internet community of practice in the PRC. *Nongjia le* (peasant-family delights) refers to an increasingly popular form of rural tourism in which village households rebuild and equip their farms as guest houses where groups of urban tourists can spend a few days enjoying country scenery, pure air and wholesome food in an authentic family atmosphere. Positioning themselves as savvy modern entrepreneurs, most of the guest house owners feel they should advertise on the Internet. Since almost none have any computer skills and still fewer have access to a computer, they hire the services of a web designer through salesmen who regularly tour the villages in search of new clients. Together the villagers and the salesmen design web pages, regularly upgraded, using a grammar of stereotypical photographs and narratives which they jointly believe will appeal to jaded urbanites. 'Now a simple click on a major Internet search-engine, such as Google, Yahoo and *Baidu*, promptly leads to thousands of *nongjiale* Internet advertise-ments' (Park 2008: 236). One would normally suppose that the regular upgrading and steady evolution of the advertisements as a genre must respond to some form of feedback from people who view the pages. Yet it turns out that almost no guest selects a guest house on the basis of the advertisements: tourists are guided by friends' recommendations or the chance spotting of a sign at the side of the road. Neither the clients nor the hosts personally visit the Web sites, yet despite all evidence to the contrary the hosts remain convinced that these Web sites are a necessary tool for promoting their trade. The peasant entrepreneurs' relationship to the Internet is continuously evolving, yet they can scarcely be described as Internet users in the conventional sense. Nevertheless, they are neti-zens of a kind, since online advertisements contribute to their collective and evolving identity; furthermore, they consider the creation and main-tenance of their web pages as a form of agency that helps redeem their rustic lack of quality, *suzhi*.

A technology, whether high- or low-tech, is a material system in which tacit understanding and explicit knowledge both play a role in naturalizing social hierarchies and encoding cultural goals and values. The philosopher of technology Andrew Feenberg refers to this material-ization of values as a *technological code*, citing as an example the design of factory machinery in early-nineteenth-century Britain: built to a scale suitable for child operators, it encoded the social and legal endorsement of child labour (Feenberg 1999: 85). Although ICTs in China were not deliberately designed to exacerbate urban–rural hierarchies, within the calculus of *suzhi*, inequalities of access to ICTs and the skills to use them still leave most villagers at a clear disadvantage—although as Park suggests, we can identify some ingenious stratagems for selective ap-propriation of the resource. The development of the power grid in China over the last forty years is another instance of technological coding that has by and large favoured towns and cities over the countryside. The original design of the Chinese electrical grid reflected official ideology in prioritizing collective production, in particular industrial production, which was largely concentrated in urban collectives. Rural electrical supply was unreliable and minimal. In the Hebei village where Wu Xiu-jie conducted her investigations, even a single 15-watt bulb for light-ing remained beyond the scope of most households well into the 1970s. With the introduction of the new economic policies, however, and the gradual reconfiguration of the ideal Chinese citizen as educated con-sumer rather than tireless and austere producer, electricity supply was reconfigured and expanded to allow, and most recently to encourage, domestic consumption even in the countryside (Wu 2008: 217–19). At first inadequate voltage made it impossible to run a TV and a sewing ma-chine simultaneously. Since 2003 one could say that a stable sociotech-nical system has at last coalesced: the electrical supply is sufficiently regular and powerful to support widespread and concurrent use of appli-ances such as TVs, washing machines, pumps or water-boiling devices. Although individual metering has made households acutely aware of the running costs, the villagers now think of themselves as *entitled* to ex-pect a regular supply of current and to complain about power shortages or failures. At the same time, they recognize that their entitlements as citizens, and as actors in the national network of electrical users, are still institutionally inferior to those of urban consumers. Not only are appli-ances sold at a higher price in rural outlets than in city stores, the goods available are usually out-of-date models, and customers have a restricted choice between 'mostly no-name products produced by small facto-ries with loose or no quality controls at all'; '"rural" equals "urban's yesterday", or even the day before yesterday' (Wu 2008: 228, 216).

As the example of successive phases of development of the power grid in China suggests, while it is commonly supposed that technolo-gies are designed to solve material problems as efficiently as possible given the current state of knowledge, what is considered to constitute efficiency in a specific context varies widely, encoding broader soci-etal values. What do we measure to calculate efficiency, and who is en-titled to what? Whereas developing suitable technology to enrol private householders as consumers of electricity was a fundamental element of the strategy of electrical companies in the late nineteenth century in Britain and the United States (Gooday 2009), in the new socialist China domestic needs were discounted in favour of industry, and only in the past few years has the functionality of the rural grid been incorporated into calculations of the efficiency of the national grid. The regulation of GM (genetically modified) crops offers another example of how chang-ing priorities can affect technological change. Moxuan Li (2010) docu-ments a series of dramatic shifts over the last two decades in Chinese regulatory policies concerning the licensing of GM crops in general and GM rice in particular. In a nutshell, the government initially pursued pro-GM policies enthusiastically, responding to the imperatives of national economic growth and rural poverty relief, coupled with a perceived need for China to meet criteria imposed by the World Trade Organization. There was then a radical shift in policy when major importers of Chinese grains or foods, including Japan and the EU, banned GM foods. At that point China signed up to the Cartagena Protocol on Biosafety, and the government began to prioritize biodiversity and environmental and consumer safety above economic growth. Meanwhile, nongovernmental organizations and groups of public campaigners such as the Red Mamas (women concerned about their children's health) also began to demand a say, expressing their sense of entitlement to participatory governance through demonstrations, boycotts, web campaigns and blogs. Having committed itself to promoting a 'high-quality' public of educated consumers, the government agreed to institutionalize a degree of public participation in regulatory policy. Most recently, however, the spectre of world starvation triggered by climate change, environmental degradation and population growth has pushed the Chinese government and public alike to shift its stance again, this time concurring on national food security as a priority and pushing ahead with the commercialization of GM rice, albeit with much more stringent testing requirements (Li 2010). Li's analysis of shifting agendas and coalitions provides a clear illustration of shifts in technological code and the calculation of efficiency and of the intermeshing of macro- and micro-level ethics through the medium of two coupled innovative technologies, biotechnology and the ICTs that are helping build a participatory public.

China today is a nation transformed and divided by technology: in the prosperous cities, many middle-class citizens dispose of similar though by no means identical technological repertoires to those of middle-class Western families, and this technological infrastructure is considered as one important factor in the production of good-quality modern citizens. In less-developed areas, and especially in much of rural China, the introduction of new technologies is slow and patchy, and this is considered one factor in their social as well as material backwardness, even though rural lives too are being rapidly and radically changed by technical innovation. In conclusion, I would like to urge that attention to technologies, and in particular to the technological repertoires associated with social roles, and to the skills and the operational sequences involved in significant social activities or transactions would offer rich insights into ordinary ethics and how they are nested in the overarching moralities of the Chinese polity.

NOTE

1. Technology studies is, by and large, encompassed within STS but could be characterized as more concerned with the philosophical or anthropological dimensions of technology. The acronym STS expands either into Science, Technology and Society or into Science and Technology Studies, depending on the political position of the practitioners involved (Fu 2007).

REFERENCES

Akrich, M. (1993), 'A Gazogene in Costa Rica: An Experiment in Techno-sociology', in P. Lemonnier (ed.), *Technological Choices: Transformation in Material Cultures since the Neolithic*, London: Routledge.

Axel, B. K. (2006), 'Anthropology and the New Technologies of Communication', *Cultural Anthropology*, 21: 354–84.

Bourdieu, P. (1973), 'The Berber House', in M. Douglas (ed.), *Rules and Meanings*, Harmondsworth, UK: Penguin.

Bray, F. (1997), *Technology and Gender: Fabrics of Power in Late Imperial China*, Berkeley: University of California Press.

Bray, F. (2007), 'Gender and Technology', *Annual Review of Anthropology*, 36: 37–53.

Bray, F. (2008a), 'Introduction', in F. Bray (ed.), *East Asian Science, Technology and Society: An International Journal*, special issue, *Constructing Intimacy: Technology, Family and Gender in East Asia*, 2/2: 151–66.

Bray, F. (2008b), 'The Technics of the America Home', in S. Montón-Subías and M. Sánchez-Romero (eds), *Engendering Social Dynamics: The Archaeology of Maintenance Activities*, Oxford: BAR International Series 1862 (Hadrian Books).

Bray, F. (2008c), 'Becoming a Mother in Late Imperial China: Maternal Doubles and the Ambiguity of Fertility', in S. Brandstädter and G. D. Santos (eds), *Chinese Kinship: Contemporary Anthropological Perspectives*, London: Routledge.

Bray, F. (ed.) (2008d), *East Asian Science, Technology and Society: An International Journal*, special issue, *Constructing Intimacy: Technology, Family and Gender in East Asia*, 2/2.

Carrier, J., and Miller, D. (1999), 'From Private Virtue to Public Vice', in H. Moore (ed.), *Anthropological Theory Today*, Cambridge: Polity Press.

Collier, S.J., and Ong, A. (2005), 'Global Assemblages, Anthropological Problems', in A. Ong and S.J. Collier, *Global Assemblages: Technology, Politics, and Ethics as Anthropological Problems*, New York and Oxford: Blackwell.

d'Onofrio, S., and Joulian, F. (eds) (2006), *Cahiers d'anthropologie sociale*, 1, special issue: *Dire le savoir-faire: Gestes, techniques et objets*.

Edwards, J. (2000), *Born and Bred: Idioms of Kinship and New Reproductive Technologies in England*, Oxford: Oxford University Press.

Feenberg, A. (1999), *Questioning Technology*, London: Routledge.

Flitsch, M. (2004), *Der Kang. Eine Studie zur materiellen Alltagskultur bäuerlicher Gehöfte in der Manjurei*, Wiesbaden, Germany: Harrassowitz.

Flitsch, M. (2008), 'Knowledge, Embodiment, Skill and Risk: Anthropological Perspectives on Women's Everyday Technologies in Rural North China', in F. Bray (ed), *East Asian Science, Technology and Society: An International Journal*, special issue, *Constructing Intimacy: Technology, Family and Gender in East Asia*, 2/2: 265–88.

Fu, D. (2007), 'How Far Can East Asian STS Go? A Position Paper', *East Asian Science, Technology and Society: An International Journal*, 1/1: 1–14.

Gooday, G. (2009), *Domesticating Electricity: Technology, Uncertainty and Gender, 1880–1914*, London: Pickering & Chatto.

Guille-Escuret, G. (2003), 'Retour aux modes de production, sans contrôle philosophique', *Techniques & Culture*, 40. Available online: http://tc.revues.org/1484 (accessed 1 August 2012).

Gusterson, H. (1996), *Nuclear Rites: A Weapons Laboratory at the End of the Cold War*, Berkeley: University of California Press.

Hughes, T.P. (1983), *Networks of Power: Electrification in Western Society 1880–1930*, Baltimore: Johns Hopkins University Press.

Ingold, T. (2001), *The Perception of the Environment: Essays on Livelihood, Dwelling and Skill*, London: Routledge.

Latour, B. (1992), 'Where Are the Missing Masses? The Sociology of a Few Mundane Artefacts', in W. Bijker and J. Law (eds), *Shaping Technology/ Building Society: Studies in Sociotechnical Change*, Cambridge, MA: MIT Press.

Latour, B. (1993), 'Ethnography of a "High-tech" Case', in P. Lemonnier (ed.), *Technological Choices: Transformation in Material Cultures since the Neolithic*, London: Routledge.

Latour, B. (2007), Interview in J.-K. Berg Olsen and E. Selinger (eds), *Philosophy of Technology: 5 Questions*, Birkerød, Denmark: Automatic Press/VIP.

Lave, J., and Wenger, E. (1991), *Situated Learning: Legitimate Peripheral Participation*, Cambridge: Cambridge University Press.

Lemonnier, P. (1992), *Elements for an Anthropology of Technology*, Ann Arbor: Museum of Anthropology, University of Michigan.

Lemonnier, P. (ed.) (1993), *Technological Choices: Transformation in Material Cultures since the Neolithic*, London: Routledge.

Lemonnier, P. (2004), 'Mythiques chaînes opératoires', *Techniques & Culture*, 43–44, special issue, *Mythes. L'origine des manières de faire*. Available online: http://tc.revues.org/1054 (accessed 1 August 2012)

Li, M. (2010), 'To See China in a Grain of GM Rice: A Study on the Governance of Biotechnology in China', PhD thesis, Science Studies Unit, University of Edinburgh.

Lim, S. S. (2008), 'Technology Domestication in the Asian Homestead: Comparing the Experiences of Middle Class Families in China and South Korea', in F. Bray (ed), *East Asian Science, Technology and Society: An International Journal*, special issue, *Constructing Intimacy: Technology, Family and Gender in East Asia*, 2/2: 189–210.

Liu, X. (2009), *The Mirage of China: Anti-Humanism, Narcissism, and Corporeality of the Contemporary World*, Oxford: Berghahn.

Lu, X. (2008), 'A Chinese Perspective: Business Ethics in China Now and in the Future', *Journal of Business Ethics*, 86/4: 451–461.

Malinowski, B. (1935), *Coral Gardens and Their Magic: A Study of Tilling the Soil and of Agricultural Rites in the Trobriand Islands*, London: Routledge & Kegan Paul.

Matsuda, M. (2008), 'Children with *Keitai*: When Mobile Phones Change from "Unnecessary" to "Necessary"', in F. Bray (ed.), *East Asian Science, Technology and Society: An International Journal*, special issue, *Constructing Intimacy: Technology, Family and Gender in East Asia*, 2/2: 167–88.

Nowotny, H. (2006), 'The Quest for Innovation and Cultures of Technology', in H. Nowotny (ed), *Cultures of Technology and the Quest for Innovation*, New York and Oxford, Berghahn.

Oates, J. (2009), 'China Wants Parental Control of All PCs', *The Register* (8 June 2009). Available online: http://www.theregister.co.uk/2009/06/08/china_bundles_censor/ (accessed 31 January 2010).

Oldenziel, R., and Zachmann, K. (eds) (2009), *Cold War Kitchen: Americanization, Technology, and European Users*, Cambridge, MA: MIT Press.

Ong, A., and Collier, S. (eds) (2005), *Global Assemblages: Technology, Politics, and Ethics as Anthropological Problems*, New York and Oxford: Blackwell.

Park, C.-H. (2008), 'Symbolic Appropriation of the Internet: Modernity, Peasant Bodies, and the Image of Familial Intimacy in China's *Nongjiale* Tourism Online Advertisements', in F. Bray (ed.), *East Asian Science, Technology and Society: An International Journal*, special issue, *Constructing Intimacy: Technology, Family and Gender in East Asia*, 2/2: 235–64.

Pfaffenberger, B. (1992), 'Social Anthropology of Technology', *Annual Review of Anthropology*, 21: 491–516.

Pfaffenberger, B. (2001), 'Symbols Do Not Create Meanings—Activities Do: Or, Why Symbolic Anthropology Needs the Anthropology of Technology', in M. Schiffer (ed.), *Anthropological Perspectives on Technology*, Albuquerque: University of New Mexico Press.

Rafael, V. (2003) 'The Cell Phone and the Crowd: Messianic Politics in the Contemporary Philippines', *Public Culture*, 15: 399–425.

Santos, G., and Donzelli, A. (forthcoming), 'Rice Intimacies: Reflections on the "House" in Upland Sulawesi and South China', in G. Weichart (ed.), *Living in Memory: Houses, History and Social/Natural Environment in Southeast Asia*, special issue of *ARCHIV für Volkerkunde*.

White, B. (2000), 'Rice Harvesting and Social Change in Java', *The Asia Pacific Journal of Anthropology*, 1/1: 79–102.

Wu, X. (2008), 'Men Purchase, Women Use: Coping with Domestic Electrical Appliances in Rural China', in F. Bray (ed.), *East Asian Science, Technology and Society: An International Journal*, special issue, *Constructing Intimacy: Technology, Family and Gender in East Asia*, 2/2: 211–34.

Yan, Y. (2003), *Private Life under Socialism: Love, Intimacy, and Family Change in a Chinese Village 1949–1999*, Stanford, CA: Stanford University Press.

CHAPTER 11

TECHNOLOGIES OF ETHICAL IMAGINATION

Gonçalo Santos

Ethics in so far as it springs from the desire to say something about the ultimate meaning of life, the absolute good, the absolute valuable, can be no science. What it says does not add to our knowledge in any sense. But it is a document of a tendency in the human mind which I personally cannot help respecting deeply and I would not for my life ridicule it.

Ludwig Wittgenstein (1929: 44)

This chapter focuses on a contemporary 'traditional' institution of grassroots charity in rural South China: the practice of mobilizing charitable donations of money and other resources to sponsor endeavours aimed at the common good. In the Cantonese-speaking 'hilly areas' of Guangdong (my research area since 1999), as in much of South China, this practice has undergone a dramatic process of expansion in the reform period. Today, most collective endeavours at the community level (including ritual activities) would not be possible without the mobilization of charitable monetary donations. These initiatives are not built upon a radical opposition between charity and kinship/community: aiding members of one's own household is not charity but contributing to the well-being of one's lineage or neighbourhood is considered a 'charitable deed' (sihn-hahng).[1] Such 'good deeds' are valued as 'hidden merits', but people also strive to make their 'good deeds' visible. Indeed, the names of donors usually need to be acknowledged in stone inscriptions or other artefacts of public recognition in lists of 'fragrant names' (fong-mihng)—a distinction that reflects the local representation of donations as honourable acts of generosity.

In this chapter, I approach local donation contests primarily as a window into the complexities of China's contemporary moral/ethical landscape—the terms 'moral' and 'ethical' will be used interchangeably in the text. Writing about China in general, Yunxiang Yan (2009) observes that the few existing studies of moral discourses and practices in specific settings provide contradictory accounts of the impact of the market-oriented reforms. While some authors emphasize developments deemed negative, such as the rise of an egotistic culture (Liu 2000; Yan 2003), others focus on more positive developments such as the continuing hold of traditional values, the growth of volunteerism or the rise of a broad sense of community (Ku 2003; Oxfeld 2004; Jankowiak 2004; Fleischer 2009). Yan (2009) himself focuses on a phenomenon—the growing number of cases of extortion of 'good Samaritans'—that points in the direction of moral decline, but his analysis is more complex. In his view, China's moral landscape is undergoing a series of multilayered and multi-directional changes that reflect a large-scale ethical shift from a collective system of responsibility and self-sacrifice to an individualistic system of rights and development (see also Kleinman et al. 2011).

This chapter provides an ethnographic qualification of this multilayered and multi-directional transformation, but the main goal of my 'micro-historical' exploration is to contribute to theoretical debates in what Laidlaw (2002) called 'anthropology of ethics and freedom'. Like most chapters in this volume, I approach the ethical as a modality of social action in the flow of everyday life. My analysis focuses on explicit ethical reflection, and its starting point is the idea that the human tendency to engage in this kind of reflective activity—including the kind of ethical reflection alluded to by Wittgenstein in the epigraph to this chapter—is a fundamentally imaginative enterprise. This approach draws support from a growing body of research in the cognitive sciences that contests the conventional view of 'moral reasoning' as a rule-following activity based on universal laws (Johnson 1995; Harris 2000). This research suggests that 'moral reasoning' is an ongoing constructive activity that relies to a large extent on the human capacity for imagination.[2] To say that 'moral reasoning' is imaginative is not to argue that it is an entirely subjective non-rational process without any constraints, but to argue that it is based on various kinds of metaphoric concepts and structures whose development and maturation is shaped by many different factors including social-cultural factors.

In this chapter, I am primarily interested in these social-cultural dimensions of the work of ethical imagination, and I focus on the role played by technology in the production and objectification of shared structures of ethical imagination. My approach was inspired by a long-standing anthropological tradition concerned with the study of techniques/technology (Pfaffenberger 1992; Lemonnier 1992). This tradition, as Bray (Chapter 10, this volume: 175) explains, 'has developed a practical and flexible analytical method for linking the material, social and symbolic dimensions of technical or technological practices and skills, regardless of whether they are high- or low-tech'. The 'technical' here includes bodily practices as well as the use of tools, and its scope goes well beyond the pursuit of material rewards. As Gell (1988: 6) famously argued, the 'technical' should be defined as 'the pursuit of intrinsically difficult-to-obtain results by roundabout or clever means'—a definition that makes no distinction, from the standpoint of 'degree of technicality', between the pursuit of material rewards through technical activity and the equally 'technical' pursuit of symbolic rewards.

My focus on technologies of ethical imagination builds on this broad conceptualization of the 'technical' and deals with a specific technological apparatus: ceremonial auctions organized by deity temple associations in rural northern Guangdong to gather funds for large-scale ritual festivals. In these auctions, people compete with one another for the acquisition of small decorative mirrors with a high symbolic value. Each mirror contains a written word referring to a specific element of the local moral code, so to acquire a mirror is to become the patron of a written word of virtue. I shall argue that these ceremonial auctions are part and parcel of a complex technological apparatus through which shared imaginary codes of conduct are systematized, objectified and made visible to larger audiences, but my account will not simply emphasize the Durkheimian effects of this technological apparatus in terms of generating moral orthodoxy and social cohesion. It will also show how this technological work of ethical imagination and moral regulation unfolds upon a deeper reality of moral disagreements that needs to be theoretically acknowledged.

In what follows, I explore these 'moral frictions' with a seemingly trivial incident that took place in the context of an auction for written words organized by a temple association in my field site in 1999. Focusing on one single case study may seem too narrow, but my account will provide a level of qualitative detail that is usually lacking in analyses of larger samples. The main character of the incident here described is a middle-aged Cantonese farmer I shall refer to with the pseudonym Bright Gold.[3] In order to tell you his story, I shall need to describe the local world of temple auctions in the context of the broader politics of 'religious revival' behind their resurgence in the post-Mao era.

A SMALL INCIDENT IN A DEITY TEMPLE IN NORTHERN GUANGDONG

I first met Bright Gold (b. 1962) in July 1999 at the very beginning of my first and longest spell of research in Harmony Cave. This is a small Cantonese 'single-lineage village' located in the relatively out-of-the-way township of Brightpath in northern Guangdong. The term 'single-lineage village' refers to a compact residential formation whose families claim descent from a founding ancestor and practice patrilocal exogamy at the group level. These villages are usually built around communal ancestral halls, and they constitute territorial corporations that maintain ritual alliances with other local and non-local lineage formations claiming to have a common origin (Watson 1985; Faure 1986).

In 2001, Brightpath had more than 110 of these villages (some of them with two or three lineages), and these villages were integrated in thirteen different 'rural administrative areas'. Brightpath also boasted thirteen associations built around temples for the worship of local gods. Each of these deity temple associations (usually involving various neighbouring villages) represents an independent cult that has no institutionalized relationship with other temples or social organizations (Dean 2003; Goossaert 2004). These associations usually have a high degree of autonomy despite falling outside of China's five officially recognized religions.[4]

Despite the impression of remoteness conveyed by its landscape of paddy fields and limestone mountains, the township has not been isolated from wider historical transformations. The local deity temples and ancestral halls may look traditional, but they were actually reconstructed as recently as the 1980s and the 1990s. The local scenery may look agrarian, but the economy is no longer strictly based on agriculture due to the impact of the market-oriented reforms. This shift to a 'post-agrarian' condition was linked to a massive wave of 'temporary labour migration' to the wealthier urban parts of southern Guangdong, where most Brightpathers work in factories or else set up small family enterprises of vegetable gardening.

These new strategies of livelihood have accelerated the monetization of the local economy and have improved the average household income—just as they have exposed the region's increasingly peripheral position in the wider globalizing economy of the province. By and large, most Brightpath migrants have remained tied to their native township and village, and their households are the basis of a new local affluent class whose emergence reflects increasing socioeconomic inequalities. The bulk of these households has made enough money to build 'modern' two-story houses or 'mansions' made of industrial materials, but a significant portion of the population lives in 'traditional' clay-brick house compounds built in the 1960s, 1970s or 1980s.

But let us go back to Bright Gold. I lived in his modest clay-brick house between July 1999 and January 2000. At the time, his household included himself, his wife and their three sons and one daughter. Bright Gold had no brothers, only four sisters (all married out of the village). Bright Gold and Full Elder Sister married in 1981, and they had their four children during the following decade—the period when electricity arrived in the village and Deng Xiaoping's reforms were launched. This was also the period when Bright Gold's parents died, leaving the couple with no childcare support to join the 'gold rush' to the Pearl River Delta region. When I moved into their clay-brick house in July 1999, they were in a difficult economic position, but their problems were not just economic.

BRIGHT GOLD PLEDGES TO MAKE A DONATION
FOR A MAJOR RITUAL FESTIVAL

Upon my arrival, I learned that Bright Gold had been seriously ill during the winter, but no one was able to tell me the details. I was simply told that his recovery had taken place a few days before a major public assembly was held on 16 March at the Temple of the Old Woman Lahm, a temple originally built during the Qing dynasty (1644–1911) and destroyed in 1958 during the Great Leap Forward. This assembly was part of the preparations for a major ritual festival announced earlier that same year. This would be the third [M] *Jiao* festival since the temple's lavish reconstruction in 1988 out of the combined efforts of twelve different villages belonging to two neighbouring rural administrative areas (a total population of 3,500 individuals).

As elsewhere in rural South China (Siu 1990; Dean 2003; Li 2001; Tam 2006; Lagerwey 2010: 95–152; Aijmer and Ho 2000: 187–236), the performance of *Jiao* festivals started being 'revived' during the 1980s together with other local practices and performative acts of popular religion.[5] *Jiao* festivals are large-scale sacrificial offerings organized on a periodic basis by local temple associations. Through a series of rituals performed by a troupe of ritual experts over a period of days, the community seeks to renew its alliance with the gods, thanking them for the graces obtained in the past and asking for further support. The exact goal, duration and periodicity of the *Jiao* are clearly stated in a handwritten memorial posted on the outer wall of the temple that includes the exact details of all temple community households. These data will be transferred to the records of the 'celestial bureaucracy' during the ritual proceedings through recitation and burning.

This expression, 'celestial bureaucracy', is important to understand the sociocultural logic behind these events. Most public representations of the world of gods, ghosts and ancestors in Chinese popular religion are informed by a 'bureaucratic metaphor' drawing on the imagery of the imperial heritage (Wolf 1974; Feuchtwang 2001). According to this metaphor, just as the world of the living was once ruled by a powerful bureaucracy of military and civil officers, so the world of the spirits is ruled by a mighty celestial bureaucracy of military and civil gods whose temple dwellings are explicitly cast from imperial palaces and buildings. This celestial bureaucracy—like its imperial counterpart—has both a central and a local dimension, but most deity cults at the community level are concerned with local gods or local manifestations of well-known deities. Fear of these gods and respect for their powers inspire attempts to influence their behaviour through worship including offerings of incense, food or 'spirit money'. These are a way of asking the gods for benevolence and for protection from wandering ghosts (a major cause of misfortune).

Jiao festivals are one of the ways through which communities make petitions to the celestial bureaucracy. The rituals themselves derive in large part from the Daoist liturgical tradition, but their development was also shaped by Buddhist and shamanist traditions, displaying significant regional variations[6] (Lagerwey 2010: 95–152; Tam 2006; Tan and Zeng 2010). Since its reconstruction in 1988, the Temple of the Old Woman Lahm has performed a so-called *Jiao* for the Population (*yahn-hau ching-jiu*)[7] every five years. The first was staged in 1989, the second in 1994 and the third was the one everyone was talking about when I first arrived in the village in July 1999.[8] This *Jiao* was scheduled for the autumn, and the afore-mentioned public assembly on 16 March was a fund-raising initiative by the temple's management committee, always composed of laypersons. This committee had been 'elected' in January with the blessing of the gods, and it included—as usual—a small group of local male notables and their followers.[9] It is not uncommon for the most prominent members of these committees to be over sixty, but age is not the only factor determining access to office. Wealth, prestige, reputation, skills and connections are as important, if not more so.

There were more than 100 men attending the 16 March fund-raising assembly at the Temple of the Old Woman Lahm. Bright Gold was one of them, and he surprised many when he pledged to donate money for the upcoming festival despite his family's well-known economic difficulties.

At the time, the late 1990s, fund-raising assemblies to mobilize donations for local temple activities were already quite common in the township (cf. Dean 2003; Tam 2006; Aijmer and Ho 2000: 187–236). Such initiatives were significantly restricted during the Maoist period, but they were quite common in the pre-Communist era. Traditionally, most local temple activities did not just rely on corporate assets (if any) but also on the ability of each temple's committee to collect two kinds of popular contributions: (*a*) obligatory 'pinched or pooled' (*gaap ge*) contributions from all households belonging to the temple community, and (*b*) voluntary 'donated' (*gyun ge*) contributions from anyone inside or outside the temple community. If the first was like a compulsory tax aimed at insiders, the second resembled charitable donations (cf. Goossaert 2004: 135–51).

This same dynamic of obligatory and voluntary contributions applies to present-day *Jiao* festivities, but there are significant departures from the 'traditional' fund-raising pattern. To begin with, obligatory payments and voluntary donations are now almost exclusively centred on cash—and less on labour or agricultural resources. Moreover, temple activities have become strongly dependent on donations because most local temples never regained the corporate assets lost during the Maoist period; and the income derived from obligatory payments only covers a meagre portion of the costs of mounting festivals. By and large, the major sources of funding are voluntary donations. In some parts of South China, donations from non-locals including overseas Chinese have become important (Ku 2003), but this is not the case in Brightpath.

BRIGHT GOLD'S PLEDGE WAS MADE AT AN AUCTION FOR WRITTEN WORDS OF VIRTUE

A major incentive behind this thriving culture of donations is the desire for divine redemption from previous moral wrongdoings (including those from past lives). This belief in the cosmic effects of monetary donations—strongly associated with the Buddhist tradition—is popular but not universally held. A more important factor is the desire to have one's economic success and generosity publicly recognized through artefacts of symbolic distinction issued by the temple's management committee. This technique of producing artefacts such as placards or stone inscriptions with the names of all donors together with their native places and the exact amounts of their donations is linked to very old traditions of religious fund-raising, ritual accountancy and memory inscription (Goossaert 2004). However, it seems clear that the contemporary concern with the symbolic recognition of acts of monetary donation has reached unprecedented dimensions and levels of commercialization.

In the context of *Jiao* festivals, the handling of donations is the responsibility of the festival's presiding committee. These committees usually resort to supplementary fund-raising strategies to accrue their budgets. In Brightpath, a popular strategy—at least since the late nineteenth century—is to organize ceremonial auctions in which temple community members compete with one another for the acquisition of a limited number of small decorative mirrors called 'mirror screens' (*geng-pihng*). Each of these mirrors contains one or a few written characters making up a word whose meaning is associated with a specific element of the local code of goodness and right action. Hence locals refer to these ritual auctions with the expression 'bidding for written words' (*biu-jih*) because what is really at stake in these contests is the possibility of being granted the title of 'major contributor' (*jyu-yuhn*) or patron of a written word of virtue.[10]

The pledge made by Bright Gold at the Temple of the Old Woman Lahm occurred in one of these auctions. We shall look more closely at the meanings of the words sold at these auctions below. Before that, I would like to explain the auctions' focus on mirrors with written words. The mirrors sold at the auctions are commonly said to have magical properties, and one reason for this is the fact that mirrors in general are thought to have magical properties as they attract good fortune and protect people from evil spirits.[11] But what primarily accounts for the magical power of the mirrors sold at the auctions is that they contain written characters that are considered sacred and magical.

This idea of the sacredness and magical efficacy of written characters was historically cultivated by all major Chinese ritual traditions,[12] and it is today quite visible in religious practices such as talismanic writing (*fuh-luhk*), in which written characters are invested with supernatural powers such as deterring evil spirits from entering the household, guarding the body/person or fulfilling personal desires (see Yen 2005). The 'words of virtue' painted on the mirrors are said to have similar supernatural powers; so to have one of these 'words of virtue' hanging on the wall of one's household is like keeping a small piece of paper with talismanic writing close to one's body: it is a magic technique to get divine protection.

When describing the auctions, village folks compare the figure of the owner, issuer and auctioneer of the written words (i.e. the temple's management committee) to a government-like organization with a 'big president' (*daaih jung-leih*) and many 'deputies' (*yuhn-sau*). The mandate of those heading this organization is not permanent and needs to be sanctioned by the temple's tutelary deities. These deities also have a say in the selection of the auctions' winning bidders: although what really matters is the size of one's bid, this mundane explanation is often complemented by a less secular narrative that depicts each winning bid as a sign of divine reward for proper moral conduct—the kind of conduct worthy of moral redemption and symbolic distinction.

In practice, this work of symbolic distinction is achieved and materialized in different ways. To begin with, the name of the winning bidder is painted on the surface of each mirror after the auction. Given that these mirrors will be on public display at the temple during the ritual festivities before being given to their patrons, there will be plenty of chances for visitors to learn about *who* is the patron of *which* written word. This information together with the final price of each word can also be found on a large sheet of red paper posted on the outer wall of the temple. There is also a ceremony to 'deliver the written words' (*sung-jih*) taking place towards the end of the *Jiao* ritual festivities. During this ceremony, each mirror is delivered to the door of its respective patron by a lion dance troupe performing a ritual show combining music, firecrackers and martial arts.

BRIGHT GOLD PLEDGED TO BECOME THE PATRON
OF TWO WRITTEN WORDS OF VIRTUE

As noted earlier, it is up to the management committee to select the words for auction, usually with the help of a trustworthy community member with ritual knowledge. The final list is said to reflect the wishes of the tutelary deities and has to be approved in consultation with representatives of the local elite. State authorities do not have a direct say in the words selected—just as they do not have a direct say in the composition of the temple's committee—but they constitute an important background actor, and they may interfere at any point. Most words selected evoke traditional concepts or expressions with strong ritual, literary and philosophical connotations, neatly recycled in light of contemporary realities. The total number of words can vary (usually not higher than forty). Most are 'single-character words' (*daan-jih*) and 'double-character words' (*seung-jih*). In some auctions, there are also traditional idioms made up of three or four characters, and the characters are sold individually. All written words are meant to be read in the local Cantonese language and not in Mandarin.[13]

The 16 March auction at the Temple of the Old Woman Lahm included thirty-seven written words: twelve 'single-character words' (see Figure 11.1) and twenty-five 'double-character words' (see Figures 11.2a and 11.2b). These lists of words are only the product of the reflective work of the ethical imagination of one or a few individuals, but they are publicly presented as divinely sanctioned products of the collective ethical imagination, approved by local state authorities. And indeed, the lists in question may be described as authoritative selective linguistic rationalizations of the locally shared structures of moral imagination. I say 'selective' because these lists of words do not exhaust the local 'space of possibles' in terms of ethical reflection and tell us little about ethical imagination in action, but we shall return to this point later.

1	丁 ding	population, male descendants	¥1,200	Harmony Cave (Team 1) - Family with mansion
2	財 choih	wealth, riches	¥1,000	Harmony Cave (Team 1) - Family with mansion
3	貴 gwai	expensive, noble	¥880	Harmony Cave (Team 1) - Family with mansion
4	旺 wohng	prosperous, flourishing	¥620	From another village - Family with mansion
5	福 fuk	good fortune, prosperity, blessing	¥580	From another village - Family with mansion
6	祿 luk	good fortune, official salary	¥460	From another village - Family with mansion
7	壽 sauh	longevity	¥350	From another village - Family with mansion
8	全 chyuhn	complete, perfect	¥500	Harmony Cave (Team 1) - Family with mansion
9	金 gam	gold	¥450	From another village - Family with mansion
10	玉 yuk	jade	¥280	From another village - Family with mansion
11	滿 muhn	full, complete, satisfied	¥480	Harmony Cave (Team 1) - Family with mansion
12	堂 tohng	main room of a building or house; term used to refer to relatives 'of the same lineage or clan'	¥420	From another village - Family with mansion

Figure 11.1 List of written words and respective prices and patrons, *Jiao* festival 1999, 'One-character words'. Total revenue = ¥7,220 (€794)

In terms of content, these lists of words are not just concerned with defining the components of a 'good life' (e.g. prosperity, descendants, luck), but also with identifying the principles of right and wrong (e.g. justice, fairness, impartiality) and the things that are worth pursuing in themselves (e.g. sincerity, happiness). In other words, to use a distinction drawn by Alasdair MacIntyre (1981), the 'virtuous' here refers not just to 'goods internal to a given practice'—things such as sincerity, fairness or justice, whose achievement is said to benefit the whole community—but also to 'goods external to practices'—things such as fame, wealth or state nobility, of which it is said that the more someone has of them the less there is for others. This all-encompassing realm

1	元亨 yuhn-hang	Prosperous and smooth; a literary reference to the first trigram of the Book of Changes	¥380	From another village - Family without mansion
2	利貞 leih-jing	Loyal and beneficial; a literary reference to the first trigram of the Book of Changes	¥420	From another village - Family without mansion
3	**勝意** **sing-yi**	**Literally successful ideas**	**¥1,250**	**Harmony Cave (Team 1) -** **Family with mansion**
4	吉祥 gat-cheuhng	Lucky, auspicious, propitious	¥580	Harmony Cave (Team 5) - Family with mansion
5	誠心 sihng-sam	Sincerity, good faith	¥780	Harmony Cave (Team 1) - Family with mansion
6	公正 gung-jing	Just, fair, impartial	¥180	Harmony Cave (Team 1) - Family without mansion
7	福德 fuk-dak	Literally prosperity and virtue, good fortune and kindness	¥620	Harmony Cave (Team 1) - Family with mansion
8	安樂 on-lohk	Peace and happiness	¥260	Harmony Cave (Team 1) - Family without mansion
9	萬事 maahn-sih	Everything; as in the idiom 'maahn-sih yuh-yi', or 'everything according to one's wishes'	¥650	From another village - Family with mansion
10	恭喜 gung-hei	Congratulations; as in the greeting 'gung-hei faat-choih', or 'congratulations and best wishes for a prosperous New Year'	¥350	From another village - Family with mansion
11	發達 faat-daaht	Flourishing, prosperous, developed	¥880	Harmony Cave (Team 1) - Family with mansion
12	百福 baak-fuk	Literally hundred good fortunes	¥380	From another village - Family without mansion
13	禎祥 jing-cheuhng	Lucky and auspicious	¥520	Harmony Cave (Team 1) - Family with mansion

Figure 11.2a List of written words and respective prices and patrons, *Jiao* festival 1999, 'Two-character words' (Part 1). Total revenue = ¥7,250 (€797)

of the 'virtuous' clashes with MacIntyre's own emphasis on 'internal goods' and evokes the social theory of authors such as Bourdieu (1998: 75–145) because for him the pursuit of 'goods internal to a given practice' is also not fully disconnected from the pursuit of 'external goods' like fortune and recognition—and vice versa.

One might think that the bids offered for these various 'goods' are not very significant in size, but this is not the case. I analysed the budget sheets of various auctions, and this analysis has confirmed my

14	招財 jiu-choih	Literally inviting wealth; as in the idiom 'jiu-choih jeun-bou', or 'ushering in riches and treasures'	¥580	From another village - Family with mansion
15	延壽 yihn-sauh	To prolong life	¥560	Harmony Cave (Team 2) - Family without mansion
16	添丁 tim-ding	To have another (male) descendant	¥880	Harmony Cave, Team 1 - Family without mansion
17	**富貴** **fu-gwai**	**Riches and honor, wealth and rank**	**¥1,300**	**Harmony Cave (Team 1) - Family with mansion**
18	福星 fuk-sing	Lucky star, mascot	¥700	From another village - Family with mansion
19	興隆 hing-luhng	Prosperous, thriving, flourishing	¥680	From another village - Family with mansion
20	永安 wihng-on	Always content, calm, peaceful and safe	¥960	Harmony Cave (Team 1) - Family with mansion
21	**生財** **saang-choih**	**To amass wealth, to make money; as in the idiom 'woh-hei saang-choih' or 'good manners bring riches'**	**¥1,100**	**Harmony Cave (Team 3) - Family with mansion**
22	順遂 seun-seui	Everything is going smoothly just as one wishes	¥480	From another village - Family without mansion
23	和氣 woh-hei	Gentle, kind, courteous, polite, amiable; as in the idiom 'woh-hei saang-choih', or 'good manners bring riches'	¥880	Harmony Cave (Team 3) - Family with mansion
24	如意 yuh-yi	According to one's wishes; as in the idiom 'maahn-sih yuh-yi', or 'everything according to one's wishes'	¥680	From another village - Family with mansion
25	**揭榜** **kit-bohng**	**To be recognized as the best; (traditional) to come first in the highest imperial examinations**	**¥2,500**	**From another village - Family with mansion**

Figure 11.2b List of written words and respective prices and patrons, *Jiao* festival 1999, 'Two-character words' (Part 2). Total revenue = ¥11,300 (€1,243)

impression—acquired through participant observation—that people are taking these ritual contests quite seriously. The 1999 auction, for example, made a total of 25,770 RMB (€2,835)—a very impressive number by local standards that represented almost 50 per cent of the festival's revenue. The amount of money paid for each word was also very impressive.

Figures 11.1, 11.2a and 11.2b show that the most expensive word was *kit-bohng*. Unlike all other words auctioned, this word could only be acquired by a household with a specific profile, that is, a household with a good reputation, economic affluence, plentiful offspring, and educational success (of the kind leading to government posts). The final bid for this word was 2,500 RMB (€275), a very significant amount of money by local standards representing four to five months' salary for a migrant factory worker. At the other end of the spectrum, the cheapest word was *gung-jing*, meaning 'justice and fairness'. This word was acquired for 180 RMB (€19), again, a significant amount of money corresponding to half the monthly salary of a migrant labourer.

These numbers show that the major players of the auctions are the successful households in the post-agrarian economy, that is, those that have already managed to accumulate enough savings to build at least one 'modern' two-story house or 'mansion'. The fact that these households are spending a significant amount of their savings in auction bids may lead one to think that they are engaging in 'irrational economic behaviour' given the local impoverished economy. However, one needs to bear in mind—to echo a point made by Geertz (1973) in his essay on Balinese cockfighting—that their savings are not being wasted but converted into something far more important than money in the local cosmologies of value. Divine protection and redemption are among these things, at least for some. Another—far more important—is divinely sanctioned public recognition and symbolic capital: the kind of public recognition and symbolic capital associated with becoming the patron of a written word of virtue. But what is most fascinating about these short-term transactional processes of capital conversion is that they are explicitly sponsoring the ritual objectification and reproduction of something that has little to do with these worldly exchanges: the local structures of ethical imagination.

It is in this sense that I refer to the auctions as technologies of ethical imagination. Through a series of complex operational sequences, the auctions are responsible for the production of a highly authoritative picture of collective ethical imagination that circulates in the local community with the approval of state authorities, conveying a strong impression of moral orthodoxy and social cohesion. And yet, as noted earlier, the written words 'sold' at these auctions are only a selective linguistic rationalization of the locally shared schemas of ethical imagination. There are significant informal disagreements about which words/concepts are left out and/or are most valuable, just as there are significant informal disagreements as to how these various words/concepts relate to specific real-life situations. There are also significant informal disagreements in terms of bidding preferences, meaning that different individuals/households are not necessarily interested in the same words/concepts for the same reasons. These qualifications do not imply that the idea of a unified framework of collective ethical imagination is an illusion or has no sociological force, as argued for example by Zigon (2009) drawing on life-history research in contemporary Russia; they only call for a theoretical acknowledgement of this deeper reality of moral disagreements.

The story of Bright Gold's active participation in the 1999 auction of the Temple of the Old Woman Lahm is useful for thinking about these 'moral frictions' because it helps bring some of these frictions to the surface. On the day of the auction, Bright Gold felt like trying his luck to celebrate his recent recovery from illness; and he did it without thinking too much about the consequences. He was interested in two specific written words: *on-lohk*, meaning 'peace and happiness', and *gung-jing*, meaning 'justice and fairness'; and to everyone's astonishment (including his own), his bids proved victorious despite the fact that he only made a single offer for each word. Bright Gold agreed to pay the following day, but after a few days, it became clear that he would not be able to make any payment at all. This was the beginning of a series of heated discussions that eventually turned into an open conflict.

BRIGHT GOLD FAILS TO KEEP HIS PLEDGE BUT DENIES ANY WRONGDOING

While all other winning bidders settled their payments immediately, Bright Gold had still not done so in July—several months after the auction—despite having been repeatedly admonished by both close relatives and the festival's presiding committee. He also failed to show up at two important temple assemblies just a few weeks before the beginning of the ritual festivities in November.

As the festival drew near, more and more people started gossiping about his lack of 'sincerity' (*sihng-sam*)—one of the written words on 'sale' at the auction. Many started referring to him derogatorily as someone who 'says a lot of things but does not do arithmetic [i.e. keep his word]' (*gong-yeh ngh syun-sou*) and someone who 'has no money to say anything' (*mouh chihn gong-yeh*). Many in his village (including close relatives) also began referring to him as a 'dead son' (*sei-jai*, i.e. a very bad boy)—one of those who brings 'loss of face' (*diu-ga*) and does not care about the maintenance of harmonious relations with his relatives and neighbours. Even his wife and children were turning their backs against him.

It was clear that Bright Gold had made a mistake. Besides making a pledge he could not honour, he also did not provide any public excuse and acted as if he had done nothing wrong. I should note at this point that in what follows my aim is not to question this assessment and prove Bright Gold right. My analytical interest lies elsewhere. Beyond the question of right and wrong, I am interested in exploring the subjective dimensions of this incident in order to suggest that the auctions' technical achievement in terms of creating an authoritative framework of collective ethical imagination builds on a deeper reality of moral disagreements. These disagreements focus not just on the question of what kinds of imaginary rules and values of conduct are important but also on the more ordinary question of how these rules and values relate to real-life situations.

Having lived in Bright Gold's house for six months and having followed his activities through regular visits and phone exchanges during the last ten years, I am convinced that his bids were genuine, that his pledge to donate money was sincere, and that his subsequent denial of wrongdoing was a post hoc reaction to public accusations. But even if one takes this sympathetic stance towards Bright Gold, one still needs to explain why he made a pledge without being certain he could keep it; my view is that his pledge was the product of wishful thinking and was based on some unrealistic assumptions.

To begin with, Bright Gold underestimated the extent to which his family was in economic difficulty. At the time of the auction, they could not even afford to eat pork with any regularity, let alone engage in public acts of charitable giving. Perhaps more importantly, Bright Gold overestimated the extent to which he was in control of his family's finances. His wife, Full Elder Sister, had already taken over the role of 'breadwinner' a few years earlier, in 1997, when she decided—against Bright Gold's wishes—to venture into the suburbs of the provincial capital to make money.

The build-up to this domestic power reversal started soon after the birth of their fourth child in 1991, when the local family-planning policy—which allowed a maximum of three children—forced them to undergo sterilization.[14] Of the two of them, Bright Gold was the one taken to the township's hygiene station, and this event would prove a turning point in the couple's life. To begin with, Bright Gold's health (including his energy levels and sexual well-being) was negatively affected by the procedure. These complications emerged at a time when the couple started to experience increasingly open divergences in their attitudes to the changing times. In clear contrast to Bright Gold, who believed that they should both remain at home practicing agriculture and taking care of the children, Full Elder Sister thought that they should focus on earning money and 'getting rich first' ([M] *xian-fu-qi-lai*). In her view, they should try their luck in the Pearl River Delta region like most of their close village relatives; but because their children were still too small, and Bright Gold's parents had already passed away, only one of them should go (ideally, the man of the household), while the other stayed in the village.

After several years of quarrels, Full Elder Sister's decision to move out of the village with their eldest son in 1997 was an act of rebellion against her husband's refusal to do what it takes to fulfil the new local ideal of a modern family provider.[15] Her decision reflected her strong personality, but she would have never been able to do it without the support of their close relatives in the village. These relatives agreed that Bright Gold's failure to 'assume responsibility' (*fuh-jaak-yahm*) as the household's breadwinner was unacceptable. In their view, Full Elder Sister's decision to leave the village was the only way forward. Of course, this move also represented a major turnaround in the couple's power dynamics. As Full Elder Sister became the family's only 'money-maker', Bright Gold had his authority significantly diminished. By the end of her first year away from the village, Full Elder Sister was commonly referring to her husband as a loser in front of their children— a behaviour that echoed the attitudes of their close village relatives.

Two years later, when the auction incident occurred, Full Elder Sister was still the one in charge of household expenses, and her take on the incident—that is, her explicit work of ethical imagination—was that the family should not give any money to the festival's committee, as this would be a waste of savings on things they clearly could not afford. She also believed that Bright Gold would eventually find a way to negotiate the payment of his bids with money coming from the monthly rental payments I was making to them as a tenant.

BRIGHT GOLD REFUSES TO PAY HIS BIDS AND QUESTIONS THE AUTHORITY OF THE TEMPLE COMMITTEE

There are of course other factors involved in this incident, and I cannot deal with all of them here. However, I would like to draw attention to a particular aspect of Bright Gold's reading of the incident because it adds significant historical complexity to the episode and helps the reader understand the rationale behind his strong-minded denial of wrongdoing. As argued earlier, this denial was a post hoc reaction that had little to do with his initial act of wishful thinking at the auction. What I shall now show is that the explicit work of ethical imagination behind this post hoc reaction was shaped by a particular biographical trajectory—one that cannot be separated from China's recent political history.

Bright Gold was one of the few villagers of his generation (growing up during the Great Cultural Revolution) who managed to graduate from middle school.[16] Several villagers told me he was strongly committed to Maoist thought during his schooling, and I believe that this commitment has not faded away. Recalling a famous speech by Chairman Mao (1965 [1945]), Bright Gold would often alert me (during fieldwork between 1999 and 2001) to the continuing need to fight for the removal of the 'big mountains' obstructing China's socialist transformation. In his original speech, Mao talked of two 'big mountains' (imperialism and feudalism) that needed to be removed by the unity, hard work and perseverance of the people; but Bright Gold added a third mountain to this list: capitalism. He thought that the post-Mao resurgence of popular religion (inspired by 'feudalist superstitious beliefs') and monetary transactions (inspired by 'capitalist worship of money') signalled a full-fledged reappearance of Mao's 'big mountains' and represented an unacceptable retreat from his virtuous teachings.

In light of these strong ethico-political convictions, it is easier to understand how Bright Gold's initial denial of wrongdoing ended up escalating into a post hoc 'revolutionary' strategy aimed at challenging the authority of the temple's management committee. This strategy is best illustrated by Bright Gold's efforts to devise a plan to expose the 'fictitious' nature of the two very entities—gods and money— at the heart of the disgracefully 'feudalist' and 'capitalist' activities of the temple committee. Bright Gold's plan was to arrange a public assembly at the temple in which he would pay his two winning bids with 'spirit money' (banknote-shaped strips of white paper used to worship gods and ancestors). By doing this, he wanted to make the point that the standard renminbi banknotes used to pay auction bids are as 'fictitious' as the 'fake paper money' burned in honour of non-existent supernatural creatures. He also wanted to argue—against the new local affluent class and the picture of ethical imagination celebrated in *Jiao* auctions—that money is not a reliable measure of virtue. In his view, the monetization of the local society and of the local moral landscape had led to increasing levels of corruption and moral decay not just among the local authorities but also among the local elites (the leading organizers of *Jiao* festivals).

Bright Gold was determined to go ahead with his plan, but his children (under the domineering influence of their mother) begged him to abandon it, arguing—quite realistically—that he would only make a fool of himself and his family. That same morning, the children tearfully asked me to lend money to their father; and after a series of complex negotiations coordinated by the temple committee, Bright Gold ended up paying his two winning bids with the financial support of myself and another local villager—each of us paying for one mirror.

When I visited Harmony Cave in November 2009 to attend another *Jiao* festival at the Temple of the Old Woman Lahm, these two mirrors were still hanging on the wall of Bright Gold's kitchen; but a few things had changed since the 1999 auction. Most importantly, Bright Gold joined his wife in 2003 to help her run their vegetable gardening business. His views on Mao's 'big mountains' have not changed, but his worries and energies are now focused on his wife's increasingly poor health and his eldest son's lack of marriage prospects. Bright Gold's reputation never fully recovered after the auction incident, not least because his economic situation has not improved, and money—as he himself often argues—has become a major indicator of virtue, among other things.

If back in 1999 Bright Gold did not find any powerful allies to support his cause, it was certainly not because his ethical positions were odd or unusual. My field notes from that period are filled with references to informal conversations during which many people showed empathy and understanding for some of Bright Gold's positions. For example, then as now, Bright Gold is *not* the only voice criticizing the post-Mao transformation of the local ethical landscape including the monetization of morality. Like Bright Gold, many of these critical voices—including those born in the current reform era—tend to look at present-day realities in light of the so-called moral and spiritual achievements of Maoism, but very few ever develop their ideas in public in a confrontational manner. In Harmony Cave, there are only two other villagers doing this, and their behaviour is also the object of frequent public mockery.

This apparent lack of open heterodoxy suggests that the collective schema of ethical imagination supporting the monetization of virtue has become so hegemonic locally that it faces little public opposition. There are many reasons for this (including important political and institutional reasons), but I only have space to mention one factor that is closely related to one of the words sold at the 1999 auction: the word *woh-hei*, meaning amiable, peaceful, polite (see Figure 11.2b). I mention this word because it points to an aspect of the local society that helps one understand the apparent lack of open disagreements: its strong emphasis on the importance of seeking agreement and claiming it even when it does not exist, for the sake of harmony and unity (Watson 1985; Santos 2006). In such a context, doing things that openly challenge the ideal of the desirability of an imagined orthodoxy renders one vulnerable to being called a 'bad person', someone who does not care about the maintenance of harmonious relations with relatives and neighbours.

TECHNOLOGIES OF ETHICAL IMAGINATION

This chapter has proposed an exploration of the 'ethical' as it manifests itself in concrete ordinary settings. Instead of defining the 'ethical' a priori as an abstract system of rules or values or as a separate realm of social life, I explored the 'ethical' as it manifests itself historically in specific practices and discourses, in specific acts of practical judgement, in specific ritual performances aimed at establishing the criteria for certain kinds of judgement.

Lambek (2010: 12–13) notes that there are two major anthropological traditions in the study of ethics and morality. One—the

Durkheimian—has been primarily concerned with rules and obligations; the other—the Boasian—has focused mostly on values and categories. Both traditions have strong roots in the Kantian dualism of man
and nature, reason and perception, freedom and constraint; and they
both tend to look at ethics as a property or function of 'abstract reason' (in the Kantian sense), approaching ethics primarily as a matter
of 'rule-following'. It was this analytical emphasis on 'rule-following'
that prompted both traditions to build their reflections around the question of universality or correctness. This approach was productive but
resulted in a theoretical stalemate between relativists and universalists:
while universalists emphasize the existence of universal moral laws,
relativists emphasize the force of particular cultural and historical contexts (see also Lukes 2008). According to Lambek (2010: 16), one can
largely avoid these analytical difficulties by seeking inspiration in the
work of Aristotle: 'Specifically, by returning to Aristotle, we can take
ethics to be fundamentally a property or function of action rather than
(only) of abstract reason'.

The material presented in this chapter has similarly approached the
'ethical' as a property or function of action, but unlike Lambek (2010),
I did not ignore the earlier anthropological concern with reasoning. I
only shifted away from the traditional focus on 'reasoning' as a rule-
following activity. Drawing on recent research in the cognitive sciences,
I argued that what is conventionally called 'moral reasoning' is indeed
more flexible and open-ended than the 'rule-following' metaphor allows: it is a constructive cognitive activity that depends to a large extent
on the human capacity for imagination. Moral reasoning is a constructive imaginative activity because it relies on various kinds of metaphoric
structures whose development and consolidation is shaped by many
different factors, including the fact that human beings are tied to specific
social-cultural environments. In this chapter, I focused only on these
social-cultural dimensions of the work of ethical imagination, highlighting the role played by technology in the production and objectification
of shared structures of ethical imagination.

Writing about traditional Chinese society, C. K. Yang (1961: 282–3)
famously argued that popular religion for common people was less a
source of moral ideals than a source of highly ingenious techniques—
what he called 'magic'—for obtaining happiness and warding off evil,

that is, for getting closer to the ideal of a 'good virtuous life'. The material here presented focused on a slightly different type of technical apparatus, though no less magical: a machine whose main goal is to imagine the contours of the notion of the 'good virtuous life' itself, a machine whose main function is to produce a picture of collective ethical imagination that appears natural and the only possible one. But my analysis did not just focus on the powerful effects of this technological apparatus as a producer of moral orthodoxy and social cohesion. I have also shown how this technical work of collective ethical imagination is built upon a deeper reality of moral frictions that cannot be separated from broader socio-cultural processes and politico-economic transformations. These moral frictions are probably more visible in contexts like China where people's engagement with history—despite the apparent lack of heterodoxy—has produced a diverse 'memory bank' of schemas of ethical imagination; but such frictions can be found in just about any context. The theoretical acknowledgement of this deeper reality of moral frictions is important because it clearly implies—as Laidlaw (2002) notes—that individuals are not mere 'slaves to custom' in their ethical engagements. But while I agree with Laidlaw (2002) that individuals have some degree of 'choice', my emphasis in this chapter—as illustrated by the ill-fated story of Bright Gold—was instead on the idea that these 'choices' are neither unconstrained nor without consequences.

APPENDIX: LIST OF CHARACTERS

Except where indicated with [M] standing for Mandarin (the official language), all Chinese expressions that follow refer to the Cantonese language. Cantonese terms are rendered in the Yale Romanization System with minor modifications due to local variations. Mandarin terms follow the standard Pinyin system.

baak-fuk, 百福

biu-jih, 標字

choih, 財

chyuhn, 全

daan-jih, 單字

daaih jung-leih, 大總理

ding, 丁

diu-ga, 丟架

fong-mihng, 芳名

fu-gwai, 富貴

fuh-jaak-yahm, 負責任

fuh-luhk, 符籙

fuk-dak, 福德

fuk-sing, 福星

gaap ge, 夾嘅

gam, 金

gat-cheuhng, 吉祥

geng-pihng, 鏡屏

gong-yeh ngh syun-sou, 講嘢唔算數

gung-hei, 恭喜

gung-jing, 公正

gwai, 貴

gyun ge, 捐嘅

faat-daaht, 發達

fuk, 福

hing-luhng, 興隆

jiao, 醮 [M]

jing-cheuhng, 禎祥

jiu-choih, 招財

jyu-yuhn, 主緣

leih-jing, 利貞

luk, 祿

kit-bohng, 揭榜

maahn-sih, 萬事

mahn-taahn, 文壇

mouh-taahn, 武壇

mouh chihn gong-yeh, 冇錢講嘢

muhn, 滿

on-lohk, 安樂

saang-choih, 生財

sauh, 壽

sei-jai, 死仔

seun-seui, 順遂

seung-jih, 雙字

sihn-hahng, 善行

sihng-sam, 誠心

sing-yi, 勝意

sung-jih, 送字

tim-ding, 添丁

tohng, 堂

wihng-on, 永安

woh-hei, 和氣

wohng, 旺

xian-fu-qi-lai, 先富起來 [M]

xi-zi-hui, 惜字會 [M]

yahn-hau ching-jiu, 人口清醮

yihn-sauh, 延壽

yuh-yi, 如意

yuhn-hang, 元亨

yuhn-sau, 緣首

yuk, 玉

NOTES

1. Except where indicated with [M] standing for Mandarin (the official language), all romanized Chinese words or expressions refer to Cantonese. The system of Cantonese romanization used in this chapter is the Yale system with minor modifications due to local variations. All Mandarin words and expressions follow the standard Pinyin system. A list of characters can be found in the Appendix just after the main text.

2. Moral reasoning is a constructive imaginative activity because it uses imaginatively structured concepts and because it requires imagination to discern what is morally relevant in situations, to understand empathetically how others experience things and to envision alternative courses of action in a particular case. This capacity for imagination has been shown to play an important role in human reasoning in general, emerging early in children's development. It is especially obvious in children's games of pretend play, but it invades and transforms their developing conception of reality itself (see Harris 2000).
3. All the names of places and persons most directly related to the area of my field research are pseudonyms.
4. Buddhism, Taoism, Protestantism, Catholicism and Islam.
5. The term 'popular religion' refers to a highly composite religious system that brings together the rituals of the Confucian, Buddhist and Daoist traditions in local practices of ancestor worship and deity cults with local shamanistic traditions and with various mantic systems for reading landscape, faces, hands and times. This term has been criticized for its elitist connotations (Lagerwey 2010: 153), but I do not address this issue here.
6. In the Brightpath region, for example, *Jiao* rituals display many elements explicitly associated with Buddhist and shamanist traditions (Tam 2006; Tan and Zeng 2010). The rituals are complex and their performance usually unfolds simultaneously in two separate altars: the 'civil altar' (*mahn-taahn*) inside the main temple building and the 'military altar' (*mouh-taahn*) set on a temporary bamboo shelter outside. Village folks often refer to these altars, respectively, as the 'muttering altar' and the 'dancing altar' because most performances in the first altar entail Buddhist recitations and most performances in the second altar include Daoist rites and shamanic acts of various kinds including theatrical dances *en travesti* (men in female roles). In addition to what goes on inside these two altars, there are also a few acrobatic shows (fire walking, climbing knife ladders) taking place outdoors at different times during the festivities.
7. The reason why local *Jiao* rituals are called '*Jiao* for the population' is not clear. Although it is tempting to link this designation to the increasing salience of 'population' in Chinese political rhetoric, this linkage is not warranted because the designation was already in use during the pre-Communist period. In all likelihood, the designation is linked to the region's long-standing concerns with epidemics and population health.
8. Since then, two other *Jiao* festivals have taken place: one in 2004, the other in 2009—always in the autumn, soon after the second rice harvest of the local double-cropping cycle.

9. The leader of this committee was a charismatic retired civil servant from Harmony Cave (he would also preside over the *Jiao* festivals of 2004 and 2009). Another Harmony Cave villager led the *Jiao* festivals of 1989 and 1994, but his mounting gambling debts in the late 1990s forced him to flee the township just before his death in 2000.

10. These ritual contests are open ascending price auctions, like those described by James Laidlaw (1995: 334–45, 349–53) for an urban Jain community in Northwest India, in which participants bid openly against one another, with each subsequent bid higher than the previous bid; the auctioning of each written word ends when no participant is willing to bid further, at which point the highest bidder is declared as the winner of the contest.

11. Nowadays, these mirrors can take the form of computer-designed framed paper certificates, but they are still referred to as 'mirrors' or 'mirror-screens' precisely because of the high symbolic value of mirrors in general.

12. The Confucian tradition, for example, is well known for its active role in the cultivation of the sacredness of the written word, and this emphasis has led it to promote 'associations for cherishing written words' ([M] *xi-zi-hui*) in the late imperial period (Liang 1997: 131–55). The Daoist and Buddhist traditions are also well known for their active role in the cultivation of the art of calligraphy (Goossaert 2004).

13. This is a reminder of the continuing existence in Guangdong of an unofficial vernacular writing tradition whose origins go back to the late imperial period (Snow 2004).

14. This experience of coercive sterilization is not exceptional in the local context. As the local birth planning policy started to get stricter in the 1990s, village couples insisted on transgressing official birth quotas, and most faced the penalty of sterilization. This is still the case today, but the policy now rarely allows more than three children (see Harrell et al. 2011).

15. Full Elder Sister told me that divorce was not a real option for her because this practice—despite being officially legal since 1950 and increasingly common in many parts of China after the 1980s—carries very negative connotations locally. If she divorced, she would have to return to her natal village and face local scorn. A better alternative would be to marry again (and move into her new husband's community), but the prospects of finding a suitable marriage partner at her age were not very high. There was also the question of who would keep their four children.

16. The overwhelming majority of the present adult literate population in Harmony Cave and surrounding villages has only attained literacy at the primary school level. In 2001, 29 per cent of all adult males of Harmony Cave were still illiterate. Moreover, the average level of education among literate

males was low: over 60 per cent had not moved beyond elementary school and a mere 8 per cent had reached senior high (none had reached university).

REFERENCES

Aijmer, G., and Ho, V. K. Y. (2000), *Cantonese Society in a Time of Change*, Hong Kong: Chinese University Press.

Bourdieu, P. (1998), *Practical Reason: On the Theory of Action*, Stanford, CA: Stanford University Press.

Dean, K. (2003), 'Local Communal Religion in Contemporary South-East China', *China Quarterly*, 174/1: 338–58.

Faure, D. (1986), *The Structure of Chinese Rural Society: Lineage and Village in the Eastern New Territories, Hong Kong*, Hong Kong and Oxford: Oxford University Press.

Feuchtwang, S. (2001), *Popular Religion in China*, London: Curzon Press.

Fleischer, F. (2009), *Between Technology of Self and Technology of Power: The Volunteer Phenomenon in Guangzhou, China*, Max Planck Institute for Social Anthropology, Working Paper 11.

Geertz, C. (1973), 'Deep Play: Notes on the Balinese Cockfight', in *The Interpretation of Cultures*, London: Fontana Press.

Gell, A. (1988), 'Technology and Magic', *Anthropology Today*, 4/2: 6–9.

Goossaert, V. (2004), *Dans les temples de la Chine. Histoires des cultes. Vie des communautés*, Paris: Albin Michel.

Harrell, S., et al. (2011), 'Fertility Decline in Rural China: A Comparative Analysis', *Journal of Family History*, 36/1: 15–36.

Harris, P. (2000), *The Work of the Imagination*, Oxford: Blackwell.

Jankowiak, W. (2004), 'Market Reforms, Nationalism and the Expansion of Urban China's Moral Horizon', *Urban Anthropology and Studies of Cultural Systems and World Economic Development*, 33: 167–210.

Johnson, M. (1995), *Moral Imagination: Implications of Cognitive Science for Ethics*, Chicago: University of Chicago Press.

Kleinman, A., et al. (2011), *Deep China: The Moral Life of the Person*, Berkeley: University of California Press.

Ku, H. B. (2003), *Moral Politics in a South Chinese Village: Responsibility, Reciprocity and Resistance*, Lanham, MD: Rowman & Littlefield.

Lagerwey, J. (2010), *China: A Religious State*, Hong Kong: Hong Kong University Press.

Laidlaw, J. (1995), *Riches and Renunciation: Religion, Economy, and Society among the Jains*, Oxford: Clarendon Press.

Laidlaw, J. (2002), 'For an Anthropology of Ethics and Freedom', *Journal of the Royal Anthropological Institute*, 8/2: 311–32.

Lambek, M. (2010), 'Introduction', in M. Lambek (ed.), *Ordinary Ethics: Anthropology, Language and Action*, New York: Fordham University Press.

Lemonnier, P. (1992), *Elements for an Anthropology of Technology*, Ann Arbor: University of Michigan, Museum of Anthropology.

Li, X. (2001), 'Xiangcun minjian xinyang: Tixi yu xiangzheng' (Country Folk Beliefs: System and Symbol), PhD dissertation, Department of Anthropology, Zhongshan University.

Liang, Q. (1997), *Shishan yu jiaohua: Ming Qing di cishan zuzhi* (*Charitable Deeds and Enlightenment: Ming-Qing Charity Organizations*), Taibei Shi, Taiwan: Lianjing chubanshi yegongsi.

Liu, X. (2000), *In One's Own Shadow: An Ethnographic Account of the Condition of Post-reform Rural China*, Berkeley: University of California Press.

Lukes, S. (2008), *Moral Relativism*, New York: Picador.

MacIntyre, A. (1981), 'The Nature of the Virtues', *The Hastings Center Report*, 11/2: 27–34.

Mao, T.-T. (1965 [1945]), 'The Foolish Old Man Who Removed the Mountains', in *Selected Works of Mao Tse-Tung*, vol. iii, Beijing: Foreign Languages Press.

Oxfeld, E. (2004), '"When You Drink Water, Think of Its Source": Morality, Status, and Reinvention in Rural Chinese Funerals', *Journal of Asian Studies*, 63: 961–90.

Pfaffenberger, B. (1992), 'Social Anthropology of Technology', *Annual Review of Anthropology*, 21: 491–516.

Santos, G. (2006), 'Os "camponeses" e o "imperador". Reflexões etnográficas sobre orizicultura intensiva e estratificação social no Sudeste da China', *Etnográfica*, 10/1: 41–70.

Siu, H. F. (1990), 'Recycling Tradition: Culture, History, and Political Economy in the Chrysanthemum Festivals of South China', *Comparative Studies in Society and History*, 32/4: 765–94.

Snow, D. (2004), *Cantonese as Written Language: The Growth of a Written Chinese Vernacular*, Hong Kong: Hong Kong University Press.

Tam, W. L. (2006), 'Local Religion in Contemporary China', in J. Miller (ed.), *Chinese Religions in Contemporary Societies*, Santa Barbara: ABC-CLIO.

Tan, W. L., and Zeng, H. X. (eds) (2010), *Yingde de Chuantong Difang Shehui yu Minzu (The Traditional Local Society and People of Yingde)*, Chengdu: Sichuan daxue chubanshe.

Watson, R. P. (1985), *Inequality among Brothers: Class and Kinship in South China*, Cambridge: Cambridge University Press.

Wittgenstein, L. (1929), 'A Lecture on Ethics', in J. C. Klagge and A. Nordmann (eds), *Philosophical Occasions, 1912–1951*, Indianapolis, IN: Hackett Publishing Company Inc.

Wolf, A. P. (1974), 'Gods, Ghosts, and Ancestors', in A. P. Wolf (ed.), *Religion and Ritual in Chinese Society*, Stanford, CA: Stanford University Press.

Yan, Y. (2003), *Private Life under Socialism: Love, Intimacy, and Family Change in a Chinese Village 1949–1999*, Stanford, CA: Stanford University Press.

Yan, Y. (2009), 'The Good Samaritan's New Trouble: A Study of the Changing Moral Landscape in Contemporary China', *Social Anthropology*, 17/1: 9–24.

Yang, C. K. (1961), *Religion in Chinese Society*, Berkeley: University of California Press.

Yen, Y. (2005), *Calligraphy and Power in Contemporary Chinese Society*, London: Routledge.

Zigon, J. (2009), 'Within a Range of Possibilities: Morality and Ethics in Social Life', *Ethnos,* 74/2: 251–76.

CHAPTER 12

POLITICAL HISTORY, PAST SUFFERING AND PRESENT SOURCES OF MORAL JUDGEMENT IN THE PEOPLE'S REPUBLIC OF CHINA

Stephan Feuchtwang

Trust in the ultimate leadership of the Chinese state, as a moral leadership to which petitions can be made, was an imperial tradition, even if it was often betrayed. The tradition, transformed by a modern state with a party at its core, continues through the letters and visits office of every base-level ministerial office. Petitioning could be called a technology of trust in government. But it is continued under hugely changed political and economic circumstances, named 'mass line'—a new technology of governing. The mass line is a Maoist legacy of party-led rule in which the party should, ideally, channel the ideas, experiments and experiences of the masses in different parts of China upwards and return them as mass-based directions and directives. Its full complement included mass organizations mobilized as political will to implement these directions through mass campaigns. Now, post-Mao, campaigns no longer involve mass mobilization. But the idea of upright moral leadership acting in the long-term interests of the people it leads is transmitted even while it was and is constantly disappointed.

The imperial institution of petition is ritually enacted in the petition and pledge to gods reputed for their responsiveness and justice. Both higher leaders and gods are imagined and expected to exemplify certain moral virtues—recognizing and righting grievances and responding to sincere appeals with rescue from misfortune and oppression—or to bestow fortune and harmonious and just rule. I shall return to this in the concluding section. Here I want to stay with the politics of trust in government.

Even in their great work of investigative exposure of the wrongs done by local officials to the poor farmers of Anhui in the 1990s, Chen Guide and Wu Chuntao (2006 [2003]) find that in every case of oppression there is also a story of local heroes who are upright champions of the law and of the official intentions of central government, people who can be found at upper levels, such as investigative journalists and senior party or state officials who seem willing to investigate and to right wrongs, though often only temporarily. They formulate their storytelling in the genre of moral tales, spiced with the irony that the virtuous cannot find ways to implement their good intentions and that the farmers are burdened by increasing bureaucracy, the imposition of spurious fees and the sham of short-lived face projects (Chen and Wu 2006 [2003]).[1] In sum, the technology of petition has undergone a great change, now involving entirely new institutions of government and the institution of mass media. That new technology embodies a new ideal of morally responsive leadership and its base. It is a transformation of the base, from the subject of imperial rule and divine mediation to the subject of mass equity and party leadership. While rituals of divination and petition to gods persist, as they do, the two technologies of petition exist side by side. This is the context for the everyday negotiations of judgement of experience in the recent past upon which this chapter dwells.

When the leadership from the very top of the party leads its followers to catastrophe, the expectation of morally upright leadership is dealt a blow and gives rise to reflections on whether and how to follow its monopoly of political rule. The greatest instance of a moral leadership leading to catastrophe was the famine that occurred during the revived campaigns of the Great Leap Forward from 1959 to 1961 (Bernstein 2006). Those who survived the famine transmit that time in verbal or non-verbal and everyday ways, such as reminding their children of the sacrifices they made for them, telling them to eat up, or doing the very opposite, indulging them in ways unheard of when they were children.

In this chapter, I shall give instances of this transmission in order to suggest that everyday morality is, among other things, a response to political events that have created moral dilemmas.[2] In other words, I suggest that everyday judgements of action and everyday actions themselves are historically saturated.

I am not the only anthropologist of China to suggest this. Jing Jun (2001), from whom I take the figure of saturation, writes that the proliferation of temples to the goddess of human fertility in Gansu in the 1980s was not only a response to the single-child policy but was also saturated with the loss of fertility caused by the famine. Judith Farquhar (2002) writes that eating practices (to which we should add, from her more recent work, the other practices of nurturing life [*yang sheng*]) convey a history of both past and present imbalances, of excess and deficiency. Maria Kett (2002) in her regrettably unpublished dissertation on a clinic in a Hebei village writes that complaints of neurasthenia were embodied perceptions, as expounded by the patients themselves, of times of imbalance since Mao died in 1976. Illness, failure and misfortune and the search for remedy or preventive actions to restore balance are not just physical; they are also metaphysical and moral responses to perceptions of times out of balance.

My argument is that during the Great Leap famine itself, quandaries of followership and of loyalty caused ethical reflection, and they have become endemic in the post-Mao era of party rule. This argument supplements my main point, which is that in China possibly more than elsewhere because of a long tradition of the ideal of sage imperial rule, but everywhere else too, ideals of moral leadership have to be included in the anthropology of everyday ethics.

KINDS OF SHAME IN THE GREAT LEAP FAMINE

In the course of the First Five Year Plan (1953–7), all residence, production, distribution and exchange in the People's Republic of China had been brought into a single organizational system. The Great Leap Forward then added the raising of domestic animals and vegetables into this system in a further collectivization. Furthermore, the distribution of cooked food itself was collectivized into dining halls. The organization of production was directed according to instructions from above that offered the possibility, through militarized and revolutionary enthusiasm and sustained hard work, of reaching a state of abundance in grain and steel and therefore in everything else a few years after. The party was the energizer of mobilization for production. Since 1949, it had brought to an end rampant inflation, epidemic diseases and corruption, led a campaign to redistribute land through local peasant associations so that every rural resident had security of land for subsistence, led a mass literacy campaign and set up a system of universal schooling and, through the forming of cooperatives, led socialist formation to a record harvest in 1957. Knowledge of party leadership and trust in it were therefore both high, even if it meant sacrifices involved in enduring hardship in order to build a better future for the next generation. Indeed, sacrifice for the next generation was part of the party's mass moral appeal.

The Great Leap Forward was a Communist elaboration of the movement for a strengthening of the national essence (*guo cui*) that had started in the last decades of the nineteenth century. What was unique, rather than continuous with previous versions of Chinese self-strengthening, was the singular organization of all life into 'the great Me' (*dawo*) of the political and domestic body. The People of the state, who were hailed as its masters, were expected to make sacrifices for that which posed as the greater self-sacrificer, the party's leadership, which expected them to give their lives to the future led by the party in a situation of political war, threatened by external and internal enemies. The powers of coercion that the single organization of production and consumption provided the party and its leadership were unprecedented. The main cause of the famine, in which between 30 and 40 million people died of starvation or illness related to acute malnutrition, was overzealous reporting of rises in productivity and the resulting delivery to the centre (the cities) of grain needed for seed and food in the countryside.

It is tempting to conclude that the politics of this expectation of self-sacrifice were those of coercive terror. There were indeed many cases in which brute force was used to discover and confiscate the tiny amounts of grain or sweet potatoes in the houses of villagers. What was later condemned as 'commandism' was indeed a reign of coercion. But in most places, including the prefecture of Quanzhou, where Wang Mingming and I conducted research on the transmission of the Great Leap event, the main threat was shame for lack of enthusiasm.

The ground for political shame was competitive manifestation (*biaoxian bisai*) of revolutionary ardour (Lü 2000: 84–5). We have to understand a politics in which the shame of being found wanting in a competition to show overachievement of set targets of production was enough for people to give, not just to risk, their lives. It was a politics of what Michael Dutton (2005) calls 'intensity', in which China was mobilized in a state of permanent exception, in which law and state administration were subordinated to revolutionary war. In this politics the people and its future were put at stake. Leadership acted not only to defend but also to represent itself as giving life to the people.[3] This shame affected cadres much more than those they led, into whom they sought to instil the same enthusiasm.[4] Through them, emulation and rivalry to outdo neighbouring teams and communes in reporting huge increases in productivity and in rooting out defeatists were influential and both infectious and coercive.

The result of lethal betrayal by this leadership of political shaming was a distrust of party-led enthusiasm. The same enthusiasm could be revived again in the Socialist Education (1963–4) and Cultural Revolution (1966–7) campaigns. But by the end of the 1970s, the constant changes of line had become first a factional then a ritualized performance of 'struggle', and the shaming was no longer effective.

In the Great Leap's famine conditions, fearful enthusiasm put local cadres into an acutely conflictual position. Revolutionary commitment had meant acting for the greater good of political life, even if secretly also acting for family and friends. White flags against the names of local cadres who failed to meet targets were a new symbol, a symbol of falling behind the expected enthusiasm and being labelled Right-opportunist. On one hand, cadres and their teams engaged in the knowing deception of reporting inflated production figures and remitting upwards bags of grain that meant starvation for its producers. On the other hand, they knew they should withhold grain and declare lower achievements than rivals submitted. It was a shame brought about by a realism that doubted the scientific validity and common sense of instructions from the uppermost leadership.

White flags were not the only coercive symbols in the political and moral technology of mass mobilization. As in the political rituals of the Cultural Revolution later, older symbols of humiliation were added, such as a paper turtle, a symbol of impotence, placed on the back and shoulders of the shamed cadre. In other words, failed enthusiasm brought cadres and their fellow villagers to the more personal shame of not being able to keep children and the old alive, which traditionally is also a political shame, a sign of the dereliction of sage rule. The extreme shame is a story told of previous famines, cannibalism. Survivors swapped and ate each other's dead children.[5] The shame of not being able to keep children is here extended to its extreme: the depth of humiliation that is cannibalism of children to preserve the possibility of bearing new offspring in the future. The shame of not being able to prevent an old person from dying a premature death, or an infant from dying of malnutrition, or a woman from being rendered infertile, is a deep humiliation, the most profound loss of face. Tact prevents other people from identifying families in which this occurred. Shame at not being able to provide for family and shame at the depths of depravity necessary for survival are not only feelings of severe moral shortcoming. They are also feelings about the failure of political leadership to save the people from depravity.

In a complement to this shame, there is pride in having had the social resources and skills to find ways to survive. Pride is reinforced by the idea that the hardship was shared and that, as one retired doctor who had administered to the starving told us, it did not take long for the party leadership to find effective policy remedies.

Tact is a moral virtue. But pride in survival verges on praise of the unscrupulous. In a village on the mountainous borderland with Tibet in the west of Sichuan province, half the population starved to death, according to the village accountant's figures. Here the story of survival is touched by another kind of shame. People say that the cunning (*jiaohua*) survived, the honest and straightforward (*laoshi*) died.[6] Whether it is called social capacity (*shehui caineng*) or cunning (*jiaohua*), being able to make and maintain relations of reciprocity (*wanglai*) on which to rely for social support in an emergency is also the condition of success now, in times of greater prosperity. As Yunxiang Yan (1996: 91–4, 227–8) has so well demonstrated, cunning verges on a capacity for a strong moral content (*renqing*), to be a human person, whereas those who are socially incapable are thought to be less than properly human. But being socially capable can turn into the most instrumental use of connections for immediate purposes (*la guanxi*) and without long-term interpersonal relationship. Either way, the selfish verges on the social.

RETURN TO MORE DIFFERENTIATED NORMS OF CONDUCT

Responses by two contrasting local cadres exemplify a 'return' to humanity after the end of the politics of mass mobilization. One is Chen Wansheng, a leading cadre during the famine in the village that Wang Mingming and I have been studying. He was in charge of the police in the brigade and one of a few leaders responsible for implementing the production campaigns of the Great Leap Forward. In 1961, the last year of the famine, as villagers were attempting to out-produce each other in both practical and ideological rivalry, a feud occurred over the theft by people of his village of agricultural implements from its larger neighbouring village. He enforced the return of the implements, but a ploughshare was still missing. Hearing that men from the larger village were planning to cut crops from his village to compensate, out of loyalty to his own villagers, he condoned the secret organization of a sworn brotherhood that would organize its defence. Officially he tried to defuse the conflict, but a fight in fact occurred and men from the neighbouring village were injured. Not long after, he helped his fellow villagers rebuild their ancestral hall as a way of comforting the old, who had been most vulnerable to the famine. In these ways he balanced his loyalties.

In 1963, he was accused, tried and sentenced to two years' imprisonment for not preventing the feud. The sentence was implemented in 1965. He claimed it was a politically motivated trial, since he was accused of organizing a faction. In fact, as he told Wang Mingming, he was in a patronage faction that could no longer protect him in 1965. The trial was for a criminal as well as a political offence. And so in his case, it was by a successful appeal to the same county court that he was granted withdrawal of his sentence from the record in 1988. Petitions to either the party's disciplinary officers or to judicial courts to reverse political and criminal verdicts were frequent in the 1980s. This was an example of the party maintaining trust in its capacity to correct itself, make up for mistakes and so maintain moral leadership; at the same time it could withdraw from moral dictatorship and allow, under the constraints of potential but not implemented condemnation, the restoration of other sources of moral guidance, such as the ancestral hall and the local temple whose restoration Chen Wansheng led in the 1980s. His sacrificing himself out of loyalty to fellow villagers gained him their respect and followership (Feuchtwang and Wang 2002: Chapters 4 and 5). For him, it was at one with what he was expected to do as a cadre: 'serve the people' (*wei renmin fuwu*).

The contrasting Chinese case is of a village cadre's far less mitigated loyalty to the party. In Ralph Thaxton's (2008) study of a village in the north of Henan province, the Great Leap collectivization, procurements and military organization of production were led by the vice director of the commune, a cadre hardened by the guerrilla wars against the Chinese puppet forces under Japanese command and then against the Nationalists. Thaxton shows clearly how this forged in him a fierce loyalty to Maoist ideals and a brutal resort to physical intimidation and secrecy. He was an organizer of shock forces to harvest grain and secure it for procurement by the state for the cities and industrialization. Yet even he had sufficient loyalty to his fellow villagers to leave corn grain in the fields that he knew would be gleaned secretly, at night. He also condoned the pre-harvest gathering of green grain for immediate consumption and some secret storage.

In the rectification that ended the Great Leap Forward in 1961, he was arrested for commandism and sentenced to reform in a labour camp, but he had returned by 1964 in time for the Socialist Education Campaign, during which he became party secretary of the brigade that included his village. He used his position to promote those who had been his supporters and get rid of those who had criticized him. Hatred of him, despite his compromises in the famine, flared up with arson attacks on his house in 1965 and anonymous letters against him in 1967, accusing him of being a capitalist-roader, even though he had been a staunch Maoist. That was the way to attack him successfully during the Cultural Revolution, and the commune leadership removed him from his post. After the Cultural Revolution, he was restored to his position. But when he retired, in the 1990s, he had still not been compensated for his removal in 1967. Rectification of the verdict, according to one of Thaxton's (2008) interviews, would have angered the villagers too much.[7]

One way or another, local cadres had to face in two directions—upward in obedience and sideways to fellow villagers' needs—and even the fiercest upward loyalists retained a modicum of this ambivalence.

Just as striking, the immediately responsible cadres and officials, including those in cities—such as one in Quanzhou who told us how he had apologized to the masses and found them 'really kind'—were openly accessible to their victims after the turn of regime from Mao (via Hua Guofeng) to Deng Xiaoping.

Chen Wansheng exemplifies a mixture of ideals, including his reinterpretation of the ideal of serving the people by rebuilding the lineage hall. In the same county, a much younger cadre, born in 1969, vice director of a county party propaganda department, takes a keen interest in what he understands to be the local culture of southern Fujian. This is his version of restoring humanity (the interview took place on 23 March 2004).

Is there incomprehension between the years of Mao and now?
Of course, everyone's experience influences his outlook. Life is contradictory. If the young stay in the village they will take part in the rituals and will find a different point of view out of that experience. Young people may seem to disagree with their elders and in cities follow new fashions. But in their bones they carry their elders' traditions [of lineages]. The surface is not the whole story.

Does knowledge of their elders' sufferings get passed on?
Although such things are talked about, they may not be taken seriously. We should also understand that there are great differences of detail. Some people treat suffering as the glory of their lives. Now in society there are people who treat past suffering as a kind of wealth [*caifu*] of experience.

How and why do people where you came from talk about the famine?
Those who talk about it are those who have become wealthy. Those who have not succeeded, do not. Only when you are successful can your talk be influential. They boast that they have got over the hard times and of how different it is now, for them.

A friend from the same department, a poet and calligrapher, added later that the worst thing about the 1950s and 1960s was the destruction of culture: 'I do not mean what is visible. It was a destruction of human relations [*ren yu ren guanxi*]. The revival of lineages is a replacement of the destroyed relations.'

When the first cadre talks of lineages, he refers to small-town and rural life as a location for the return to humanity. But when he speaks of cities and of the way people evaluate the more immediate, historical past as distinct from cultural past, he seems to be much more cynical. Once it was the power over food and collective organization; now it is success in having overcome a past of suffering and having gone on to accumulate wealth that gave you a right to be heard, both lacking human, moral depth.

In the same conversation, they drifted off into talk of the county's status in official measurements of advancement: gross domestic product and other rates of economic growth. This is the more concrete substance of the official discourse of development, which has replaced the language of sacrifice to the party. It indicates the amorality of sheer economic growth, in which the allusion to 'fashion' and urban life is simply the taking advantage of opportunity and luck. But on the other hand, increasing material well-being returns us to the moral project of party leadership for the material benefit of the people, though now through different means. In other words, for many, the shames of the Great Leap famine and the ritualized exhaustion of mass mobilization have led to two projects of moral reconstruction, a turn to older institutions of moral leadership and a somewhat removed and lowered expectation of party leadership managing an economy that will enable security of income and well-being.

For a view of party leadership, material well-being and moral-political unification of an increasing pride in China's success in the world, I turn now to a young woman, a university student in London in 2008, prompted by recalling the height of her father to talk about the famine:

> My father was as short as me. He suffered from insufficient nutrition because of the famine when he was a boy. Also when I wasted food or was choosy about food; they would always talk about the hardship during the famine.

But her sense of distance from the past was more emphatically political than others, articulating a change in relation to the party-state:

What effects do you think the famine has on today's life and society and younger generation people like you?

China is a socialist country where the people have continuing trust in the
Party. Therefore, in exchange, the Party should be more responsible
for the masses. Also, when coming to a natural disaster like that, the
government should certainly have called for aid from international
sources once they realised that the incident was beyond their ability
to deal with it. I think the famine warned us of the flaws of collec-
tivisation, that we should not have extensive centralised agricultural
activities which would eventually end up with deficiency. For the
new generation like us, as most of us are the only child, they (the
parents) have great influence on us. However, we are not like our
parents who had unquestionable faith in the government. Instead,
we are critical of government decisions.[8]

Even without such articulation, the attention to food can itself be a vector
of historical judgement. Grandparents, the generation that experienced
the Mao years, are frequently in charge of their few or single grandchildren. They, in lieu of the parents hard at work to earn enough to invest
in the best possible upbringing and schooling of their child, indulge
them with the most desired food. At the same time, parents also advise
their pregnant daughters on a more balanced diet (Jing 2000). This is a
time of both imbalance and the wish and means to rebalance the circuits
of life and its energies (*qi*). Children are told to eat up, indulged, fat-
tened to obesity, even while having a single child who is healthy is so
important. Anxieties and indulgences convey without words a past of
deprivation.

One articulation of this implicit reference to the past is the phrase
chi ku, 'to eat bitterness'. It refers to a past when China was the
land of famine and known in the Western world for this through the
charitable efforts of Christian and secular relief efforts responding to
the Incredible Famine of 1876–9 (Edgerton-Tarpley 2008). In Maoist China it referred to the pre-1949 past through the performance
of 'speaking bitterness' (*suku*), one of the main means of rousing
emotions for mass mobilization against class enemies, the oppressors
before Liberation. It also means dwelling on the past in ways that
the young no longer want to do. And finally it means being frugal, as
an American Chinese anthropology doctoral student during fieldwork
was said to contrast with her Chinese cousins who would not save for
their future.[9]

The young postgraduate student from the mainland with the short father, on the other hand, turns towards the sacrifice that parents made for their children and away from their sacrifice of themselves and their children for the greater whole represented by the party.

THE INVERSION OF SACRIFICE AS OBLIGATION

The famine came at the height and completion of collectivization, a peak of the party's power to command. During the height of the Maoist command system, during collectivization, when burial grounds were to be cultivated, in some parts of China the wood from the coffins in the graves was used for fires or construction. During subsequent campaigns against 'the four olds', ancestral halls and temples were torn down, scorning and preventing care for the ancestral dead and for local protector gods, as well as the demons and ghosts they could command and put in place. Mao's greatest supremacy was a time of the greatest number of unceremoniously buried dead, forgotten ancestors; he was the chief and only demon controller. Since Mao's death there has been a revival of rituals for the dead and of proper burials in the countryside, against the party's urging cremation. There has also been a restoration of rituals addressed to local gods, sometimes with the addition of Mao but then only as one of many gods, not supreme. Ancestors and gods have been restored in people's visualization of responsive power.

To illustrate this turn, I borrow from Jing Jun (2003) a highly illuminating sequence. As part of the project of building the Sanmenxia dam on the Yellow River, villagers in Shaanxi whose villages would be flooded were asked in 1957, just as the Great Leap was beginning, to volunteer to move to new settlements in far western regions of Gansu and Ningxia. The first batch that went was of willing volunteers. But the land of the new settlements was semi-desert, and some of the resettled went back to their villages, unable or unwilling to face the harsh and unpromising conditions into which they had been induced. Trust in the government sank. Nobody else volunteered. Their local cadres were dismissed. Instead, militiamen pulled the villagers' houses down and residents were forced to move.

The barren land to which they had to move caused battles over water between them and the farmers who were already there. Many trekked back in the direction of their villages in Shaanxi, begging, the older and weaker starving to death. Others followed the same route in the 1980s, avoiding the roadblocks set up by the police to impede them.

What caused this reform-era return to their villages was an intensification of feeling that they had been wronged by the state. This feeling must already have been there, but now the controls were loosened. The immediate cause was news that the level of the reservoir had, for technical reasons, been lower than planned and that their villages had not been flooded but had been turned into state and military farms. The returnees formed squatter villages and stole from the state farms. They also petitioned for the return of their villages to them, and in this they were supported by a member of the State Council. Of many protests, the one Jing Jun singles out for bringing about their eventual success was held on Qing Ming, the day for cleaning graves of parents and more distant lineal kin. Among its slogans were these: 'Return to homeland, Sacrifice to ancestors' and 'We would rather become ghosts in the reservoir area.' As Jing Jun (2003: 125) points out, this was a deliberate displacement of the masses' indebtedness to the party onto indebtedness to ancestors and to older senses of belonging, and it was saturated with the memory of the first trek back during the famine in which the old had indeed become ghosts, dying on the way.

Understand this together with the continuing, traditional importance of food as gift, as offering and as feast. In particular we must understand the reciprocity of *yang* as nutrition, which as Charles Stafford (2000) has pointed out includes the nurturing of relationships— reciprocally between older and younger generations, gods and followers, mothers and children, ancestors and descendants, as well as laterally in relationships with graded emotional attachments. One informant in the far north-eastern village of Xiajia told Yunxiang Yan (1996: 94), stressing the importance of networks of relationships for supporting survival and life, 'No matter the dynasty, we ordinary people are always the victims and have no one to rely on except our own relatives and close friends [*shizai qinyou*]. I lost my mind once and devoted myself completely to the collectives, but after the three difficult years [of the famine], no more!' In other words, he had abandoned the moral discourse of self-sacrifice to the greater good led by the party in favour of an older moral discourse of mutual, interpersonal reciprocity.

Reliance on mutual support and favour was the secret to surviving the famine and is now the means of setting up arrangements of trust to make money and to support self and family.

A CONTEMPORARY PROLIFERATION OF MORAL DISCOURSES FROM DIFFERENT TIMES

When the calligrapher and poet, cited earlier, who was also an official in a county seat in the prefecture of Quanzhou, said that the famine destroyed human relations (*ren yu ren guanxi*); when John Flower was told that 'the cunning [*jiaohua*] survived, the honest and straightforward [*laoshi*] died'; or when Felix Wemheuer was told that before the Anti-Right Opportunist campaigns in the Great Leap Forward 'Chinese people had human feeling [*yijian Zhongguoren hen laoshi*]'[10]; the people making these remarks implicitly ask whether there has been a recovery of honesty and humanity. They do not claim with any certainty that there has been.

For most people these are much more prosperous times, and at the same time, the economy is far more diversified and social life even in the countryside is far more urbanized. Cities or large towns are within close travelling distance. Family and other 'human' relations are therefore being reworked in these completely new conditions. For most Chinese, the present is a contrast with a past of hunger. For those who care to recall them, the years of the Great Leap famine stand out as the time when people 'just thought about surviving through to the next day, making it through one day at a time—you did everything for the sake of your stomach'.[11] The legacy of stomach fixation may be a certain sense of priorities and a necessary ruthlessness in the seizing of opportunities in a commercialized economy of uncertainties, as well as the need to repair family and other human relations.

To seek upright cadres, or ex-cadres who retain political clout and are prepared to stand out, such as Chen Wansheng, is still possible in a sea of opportunism.[12] It would be foolish to suggest that most of those who seek rectification of grievances are implicitly recalling the Great Leap famine. But the restoring of what people considered to be 'human' has had an effect on the moral discourse of seeking redress even through the old mass line institution of the offices for letters and visits, *xingang ke*. A frequently used term for these petitions and for the kowtows to higher officials by delegations of submitters is the old imperial term 'to plead' (*qingyuan*). In a case study of one such submission, Xiang Biao points out that the pleaders identify themselves with the state or country (*guojia*) in relation to state officials who are instruments of the state, quite unlike petitioner subjects of the emperor as the Son of Heaven. But tactically by their submission, they place government officials in a superior position and in doing so hope to arouse in them sentiments of sympathy as well as duty.[13]

Ironically, though, submission of letters and petitions for visits and the righting of wrongs can only work if they go against the expected official norm and the law by 'troublemaking' tactics: en masse rather than single submissions, skipping levels of governments and refusing to attend to local government recommendations to pursue their cases through the courts. Local governments are now assessed by their performance in dealing with petitions, so petitioners know that making trouble is effective. In these ways the old mass line institution has come into its own in the current post-Mao era (Chen 2008). A study of one such office was conducted in the city of Shenzhen (Thireau and Hua 2005). The great majority of the letter writers were rural migrant workers, feeling powerless in relation to their bosses, complaining that they are overworked, forced to do overtime and not paid for the extra hours or that their basic pay is delayed, that the conditions are dangerous and that they receive no compensation when they are injured. They appealed through the office to protectors to come and investigate their complaints. Their modes of address (Thireau and Hua 2005: 93) are highly significant of the traditions according to which they attribute moral authority to those who should and they hope will protect them from unscrupulous bosses:

- 'uncles', 'fair judges' and 'protective god'—these come from the traditions of kin who mediate in familial disputes and of the mythical heroes and deified figures of good magistrates in imperial times such as the good, investigative judge Bao Gong;
- 'comrades', 'directing comrades' and 'servants of the people' refer to the ideals of party leadership instilled during the Maoist period and continue to this day;
- 'father and mother of the people' refers to both the good, uncorrupted, imperial magistrate and to the local party cadre who remains close to the masses.

Several letters refer to their bosses in the same way that the party historians did to the exploiting landlords and capitalists that the revolution was supposed to have overthrown (Thireau and Hau 2005:100). To these are added the poignant and emotive appeals to humanity, of being treated like buffaloes, slaves and machines, appealing to both traditional concepts of human personality and feeling (*renqing wei*) and to more recent, international human rights (*rengequan*) (101). In reverse, the exploiters are referred to as animals and demons.

These letters reveal a great and significant variety of modes of address to higher authority, indicative of a multiplication of moral discourses, including a Maoist legacy of addressing the higher authority of the party-state. But at the same time, they include by implication the examples we have seen in the case of Chen Wansheng and his village. They mix together engagement in other kinds of temporality, of familial reproduction, genealogical continuity, sacrifice for children and grandchildren and the self-reliance that is achieved through the making of interpersonal relations, with the temporality of historical progress led by the party. Their interplay is occasion for everyday reflections on what it is to be good and whom to trust as a moral exemplar. And their interplay is effective. Lily L. Tsai (2007) has shown that it is not the conduct of village elections nor relative economic development that induce local cadres to invest local revenue in public goods, such as drinking water and other utilities, but the incidence of what she calls 'solidary groups': institutions in which local cadres and fellow villagers are joined. Where such institutions exist—her examples are temples, festivals and lineages—and more or less coincide territorially with administrative boundaries, cadres can not only be held to account in the institutions themselves; they can also, in the terms I have introduced, be held to 'human' account in the provision of public goods.

CONCLUSION

I think that I have shown the simultaneous deployment of at least two technologies of human relations and moral judgement, each of them replete with recent history and both of them politically transformed. One is the deployment of gifts in interpersonal relations, first of all between generations in families but also in the cultivation and maintenance of wider webs of relations. Accounting for such deployment is done through a calculus of reciprocity which is ancient but which has been transformed in changing balances of conjugal, patrilineal and affinal kinship and more broadly of the moral standards of creating, maintaining and curtailing interpersonal relations that have become singularly important. The other is the quality of sacrifice, conveying a recent history of the older generations as givers, their generosity and whether it has been reciprocated, their humanity or their boasting, cunning or selfishness. Both centrally involve food, daily meals, banquets or special cakes on special days in a calendar or a lifetime. The food and its accompaniments convey two judgements. One is the quality of respect or snub, affection or coolness and tact in the judgement of givers, recipients and observers; the other is the affection for children and grandchildren and the anxious expectation of reciprocal affection.

The importance of interpersonal trust and mutual support, conveyed through food and, of course, favours, has increased because of the recent history of sacrifice. But it is now also set in the context of elaborate legal, contractual relations and extended administrative bureaucracies. They offer other techniques of conveying judgement, of registering and appealing against failures to be just. One of these is petition. This technique is also historically and politically inflected through its function as an institution of the mass line that has become a powerful means of self-organized and semi-legal mass action, of moral protest and the realization of the rule of law.

The two technologies of food gift and of petition are joined in food offerings to gods as pledges, accompanied by written or spoken promises and pleas. The two—promise and plea—enact a relation of reciprocity and recognition in veneration of authority. The plea follows an offering of food, principally rice, accompanied by incense and spirit money, and it promises a further such offering. The plea expects a return gift, just as the protocol and rite of tribute to an emperor expects in return a feast and gifts, plus the encompassing protection of the sovereign (Feuchtwang 2007; Gibeault 2007). Veneration and wish in the form of a plea and an expectation of return re-states the ideal of sage rule, in which the god is a figure of that rule. This relationship of authority is one of mutual recognition, in which the human formed in relations of kinship, household and territorial community recognizes and is recognized by a supreme human and moral authority. That same relationship is now juxtaposed with and infused with the more historical and recent transformations of this authority, mass line and legal rectitude, in which relations of family and neighbourhood and interpersonal networks of trust and respect can be and are mobilized by the governed in political society (Chatterjee 2004).

Thus, in the ordinary actions of domestic life and the creation and maintenance of interpersonal relations, in the less-frequent visits to temples and in the occasions of petitioning and mass protest, Chinese citizens exercise a repertoire of quite different discourses for moral judgements and actions.

NOTES

1. 'Face projects' are performances and constructions to show visiting officials that local officials have conformed to a current policy.
2. All the material presented here is either attributed or is the result of research conducted by and with Wang Mingming, funded by a generous grant from the UK Economic and Social Research Council (ESRC), reference number R000239521.
3. Michael Dutton (2005) convincingly argues that at the core of Maoist politics is the question 'who is our friend and who our enemy' where the collective first person is the people. This is the question that Carl Schmitt argued to be at the core of sovereignty and politics (see Hirst 1999). Dutton presents Maoist politics as a case study of Schmitt's theory.
4. *Ganbu*, the Chinese term for what is usually translated as 'cadres', are members of the Chinese Communist Party; this usage is often extended to all officials of government, who are usually members of the Party.
5. Such stories, quite possibly based on fact, were told after the so-called Incredible Famine caused by drought in four provinces of northern China 1876–9 (Edgerton-Tarpley 2008: 211). As Edgerton-Tarpley remarks, cannibalism was by far the most frequent subject of the recollections transmitted verbally over two generations since then and recorded in stone inscriptions shortly after the event, but it also had precedents in the literature of strange stories and sections of local records devoted to the abnormal (2008: 212, 222–5).
6. Many thanks to John Flower for this information (personal communication, Oxford, 1 July 2005).
7. I thank Ralph deeply for allowing me to read a 2005 typescript of his book (Thaxton 2008).
8. Thanks to Li Sha for this interview, taken with his permission from his dissertation for the MSc China in Comparative Perspective 2008.
9. Thanks to Willa Zhen, personal communication, November 2009.

10. Reported at a workshop at Brandeis University, 18 April 2005.
11. This is how a woman in the village of Shaocun, in a relatively poor part of Zhejiang province, remembered being a young girl in the famine. Many thanks to Daniel Roberts for allowing me to use this telling quote from his PhD dissertation, the London School of Economics (LSE).
12. Seeking one's fortune was often referred to as going down into the ocean—*xiahai*.
13. Many thanks to Xiang Biao and his presentation of the case study at LSE, 27 November 2009.

REFERENCES

Bernstein, T. P. (2006), 'Mao Zedong and the Famine of 1959–60: A Study in Wilfulness', *China Quarterly*, 186: 421–45.

Chatterjee, P. (2004), *The Politics of the Governed: Reflections on Popular Politics in Most of the World*, New York: Columbia University Press.

Chen, G., and Wu, C. (2006 [2003]), *Will the Boat Sink the Water? The Life of China's Peasants*, trans. Zhu Hong, New York: Public Affairs.

Chen, X. (2008), 'Collective Petitioning and Institutional Conversion', in K. O'Brien (ed.), *Popular Protest in China*, Cambridge, MA: Harvard University Press.

Dutton, M.R. (2005), *Policing Chinese Politics: A History*, Durham, NC, and London: Duke University Press.

Edgerton-Tarpley, K. (2008), *Tears from Iron: Cultural Responses to Famine in Nineteenth-century China*, Berkeley and London: University of California Press.

Farquhar, J. (2002), *Appetites: Food and Sex in Post-Socialist China*, Durham, NC, and London: Duke University Press.

Feuchtwang, S. (2007), 'On Religious Ritual as Deference and Excessive Communication', *Journal of the Royal Anthropological Institute*, 13/1: 57–72.

Feuchtwang, S., and Wang, M. (2002), *Grassroots Charisma: Four Local Leaders in China*, London and New York: Routledge.

Gibeault, D. (2007), 'L'autorité comme échange: La Chine', unpublished paper.

Hirst, P. Q. (1999), 'Carl Schmitt's Decisionism', in C. Mouffe (ed.), *The Challenge of Carl Schmitt*, London and New York: Verso.

Jing, J. (2000), 'Food, Nutrition and Cultural Authority in a Gansu Village' in J. Jing (ed.), *Feeding China's Little Emperors: Food, Children and Social Change*, Stanford, CA: Stanford University Press.

Jing, J. (2001), 'Male Ancestors and Female Deities: Finding Memories of Trauma in a Chinese Village', in M. S. Roth and C. G. Salas (eds), *Disturbing*

Remains: Memory, History, and Crisis in the Twentieth Century, Issues and Debates vol. 7, Los Angeles: The Getty Research Institute.

Jing, J. (2003), 'Dams and Dreams: A Return-to-homeland Movement in Northwest China', in C. Stafford (ed.), *Living with Separation in China: Anthropological Accounts*, London and New York: RoutledgeCurzon.

Kett, M. (2002), 'Accommodating the Self: Health, Wealth and Wellbeing in a Suburban Chinese Village', PhD dissertation, University of London, School of Oriental and African Studies.

Kipnis, A. (2008), 'Education and the Governance of Child-centred Relatedness', in S. Brandstädter and G. Santos (eds), *Chinese Kinship: Contemporary Anthropological Perspectives*, London and New York: Routledge.

Li, S. (2008), 'A Silent Famine: A Study of China's 1959–61 Famine in a Comparative Perspective with Ukraine and North Korea Famines,' unpublished MSc dissertation, London School of Economics.

Lü, X. (2000), *Cadres and Corruption: The Organizational Involution of the Chinese Communist Party*, Stanford, CA: Stanford University Press.

Roberts, D. (2012), 'The Family in Changing China: An Account of Kinship Ideologies and Practices in Rural North China', unpublished PhD dissertation, London School of Economics.

Stafford, C. (2000), 'Chinese Patriliny and the Cycles of *Yang* and *Laiwang*', in J. Carston (ed.), *Cultures of Relatedness: New Approaches to the Study of Kinship*, Cambridge: Cambridge University Press.

Thaxton, R. (2008), *Catastrophe and Contention in Rural China: Mao's Great Leap Forward Famine and the Origins of Righteous Resistance in Da Fo Village*, Cambridge: Cambridge University Press.

Thireau, I., and Hua, L. (2005), 'One Law, Two Interpretations: Mobilising the Labor Law in Arbitration Committees and in Letters and Visits Offices', in N. J. Diamant et al. (eds), *Engaging the Law in China: State, Society and the Possibilities for Justice*, Stanford, CA: Stanford University Press.

Tsai, L.L. (2007), *Accountability without Democracy: Solidary Groups and Public Goods Provision in Rural China*, Cambridge: Cambridge University Press.

Yan, Y. (1996), *The Flow of Gifts: Reciprocity and Social Networks in a Chinese Village*, Stanford, CA: Stanford University Press.

CHAPTER 13

ETHICAL SHIFTERS IN THE CHINESE HIV/AIDS EPIDEMIC

Jing Shao and Mary Scoggin

Ethnographic examination of the HIV/AIDS epidemic in China allows us to see something new as moral worlds emerge in contemporary
China, supported and contested by ordinary 'ethical acts'. As the epidemic developed through commercial harvesting of human plasma in
rural central China in the 1990s, it produced not just illness, fear and
victimhood, but also solidarity, activism and a new sense of responsibility attached to the individual body, the separable cells within it and even
the distinct viral strains that move between bodies. This chapter places
new developments into the larger context of biosocial, economic and
political relations. We argue that this new sense of responsibility on the
part of HIV carriers reflects an expanded awareness of the individual's
own potential for agency. This awareness, in turn, has emerged within a
larger context of 'global' trends governing the distribution of agency and
rights, stemming not only from international sources (or 'liberal' ideologies of agency as discussed in Laidlaw 2008) but also from policies and
ideological efforts on the part of many layers of Chinese government
and society. The multilayered effect is a reflection of a new way that
farmers, migrant workers and an expanding list of others including sex
workers and drug users can negotiate moral status.

In this chapter, we show how certain units of meaning within the
social discourse of HIV (concepts, terms and ways of speaking) are
'shifters' that bear existential relations with the objects they represent
in context (Jakobson 1990: 338). Participants use these shifters in order

to position themselves as actors within a moral discourse; indeed, just as primary indexicals such as 'I' or 'you' must refer to an existential context of speaking, reference to channels of infection, 'types' of HIV viral strains and identity with certain communities must relate to a body of knowledge and propositions that form the background for such positions. Use of these units of meaning composes parts of a 'code', in the Jakobsonian sense. Unlike more formally acknowledged codes such as languages or even dialects, topic-specific moral propositions and stipulations under discussion here are far less tangible to inspection or introspection in a formal sense. They are particularly important, however, to participants who are invested in the moral status of HIV, including researchers, activists and especially patients. The ethnographic work we present here allows us to observe this code in action. One of us, Jing Shao, is referred to by the pronominal 'I' in the following ethnographic account. This pronominal 'I' also crucially and performatively constitutes the ethical position of the ethnographer in vivo. Scoggin and Shao collaborated on writing and research for this chapter, and the authorial 'we' reflects at least this small collectivity.

A SEPARATE EPIDEMIC

The outbreak of HIV infections in rural central China was first characterized as a 'separate epidemic' (Wu, Rou and Gui 2004) in terms of its demography. Early in the 1990s, the local government in Henan actively promoted commercial plasma collection in the province and encouraged rural residents to sell plasma as a way of supplementing their agricultural income. Thus, the outbreak was organized by the definition of farmers as a governed population and could be not associated with any epidemiologically relevant risk behaviour on the part of the individual. If anybody was to blame for the outbreak, it was the government and the collecting facilities that relaxed safety procedures and allowed contamination to take place. This was indeed why the epidemic in rural central China was kept a secret for such a long time. The Chinese government tacitly acknowledged this when it abruptly shut down all the plasma-collecting operations in Henan province in 1995. At that time, however, knowledge about HIV infections among donors was kept a secret, and the ban only served to drive plasma collection underground and to neighbouring provinces, allowing the epidemic to spread farther and faster. This phase of the HIV/AIDS outbreak in China was, first and foremost, a tragic case of massive blood contamination that primarily claimed blood and plasma donors as its victims. The Chinese government broke its silence about the epidemic in 2004 in the wake of a large number of deaths among strong-bodied farmers, following the quick progression of what they themselves thought of as a mysterious killer disease, and long after the existence and the severity of an HIV epidemic in the region first came to light in foreign media (Rosenthal 2000). In the summer of 2003, the government piloted its antiretroviral treatment in a few of the most severely affected villages. Little effort was made to select and prepare the infected villagers. Many who desperately started treatment quickly abandoned it as soon as the initial side effects began to appear. Some even suspected that the treatment was offered to hasten their deaths. These victims have an active interest in controlling the meaning of HIV within a moral code.

Below, we can observe Zhongmin (pseudonym), a 48-year-old 'former commercial plasma donor', deploying the HIV moral code and reinforcing Jakobson's description of how shifters work by describing his HIV status via reported speech, thus delivering a 'message about a message' (Volosinov in Jakobson 1990: 387).

ZHONGMIN'S GAMBIT

I was quite startled when Zhongmin said to me, 'They say our kind of virus does not transmit through sex.' I first met Zhongmin in 2003, at his wife's wake in their small house in a village in Henan, China. Hers was the third life claimed by HIV in his extended family. She was buried around midnight in the field not far from the village. The next morning, Zhongmin returned to his wife's grave, a fresh mound of earth displaced by the coffin buried underneath. The field was bare after the harvest in October. I went with him and could see more mounds dotting the fields. All five of his younger brothers had been infected through plasma donation, and so were three of the four women who had married into this family, along with one young child born with the infection. Two brothers had died the previous year, one before anybody in the village had any inkling that so many among them had been infected with HIV, a virus that had seemed so remote from their own lives. Some in the village had learned about the deadly virus in the media, characterized as a disease that spreads among homosexuals in foreign countries or drug users in southern China. There were many more families in the village like his, and many more villages like this one in Henan in neighbouring provinces of rural central China.

Zhongmin's report invokes a moral code with the opening 'they say'. He then distances 'our kind of virus' from the other kind, alien to him. Here Zhongmin is less concerned about how he acquired the virus and more interested in commenting upon his current status as sexually active. Less than a year after his wife's burial, at the time of our conversation, Zhongmin had already developed a steady relationship with a young woman eighteen years his junior. She was married and lived in town where she had a job. He had an HIV-related national policy to thank for his current job in a furniture store in town, because its owner could get tax breaks by registering the store under an HIV-positive former commercial plasma donor. Zhongmin showed up at the store for a few hours every day, sporting a business suit, a tie and a trim moustache, and he was paid a small salary. He was, as far as I could tell, passionately in love and proud of the fact that his charms trumped a tremendous social gap; his lover was willing to leave her younger and securely employed urban husband for him. The fact that the husband would also be HIV negative went unmentioned. 'I heard that the antiviral treatment is bad for kidneys,' he said. 'You mean your external kidney?' I joked, using the Chinese euphemism for testicles. He acknowledged this and said, 'I know I might die soon, but I want to have lived to the fullest when I do.' 'Do you use the condom when you are together?' I asked. 'No,' he held up his hand, 'we've had sex at least five hundred times, and have not used a condom even once.' 'How can you be so irresponsible?' I was getting angry. 'But she insisted not to,' he replied. 'But why? Isn't she aware that you are HIV positive?' 'She is, but she thinks that you only use a condom for commercial sex, and ours is not.' I did not have a chance to ask her whether she also thought that his kind of HIV did not transmit through sex.

Behind Zhongmin's assertion, there is, in fact, an active campaign that deploys a very similar moral code. Dr Gao Yaojie, a retired gynaecologist from Henan and one of the prominent figures in AIDS activism in China, courageously and tirelessly condemned the ruthless harvesting of 'source plasma' by China's fractionation industry and the complicity of her provincial government, which led to the outbreak of

HIV infection among rural donors. She has also long contended that the promotion of 'contraceptive condoms' will not stop the spread of AIDS in China as long as it diverts public attention away from the scandalous 'blood plague' resulting from plasma harvesting. From her perspective, this plague is not over, for not only has the government been covering up the true scope of the epidemic in Henan and other central provinces, but the collection of plasma has moved to other rural areas of China, which can still spark new outbreaks if it has not already done so. Official epidemiological estimates conceal more often than they reveal, she insists, given their dismal track record.

Although widely admired for her fearlessness and dedication, Gao has also compromised her effectiveness as an activist by her steadfast refusal to acknowledge the broadening HIV epidemic in China. Gao argues that in China the epidemic is a political disease, while for the rest of the world it is one of moral delinquency. If the same ethical failures and associated HIV cases are found in China, it simply is not relevant to her campaign because that is by definition a different disease. For her, transmission route is the distinction between innocence and guilt for the infected. By implication, injecting drug use and 'promiscuity' are offences against the moral code, punishable by HIV infection.[1] As a consequence of her narrow definition of the HIV epidemic in China, many of her dire projections are dismissed. Nevertheless, for tens of thousands of HIV-infected rural people, she remains an indispensible pubic figure who gives voice to their muted suffering. This is in part because her harsh judgement on HIV transmission other than through blood donation upholds the dignity, moral purity and ethical agency of the victims of the 'blood plague'.[2] The fact that she is only concerned with the stigmatization of innocent victims, and not the separate 'dirty disease', also flies in the face of the pragmatic, perhaps somewhat self-serving public health campaigns of inclusive compassion and moral tolerance for anyone infected with HIV.

Gao's prescriptive sexual morality, which she believes is preserved in the rural, traditional and therefore properly Chinese social setting, certainly supplies moral support for rural people who were desperately salvaging and hanging onto lives devastated by HIV infection. But it is a wishful step to take her position against the condom as an invitation to think that the type of HIV in their blood can only be transmitted through blood and not sex. Zhongmin, who was obviously guilty of 'promiscuity' by Gao's standard, can find an easy way out of an ethical dilemma by believing that the virus circulating in his blood did not have the vicious virulence to transmit heterosexually. By virtue of his original victimhood, he sees a saving grace imputed to his contaminated blood.

VIRAL TYPES AND MORAL FACETS

At about the same time that the pernicious epidemic of HIV was spreading in Henan, a group of virologists in Boston was testing the idea that different HIV viral strains might underlie patterns of the epidemic defined by their specific routes of transmission in different parts of the world. The idea was first proposed by Max Essex, a veteran virologist and a key player in HIV research at Harvard University. Drawing upon his extensive experience working on the epidemic in Africa and South Asia, where predominant viral strains were different from those found in North America and Europe, he hypothesized that this difference could explain the fact that in most 'industrialized countries', the epidemic was largely confined to homosexual populations and injecting drug users, while in most 'third world countries', the epidemic was driven by heterosexual contact (Cohen 1995; Pope et al. 1997; Soto-Ramirez et al. 1996). This idea gained steam particularly in research conducted in Thailand (see Shao and Scoggin 2009); and in 1996, Dr Richard Marlink (Marlink and Swan 1996), executive director of the Harvard AIDS Institute, referred to subtype B as a 'cosmopolitan subtype' as it was primarily found in big cities 'in the industrialized world' and argued that the '"heterosexual epidemics" of sub-Saharan Africa, India or southeast Asia' could be explained by 'biological difference in the subtypes'. Marlink suggested that the world, or rather 'the industrialized world', should be warned of a second heterosexual epidemic of HIV by a different virus, and develop vaccines with the foresight of targeting those non–B subtypes.

Back in Henan, informed by forays through Boston and Thailand, we see that the HIV-infected population seems to have remained a Thai B province (see the following paragraph) in China's evolving HIV epidemic, at least in so far as the molecular epidemiology of the 'former commercial plasma donors' is concerned. The international scientific probe into possible connections among the infectivity of viral subtypes, risk behaviour and epidemiological patterns presents a split that is consistent with Gao Yaojie's discrimination between a 'Chinese' epidemic limited to blood harvesting and a 'cosmopolitan' epidemic linked to drug use and sexual behaviour. However, the moral map of international activism that has resulted is at variance with Gao's; conduct that in her view is immoral becomes the focus of international preventive efforts. In Gao's view, Chinese national and local governments are happy to accept this view in the practical organization of relief efforts precisely because it enables them to conceal their own role at the root of the epidemic in China.

At an international workshop at Nanjing University in May 2007, several presentations on the HIV molecular epidemiology in China were given by Chinese researchers who had previously worked at a leading AIDS research centre in New York. Their research indicated that a new and fast-growing epidemic of HIV infection through sex was emerging in Yunnan and Guangxi, the two southern provinces which had already seen high rates of infection among injecting drug users along the routes of overland trafficking of heroin from the Golden Triangle region in South Asia. Moreover, the new heterosexual infections were predominantly of an HIV strain different from the ones already circulating among the population of injecting drug users. This 'heterosexual' subtype, labelled 'circulating recombinant form (CRF) 01_AE', had been previously known as 'subtype E', while among injecting drug users a mosaic of other recombinant forms were detected, suggesting an ongoing epidemic with multiple viral strains (Y. Zhang et al. 2006). With the advent of molecular epidemiology, distinct outbreaks of the HIV epidemics are now characterized not only by patterns of risk behaviour, demographic features, and geographic sites, but also by detectable variability in viral genetic profiles. Could there be, then, a grain of truth in Zhongmin's claim that their kind of virus was different and did not transmit heterosexually, or at least not as easily? As it turns out, plasma donors such as Zhongmin were infected exclusively with a distinct viral strain, subtype B' of HIV Type 1. This strain, also known as the 'Thai B subtype', was predominant among HIV-infected injecting drug users in the border areas of Yunnan province early in the 1990s, exactly the time of intense plasma collection in central China. The same strain has been traced by genotyping ultimately to the injecting drug users in Thailand (Graf et al. 1998; Su et al. 2003; Weniger, Takebe, Ou and Yamazaki 1994; L. Zhang et al. 2004). In the overall HIV genetic scenario in

China, however, Thai B has become distinctively 'archaic'. Newer and far more varied viral strains have long replaced Thai B in other parts of the country, among other epidemiological 'sub populations' such as commercial sex workers, injecting drug users and men who have sex with men (Laeyendecker et al. 2005; Qiu et al. 2005; Yu et al. 1999; Yu et al. 2003).

Zhongmin's village was one of the heaviest hit and among the best known in Henan. Many of his fellow villagers participated in numerous clinical trials and have had their blood drawn for epidemiological investigations. Some may have learned about the association of viral subtypes with different routes of transmission and subpopulations at risk from these encounters. Instead of speculating about where Zhongmin got the idea that his virus could not transmit sexually, we want to understand how such an idea works in a larger discourse. His own experience, together with that of many others in his village with the patterns of infections, sickness and deaths in the HIV epidemic, we suggest, became the basis of a folk and local epidemiology. As a description of how they were infected with HIV, his idea had much more than a grain of truth; few if any in his immediate social world acquired the virus through sex. Statistical evidence for the sexual transmission of HIV, by contrast, became remote and powerfully overshadowed by the preponderance of infections that occurred as a result of blood-to-blood transmission in plasma collection. Many of the 'serum-discordant' couples in the villages were unions of young HIV-positive widows bringing their orphaned children to marriages with older bachelors who had little prospect otherwise of finding wives to bear children for them.[3] Many of these couples remained happily 'discordant'. With the relaxation of vigilance in population control in these villages, quite a few HIV-positive husbands had impregnated serum-negative wives in order to have a son out of quota. Their greatest frustration so far had been disappointment with the birth of yet more girls.

Villagers knew how they had become infected with HIV. For these 'former commercial plasma donors', poverty figured prominently in their own kind of epidemiology; they were driven by poverty to sell their plasma, and poverty continues to shape their experience with the disease. Poverty and the difficult ethical decisions that accompany it were not new to these villagers. Henan as a province has long suffered a reputation for serving as the setting for desperate responses to privation.

Even as a purely economic activity, facilitated by global technology and actively organized by government, villagers faced moral censure from the beginning because they had been 'willing to sell blood for money' (Shao 2006: 554–5). They began by telling themselves (with the help of 'scripts' provided for them by respected agents in the endeavour, including entrepreneurs, village leaders and government information outlets) that they were not selling blood; they were managing plasma in a commercial exchange that was to benefit them. They were not 'lazy', as journalists and even activists sometimes hinted; they were propelling themselves into the modern world of renewable capital. If these distinctions were sometimes slippery and not completely persuasive, the distinction between what they had been doing and sex was not. Villagers are adamant about the latter distinction.

A foreign official from an international organization visited a new clinic built and staffed by the government for the officially designated 'AIDS villages' in Henan, and when he met with a group of select villagers to coax the villagers into using the condom, it became an opportunity for buffoonery. 'Is this how you should wear it?' asked one villager as he stretched the condom to try to put it on his own head. The villagers rejected responsibility for preventing 'super infections' (Simon, Ho and Karim 2006) through sexual transmission. Most of the HIV-positive villagers fortunate enough not to have lost their spouse to the disease were in serum-concordant marriages. Knowing they were HIV-positive, they were most concerned with bringing up their young children, seeing through their marriages and perhaps enjoying the luxury of living long enough to hold a grandchild. Even preserving their own doomed lives was a frivolous concern.[4] To them poverty provides the moral distinction of victimhood, a distinction often denied them in the aloof professional epidemiology of the HIV epidemic.[5]

The 'folk' belief about transmission on the part of rural victims in China comes very close to the 'biosocial' underpinning of the experiment by Essex's group of virologists in Boston. For the HIV-infected plasma donors, the biological distinction of their particular infection granted by science gives tangible and credible substance to their moral innocence in the epidemic. The distinction between subtypes is relevant within the scientific community primarily as background for treatment or immunization development, but for the already infected villagers, this distinction is magnified. An increased efficiency of one method of transmission for other strains is interpreted as a lack of efficiency for that method in their own. Exonerated of moral responsibility for their own infection, rightly or not, they have also found a way to distance themselves ethically from the responsibility to prevent continuing infections. The biosocial distinction of the mechanics of this epidemic was central to Zhongmin's position as he preserved the moral virtue of his exuberant sexuality, as distinct from the economic nature of his virus, for better or for worse.

FROM BLOOD TO SEX

According to the now well-received wisdom of epidemiology, HIV is poised to expand when women as a population (that is, 'passively') serve as the bridge between isolated high-risk groups, such as injecting drug users and commercial sex workers, and the general population (China CDC and UNAIDS 2004). Among the epidemiological indicators vigilantly monitored are the decreasing male-to-female ratio of reported cases of infection and the incidence of maternal transmission. Studies have shown that there is an alarming convergence of several important social epidemiological factors: a well-established though technically illegal commercial sex industry across China in both urban and rural areas (Xia and Yang 2005), increasing spread of drug use, huge internal migration of labour and a raging 'sexual revolution' that facilitated and was evidenced by the climbing prevalence of sexually transmitted diseases (Parish, Laumann and Mojola 2007; Qu et al. 2002; Wong et al. 2007). However, significantly accounting for the sharp increase of female cases of infection in the CDC and UNAIDS report of 2004 was the inclusion of those previously undetected or unreported infections among female plasma donors in rural central China. For them, the mode of infection was not sex. But their contribution to shrinking the overall male-to-female ratio of reported cases infection has justified and propelled a more recent shift to the aggressive and more pragmatic focus upon sex in HIV/AIDS prevention in China informed in part by global experiences and strategies (Qian, Vermund and Wang 2005; Wu, Sullivan, Wang, Rotheram-Borus and Detels 2007).

The reported association that Zhongmin's lover made between condom use and commercial sex work becomes poignant in this context. The once-prominent outbreak in rural central China, one with 'distinctive Chinese characteristics' as its political context, has now all but receded from national attention and has become an unfortunate accident that does not fit well into the epidemiological orthodoxy of how the epidemic breaks free from the isolated high-risk groups to permeate the population mainstream through sex. The aversion to condoms expressed by many HIV-infected villagers should be understood as a protest against an epidemiology that threatens to erase their distinction as victims and presents them instead as carriers of a virus that tarnishes their moral reputations.

The expansion of the HIV/AIDS outbreak after it was detected in 1995 did not have anything to do with the biological properties of one particular subtype, but it had everything to do with a total disregard of the value of lives implicit in the government's concealment and inaction. Both local and national governments saw the agricultural population as a burdensome 'surfeit' (Anagnost 1995). It is in this context that we can fully appreciate Gao Yaojie's unrelenting crusade on behalf of these victims to set the record straight with the government for this outbreak, even to the exclusion of other HIV outbreaks in other parts of China, through other routes of transmission. Nevertheless, her moral position is in essence in complete agreement with her enemies, such as the public health official in Henan who boasted about the pristine quality of the plasma that they were able to supply, when they worked to attract plasma fractionation businesses to their 'overpopulated' province. The difference between them lies in the distinction between accidentally contaminated blood and innocent blood contaminated by indifference and greed, as well as who will take responsibility for the contaminated blood of innocent people. This distinction is hard to maintain on a biological level, but it is nevertheless important for the HIV-infected plasma donors in certain contexts. Contexts, however, are by their very nature shifting. Next we demonstrate biosociality as an outcome of ethical action in a different ethnographic context.

SHIFTING SOLIDARITY

Who are our enemies? Who are our friends? This is a question of primary importance for the Revolution.

Mao Zedong, 1926

Mao's subject-based theory of politics resembles no theorist more so than Carl Schmitt (Schmitt 1976), who not only defined 'friend' and 'enemy' as the specific nature of the political, but also insisted that 'only the actual participants can correctly recognize, understand and judge the concrete situation and settle the extreme case of conflict' (27). Solidarity and alienability compose a 'duplicity' that, like other symbolic categories, requires 'the discrimination of shifters' on the part of participants of the message (Jakobson 1990: 389).[6] This is precisely the complex assignment that HIV carriers navigate in the context of their social and political position.

Villagers asserted an individual ownership over their bodies when they sold blood, and later their status as HIV carriers again changed their relation with own bodies, engendering active forms of management of the virus, creating new relations with each other and, in some cases, with the state and with global organizations. In the earlier stages of the epidemic, fear, initially of imminent contagion, ruptured the close-knit social fabric, even ties of blood, in the villages. Once large numbers of donors were tested by the government and the true source of contagion was identified and understood, fear of this sort abated. In its place are bonds of solidarity among infected donors created within and beyond these rural communities officially designated as 'AIDS villages'. Many examples display the facilitation of kin-like solidarity. Acting on a tip about the recent death of a former donor in another remote village, K (abbreviation for his name in my notes) organized a trip to give tests to thirty villagers who had donated plasma, but none turned up positive. On the way back in the crammed minivan we hired for the trip, we began to suspect that the Abbott Lab HIV-1 rapid test kits we received from a nongovernmental organization were not accurate because we had not refrigerated them properly. K asked the driver to pull over and said, 'This is easy to sort out. We can test the test kits on one of us.' Everyone in the vehicle except me and the driver knew themselves to be positive. A lot was drawn to decide who would suffer the finger prick. When the drop of blood and the reagent produced the positive sign, two stripes on the test trip, we cheered affably and nonchalantly flipped the strip out of the window.

In Zhengzhou, capital of Henan province, there is a shelter in a residential building across the street from the provincial infectious diseases hospital. The shelter is unmarked; its use as a sanctuary providing temporary room and board for rural HIV-positive patients seeking treatment at the hospital as well as their families is kept a secret from its neighbours in the building. Through word of mouth, many HIV-positive residents come and visit, seeing the shelter as a place where they could relax and drop their vigilance against revealing their status. I was travelling with two graduate students to a village in Henan, and on our way we stayed at the shelter for a night. At dinner, one student asked, with awkward tentativeness, who among the people at the big table were positive. They burst out laughing and said, 'Everyone except you!' The student, who had previously only seen pictures of AIDS patients, was surprised that she could not tell that someone was positive by sight. One visitor explained, 'You cannot tell from our appearance if we are positive or not, unless we are really sick. But we are all closer than family, because we have the same kind of blood, HIV infected blood.'[7]

Recently, we were told, the shelter had seen many more young people diagnosed with HIV infection. They were simply too young to have sold plasma early in the 1990s and must have acquired the infection otherwise. Perhaps they have been infected via sex or drug use, but the staff at the shelter has no policy or practice of prejudice against them. Increasingly, perhaps, shared blood is what counts. This form of solidarity is not based upon genes or viral strains, but on a suprabiological connection. The virus, integrated with its human hosts on the subcellular plane and defined variably on the level of populations, acts as a specific and immutable marker in social networks. It is a sign of damage on the individual body, but it is also embraced and managed as channel for productive social relations.

CONCLUSION

The Chinese state (in the form of specific interested state agents) in the early 1990s assumed biopolitical dominion over the Chinese population and was prepared to procure and parcel out value in the sale of blood. This required that individual members of that population would actively participate in circulating it using 'modern' market methods. We argue that the state did not anticipate dismantling that dominion through delegation of the act of separating blood from body, but, rather, expected a Foucaultian assumption of governable mass population and a corresponding kind of economic 'volume expansion' analogous to the endlessly renewable production of blood in the human body. However, the same economic transformation that pointedly 'granted' individuals economic rights to their own bodies also activated assumptions within the individual minds that accompanied this transition. The division between the two, mind and body, occurs here not by Cartesian sleight of hand but by physical and technological acts of disembodiment in economic transaction. Viewed two decades later, the problem is a matter not only of who should acknowledge blame for the large-scale introduction of the HIV virus into the Chinese population, but also of how far to recognize the distribution of responsibility and the ownership of bodies, blood and viruses now.

The economic use of human blood in China, which forms the backdrop of our ethnography, is viewed here in its circulation in the liberalized economy in China both as commodity and as capital. While the case studies examined here are unique, our position is that the activity we examine links even tightly sealed communities (as suggested by the whispered rumours about the 'AIDS villages' of China) to global action. The HIV/AIDS epidemic is global because of structures of sociality held in common, including the global market, the scientific research community and a vast, largely untraceable communication network. 'Everyday ethics' is precisely the meeting point between these seemingly disparate global and local levels of action. We argue that the very topic of HIV/AIDS, brought to the level of awareness through the global epidemic, acts as a 'shifter' in everyday discourse (Jakobson 1990; Silverstein 1976). Everyday ethics in this multilayered and globally diffuse scenario stems from 'ordinary language' on the part of every participant. As soon as a villager, patient, activist, government agent or researcher (including the anthropologist) engages in HIV/AIDS discourse and/or action, he or she must also assume an ethical position—just as whoever speaks must assume a pronominal position, an 'I'—not only navigated as already 'there' but potentially transforming and changing through the engagement. These facts are reflected here not only by a very specific impact of international viral research findings, but also in the generally shifting economic and political values at work. In terms of speech acts, participants employ terms such as 'plasma' (as distinct from blood) and 'viral type' (signalling specific, morally sanctioned or censured behaviours) that help activate existential states, most crucially those related to ownership, alienation, responsibility and virtue. These speech acts, when brought to awareness and employed to structure and justify individual or collective action, represent a new ethical position 'instantiated in agency', as Stafford has suggested in the introduction to this volume. This agency, like any speech act, does not occur in a philosophical vacuum but is dependent upon social circumstances and coordinated in specific behaviour that is examined and engaged ethnographically.

The strange, criss-crossing connections and contradictions we encounter in this far-ranging ethnographic travel brings to mind Dan Sperber's image of culture as disease, with varying degrees of 'susceptibility', and anthropology as epidemiology tracing its tracks (Sperber 1985). Anthropologists, too, often like to claim distance from ethical or moral questions (Fassin [2008] cites many examples). Unlike HIV carriers, however, the argument amongst anthropologists is not about whether or not they *can* legitimately avoid ethical positions but whether they *should* (D'Andrade 1995) or *should not* (Scheper-Hughes 1995). Ethical risks are especially highlighted in medical anthropology and particularly in HIV/AIDS research, where 'ethical variability'—meaning separate sets of standards and expectations for research and policy based upon culture, resource levels or other possible manifestations of difference—contributes to the exploitive targeting of human subjects in developing countries (Petryna 2005). Our view is that no one has a complete realm of choices about taking an ethical position, but each must present a position within a distribution of responsibility (Laidlaw 2008). While researchers can approach the epidemic with a purely ontological view, and even if they should attempt to do so, the act of invoking it requires the assumption of an ethical gambit. Whether distancing ourselves from ethical responsibility or conversely embracing a moral goal, we cannot avoid indexing that 'take'. Overdetermined by tensions from multiple sources, distinct aspects of the epidemic act as shifters, requiring not only recognition but participation just by rising to the level of social awareness. It may or may not matter that we, for example, have specifically condemned the greed of state capitalists and the dehumanizing effects of global technologies in this chapter, or that at the time of the conversation I was angry at Zhongmin for not protecting his lover and for possibly exposing her husband to HIV, and he knew it. In the course of engaging in discourse, any participant who uses the terms of the debate takes up a role in the fight, willing or not. Recognizing this sort of engagement is not any more of an obstacle to working in the field than carrying the virus is to talking about it. Either way it is but part and parcel of the process of discourse, and it needs to be navigated, we think, in a deliberated way. For us this engagement played a role in discovering and participating to some extent in the new bonds of productive solidarity that HIV carriers create on the basis of 'blood'.

NOTES

1. Dr Gao Yaojie has made her views widely known by speaking publicly on many occasions, by publishing several popular books on the 'blood plague' and a long-running a newsletter, which she distributes in many of rural communities devastated by the epidemic, and more recently by publishing a blog on the Internet (see, for example, the transcripts of a talk she gave to an audience of medical students in Shanghai; Gao 2005).

2. Although it does not fit well with the broad-based politics of inclusion enacted by many international and nongovernmental organizations, I emphasize that Dr Gao Yaojie's sense of morality and sympathy for the 'more innocent' victims is often evident in the activism of these organizations.

3. The term 'serum discordant' is in general use in epidemiological literature to designate couples of whom only one partner is HIV-positive.

4. According to the scientists I interviewed recently, 'super infections' result from immunological impairment by HIV and are a source of frustration in vaccine development, as new 'circulating recombinant forms' of HIV are often formed intra-cellularly in human hosts exposed to and infected by different viral strains.

5. For an excellent analysis of dissident views on AIDS in South Africa, see Fassin (2007).

6. We round out the political spectrum here, from Communist to fascist to Russian Jewish American émigré!

7. On kinship and organ donation and the refiguring of blood ties, see Sharp's (2006) *Strange Harvest*. Janet Carsten's (2000) edited collection *Cultures of Relatedness* is also interesting on substance and kinship.

REFERENCES

Anagnost, A. (1995), 'A Surfeit of Bodies: Population and Rationality of the State in Post-Mao China', in F. D. Ginsburg and R. Rapp (eds), *Conceiving the New World Order: The Global Politics of Reproduction*, Berkeley: University of California Press.

Carsten, J. (ed.) (2000), *Cultures of Relatedness: New Approaches to the Study of Kinship*, Cambridge: Cambridge University Press.

China CDC and UNAIDS (2004), *A Joint Assessment of HIV/AIDS Prevention, Treatment and Care in China*, Beijing: China CDC and UNAIDS.

Cohen, J. (1995), 'Differences in HIV Strains May Underline Disease Patterns', *Science*, 270/6: 30–1.

D'Andrade, R. (1995), 'Moral Models in Anthropology', *Current Anthropology*, 36/3: 399–408.

Fassin, D. (2007), *When Bodies Remember: Experiences and Politics of AIDS in South Africa*, Berkeley: University of California Press.

Fassin, D. (2008), 'Beyond Good and Evil? Questioning the Anthropological Discomfort with Morals', *Anthropological Theory*, 8/4: 333–44.

Gao, Y. (2005), 'AIDS Villages and "AIDS Orphans"', in G. Yanning (ed.), *'Social Immunity' against HIV/AIDS* (In Chinese), Shanghai: Fudan University Press.

Graf, M., Shao, Y., Zhao, Q., Seidl, T., Kötler, J., Wolf, H., et al. (1998), 'Cloning and Characterization of a Virtually Full-length HIV Type 1 Genome from a Subtype B'-Thai Strain Representing the Most Prevalent B-clade Isolate in China', *AIDS Research and Human Retroviruses*, 14/3: 285–8.

Jakobson, R. (1990), 'Shifters and Verbal Categories', in L. R. Waugh and M. Monville-Burston (eds), *On Language: Roman Jakobson*, Cambridge, MA: Harvard University Press.

Laeyendecker, O., Zhang, G. W., Quinn, T. C., Garten, R., Ray, S. C., Lai, S., et al. (2005), 'Molecular Epidemiology of HIV-1 Subtypes in Southern China', *Journal of Acquired Immune Deficiency Syndrome*, 38/3: 356–62.

Laidlaw, J. (2008), 'Agency and Responsibility: Perhaps You Can Have Too Much of a Good Thing', in M. Lambek (ed.), *Ordinary Ethics: Anthropology, Language, and Action,* Bronx, NY: Fordham University Press.

Marlink, R., and Swan, N. (1996), 'Heterosexual HIV Transmission', *Radio National Transcripts*, vol. 2008, Sydney: ABC Radio National Online.

Parish, W. L., Laumann, E. O., and Mojola, S. A. (2007), 'Sexual Behavior in China: Trends and Comparisons', *Population and Development Review*, 33/4: 729–56.

Petryna, A. (2005), 'Ethnical Variability: Drug Development and Globalizing Clinical Trials', *American Ethnologist*, 32/2: 183–97.

Pope, M., Frankel, S. S., Mascola, J. R., Trkola, A., Isdell, F., Birx, D. L., et al. (1997), 'Human Immunodeficiency Virus Type 1 Strains of Subtypes B and E Replicate in Cutaneous Dendritic Cell–T-cell Mixtures without Displaying Subtype-specific Tropism', *Journal of Virology*, 71/10: 8001–7.

Qian, Z. H., Vermund, S. H., and Wang, N. (2005), 'Risk of HIV/AIDS in China: Subpopulations of Special Importance', *Sexually Transmitted Infection*, 81/6: 442–7.

Qiu, Z., Xing, H., Wei, M., Duan, Y., Zhao, Q., Xu, J., et al. (2005), 'Characterization of Five Nearly Full-length Genomes of Early HIV Type 1 Strains in Ruili City: Implications for the Genesis of CRF07_BC and CRF08_BC

Circulating in China', *AIDS Research and Human Retroviruses*, 21/12: 1051–6.

Qu, S., Liu, W., Choi, K.-H., Li, R., Jiang, D., Zhou, Y., et al. (2002), 'The Potential for Rapid Sexual Transmission of HIV in China: Sexually Transmitted Diseases and Condom Failure Highly Prevalent among Female Sex Workers', *AIDS and Behavior*, 6/3: 267–75.

Rosenthal, E. (2000), 'In Rural China, a Steep Price of Poverty: Dying of AIDS', *The New York Times* (28 October): 1.

Scheper-Hughes, N. (1995), 'The Primacy of the Ethical: Propositions for a Militant Anthropology', *Current Anthropology*, 36/3: 409–40.

Schmitt, C. (1976), *The Concept of the Political*, New Brunswick, NJ: Rutgers University Press.

Shao, J. (2006), 'Fluid Labor and Blood Money: The Economy of HIV/AIDS in Rural Central China', *Cultural Anthropology*, 21/4: 535–69.

Shao, J., and Scoggin, M. (2009), 'Solidarity and Distinction: Contamination, Morality and Variability', *Body and Society*, 15/2: 29–49.

Sharp, L. A. (2006), *Strange Harvest: Organ Transplants, Denatured Bodies, and the Transformation of Self*, Berkeley: University of California Press.

Silverstein, M. (1976), 'Shifter, Linguistic Categories, and Cultural Description', in K. H. Basso and H. A. Selby (eds), *Meaning in Anthropology*, Albuquerque: University of New Mexico Press.

Simon, V., Ho, D. D., and Karim, Q. A. (2006), 'HIV/AIDS Epidemiology, Pathogenesis, Prevention, and Treatment', *Lancet*, 368: 489–504.

Soto-Ramirez, L. E., Renjifo, B., McLane, M. F., Marlink, R., O'Hara, C., Sutthent, R., et al. (1996), 'HIV-1 Langerhans' Cell Tropism Associated with Heterosexual Transmission of HIV', *Science*, 271/5253: 1291–3.

Sperber, D. (1985), 'Anthropology and Psychology: Towards an Epidemiology of Representations', *Man*, 20/1: 73–89.

Su, B., Liu, L., Wang, F., Gui, X., Zhao, M., Tien, P., et al. (2003), 'HIV-1 Subtype B' Dictates the AIDS Epidemic among Paid Blood Donors in the Henan and Hubei Provinces of China', *AIDS*, 17/17: 2515–20.

Weniger, B. G., Takebe, Y., Ou, C. Y., and Yamazaki, S. (1994), 'The Molecular Epidemiology of HIV in Asia', *AIDS*, 8 Suppl 2: S13–28.

Wong, S.P.Y., Yin, Y.-P., Gao, X., Wei, W.-H., Shi, M.-Q., Huang, P.-Y., et al. (2007), 'Risk of Syphilis in STI Clinic Patients: A Cross-sectional Study of 11 500 Cases in Guangxi, China', *Sexually Transmitted Infections*, 83/5: 351–6.

Wu, Z., Rou, K., and Gui, H. (2004), 'The HIV/AIDS Epidemic in China: History, Current Strategies and Future Challenges', *AIDS Education & Prevention*, 16: 7–17.

Wu, Z., Sullivan, S. G., Wang, Y., Rotheram-Borus, M. J., and Detels, R. (2007), 'Evolution of China's Response to HIV/AIDS', *Lancet*, 369/9562: 679–90.

Xia, G., and Yang, X. (2005), 'Risky Sexual Behavior among Female Entertainment Workers in China: Implications for HIV/STD Prevention Intervention', *AIDS Education & Prevention*, 17/2: 143–56.

Yu, X. F., Chen, J., Shao, Y., Beyrer, C., Liu, B., Wang, Z., et al. (1999), 'Emerging HIV Infections with Distinct Subtypes of HIV-1 Infection among Injection Drug Users from Geographically Separate Locations in Guangxi Province, China', *Journal of Acquired Immune Deficiency Syndrome*, 22/2: 180–8.

Yu, X. F., Wang, X., Mao, P., Wang, S., Li, Z., Zhang, J., et al. (2003), 'Characterization of HIV Type 1 Heterosexual Transmission in Yunnan, China', *AIDS Research and Human Retroviruses*, 19/11: 1051–5.

Zhang, L., Chen, Z., Cao, Y., Yu, J., Li, G., Yu, W., et al. (2004), 'Molecular Characterization of Human Immunodeficiency Virus Type 1 and Hepatitis C Virus in Paid Blood Donors and Injection Drug Users in China', *Journal of Virology*, 78/24: 13591–9.

Zhang, Y., Lu, L., Ba, L., Liu, L., Yang, L., Jia, M., et al. (2006), 'Dominance of HIV-1 Subtype CRF01_AE in Sexually Acquired Cases Leads to a New Epidemic in Yunnan Province of China', *PLoS Medicine*, 3/11: e443.

AFTERWORD

CHAPTER 14

THE DRIVE FOR SUCCESS AND THE ETHICS OF THE STRIVING INDIVIDUAL

Yunxiang Yan

At the outset of his introductory chapter, Charles Stafford presents a two-point guide to the contributions in this volume. First, in an attempt to break the collective spell in anthropology that prioritizes the aggregated view of action and turns individuals into a group unit of culture or morality, most chapters focus on the individual and the agentive side of his or her moral life. Second, extending the notion of ordinary ethics borrowed from Michal Lambek, the authors collectively explore the routine working of ethics in both social action and discourse—in some cases explicit ethical reflections—in the everyday life of ordinary Chinese people.

I entirely concur with Stafford on these two points and wish to add that they are particularly important for the study of morality and ethics in China because of a dynamic and constitutive feature of the Chinese notion of the person, known as *zuoren* in the Chinese language. The literal translation of *zuoren* is 'to make oneself a person' or 'to become human', as Chih-yuan Wang discusses at the very beginning of his chapter in this volume. The semantic and social implications of this notion, especially in the discourse on Confucian humanism (see e.g. Tu 1985) are simply too rich to be reviewed here; suffice it to note that the Chinese person is not born as a full person who is entitled to a set of natural rights. Instead, the Chinese individual can only gradually become a person through a process of self-cultivation, or *zuoren*, in which everything one does and says contributes to the end of becoming a moral person.

The process is therefore highly individualistic, habitual and implicit. However, the achievement of humanity, or how good a moral person one has become, relies mostly on the relationship with one's family, kinship, community and society at large. At any moment in Chinese history, there is always a set of standards of the good person towards which Chinese individuals strive and by which others are evaluated both formally and informally, including by gossip. In this sense, *zuoren* is a highly social, goal-oriented and explicit process.

Reading these chapters reminds me of the recent call by Daniel Miller for more and better studies of the individual: 'The understanding of the individual is something that should be part and parcel of the domain of anthropology even when we are working in a society which seems almost entirely opposed to individualism' (Miller 2009: 3). The simple fact that anthropologists almost invariably work with flesh-and-blood individuals and work through individual presentations by informants makes a compelling case to understand the people under study as individuals, instead of merely as a representation of an abstract collectivity or culture. Particular inspiring is Miller's ambition to find a way to account for both society and individuals simultaneously: 'The point is that we are not simply telling a story about a person. The individual is used analytically to display a pattern of relationships that convey a sense of the cultural order the person lives by' (Miller 2009: 12). In a similar vein, the preceding chapters progress further by exploring the moral landscape in China through the prism of individuals and their ethics.[1]

What kinds of cultural order may we discern from the rich stories about the ordinary ethics of Chinese individuals presented in this volume? Understandably, readers may come up with different answers to this question, particularly so when the ethnographic accounts are set at the level of the individual. But what strikes me most is that the urge to succeed and the accompanying anxiety, constituting what I will refer to here as the *drive for success*, either directly trigger or help to cause many of the ethical reflections, discourses, judgements and actions among the individuals presented in the volume. Although the drive for success is arguably relatively new in China, to a great extent it has negated or altered many of the previously dominant moral values and makes its way into the core of being a moral person, that is, the process of *zuoren*. Driven by the urge for success, the individual strives by all possible means to make it out there, to deal with his anxieties and to strike a balance in the torment between conflicting moral visions and values, resulting in a noticeable change in China's moral landscape, that is, as I will call it, the ethics of the striving individual.

In the following pages, I will first highlight the impact of the drive for success on Chinese individuals and their ethical responses to the newly emerging pressures through refashioning themselves as the striving individual, for example, as shown in the ethnographic accounts in Chapters 3 and 4. Next I will briefly examine other aspects of the ethics of the striving individual, focusing on their ethical struggle to cope with the anxieties of success, which at times can be oppressive. In the third section, I connect the ethics of the striving individual to the larger context where a double-transformation is ongoing in Chinese society—namely, the rise of the individual and the individualization of society—together with a shift from a collective ethics of duties and self-sacrifice to an emergent ethics of individual rights and self-development. The notion of the striving individual is further explored in light of Nikolas Rose's (1998) study of the enterprising self and Ulrich Beck's (1992) individualization thesis.

THE DRIVE FOR SUCCESS AND THE MAKING
OF THE STRIVING INDIVIDUAL

The majority of ethnographic chapters in this volume, nine out of twelve, examine the moral experiences of individuals in (or from) a rural context where, ironically, success is primarily defined by one's ability to leave the countryside, or at least to escape the hard physical labour of agriculture. In his fine study of the ordinary ethics embedded in the parent–child relationship in a Anhui village, James Johnston (Chapter 3) describes the ethical dilemma between the centrifugal morality that pushes the individual to leave the parents and village home in order to make it out there in the city and the centripetal morality that requires the individual to return home during holidays and to fulfil other filial obligations in the village. At a deeper level, Johnston notes, the pushing force of making one's life successful in the outside world prevails because the obligatory family gathering during the Chinese New Year is a celebration of the children's past efforts to leave the village as well as of the prospects of their permanent escape from village life. This is because villagers born at the bottom of the social hierarchy are convinced that the only path out of their situation (*chulu*) is to leave for the city, and, among the limited options for leaving, education is the best. 'Our only path out of the village is to study; it's only by studying hard that our lives will be great,' states a 15-year-old girl from the village where Johnston conducted his field research.[2] To realize this dream, children as young as ten must leave their parents to attend boarding school in the local township, and those who can make it successfully through middle school and on to college will continue to move farther away from the village and their parents, hopefully to become permanent urban residents. When the annual family celebration requires that they temporarily return home, the young generation feels the dilemma because they do not want to waste time and resources to go home, possibly undermining their fight for success, and they have difficulties connecting parental expectations to return home with the parental teachings to achieve success.

It should be noted that the parents might perceive this ethical difficulty differently because only the return of their success-driven children, especially those who have established themselves in the cities, during the festivities can display the parents' success to both fellow villagers and their ancestors. Perhaps the ethical tensions between the centrifugal and centripetal values do not exist for the parents. By focusing on the young villagers, Johnston arguably underplays the generational differences between a more individualistic understanding of success and the remaining influence of the collectivist understanding of success for the sake of glorifying ancestors (more on this towards the end of this chapter).

Ethnographic evidence in Chapter 4 shows that despite modern changes in marriage and family that accord young rural women the freedom to choose not only their mate but also a life of their own, they still perceive finding a good husband as the only option in life and, more importantly, as a measure of their being a good person. On several occasions, I-chieh Fang notes that the femininity and moral worth of these young female migrant workers are judged by the social status of their husbands, as reflected in the husbands' job, title, salary, family background and appearance. In this sense, a young woman does not have her own success, much less a life of her own. This is a serious setback from the early women's liberation movement at the turn of the twentieth century. As failure to find a good husband is now regarded as the responsibility of the individual, instead of the parents, these young women strive to find a perfect match. They take good care of their physical appearance because beauty is the key to attracting the ideal man; they keenly protect their purity and do not want to start a relationship unless it will lead to marriage; yet they do not object to premarital sex or cohabitation if it is a bridge to marriage.

Why is finding a good husband so important to these young female migrant workers? Fang offers a multifaceted explanation but emphasizes above all individual emotional and financial needs. Many of these young female migrant workers arguably suffer from a kind of affect deficiency because in childhood they were left behind in the village by their parents, who spent most of the year working in the cities. By the time they became migrant workers, the new urban environment (at least theirs) was filled with distrust, indifference, deception and danger. To survive they learned to lie—for example, to lie about their age, to use fake identity cards, to make up false resumes or to simply cook up new identities if necessary—while they were often the victims of counterfeit goods and the counterfeit culture at large.[3] As part of this environment, they became aloof, distrustful and calculating on the one hand and desperately searching for intimacy and protection by way of marriage so as to enjoy a worry-free and happy life on the other.

Admittedly, the individuals—rural children and young women—presented in Chapters 3 and 4 are fighting to succeed from the bottom of the social pyramid, and they have a very long way to climb up the social ladder to reach wealth and status. Yet those in China at higher levels of the pyramid appear to be under the same, if not more, pressure and anxiety, for example, the overworked white-collar professionals who must work extra hard to compete with the younger cohort (Hanser 2001; Hoffman 2010). The only difference is that at the lower levels, the struggle for success seemingly is based more on individual diligence (such as studying hard) and controllable variables (good test scores or perfect husbands) instead of the complex networks of social capital and political power. The relative simplicity at the bottom level, however, may also more clearly reveal the costs, such as the emotional cost of separation from one's family members, the quality of childhood[4] or the moral costs of engaging in unethical behaviour. Although Fang and Johnston choose not to explicitly examine these issues, their ethnographies still offer a glimpse of the dark side of the drive for success.[5]

In my opinion, although motivations to achieve have never been in short supply in Chinese culture, the drive for success is a relatively new development in the moral landscape of China. The key difference lies in the goal of achievement: is it for the person as an individual or by the person on behalf a collectivity? Until the 1980s, a cultural imperative of curbing self-interest and submitting the ego to a collectivity—be it family, kinship, community or the state—served as the guiding principle in the cultural construction of the person. The agentive side of one's moral life was first and foremost geared towards the goal of making oneself part and parcel of this collectivity, and therefore one's achievements in real life were made to glorify the collectivity, instead of oneself as an individual.[6]

This proper moral life was prescribed in traditional Confucian ethics as the journey to reach the level of *ren*, which has been commonly translated in English as benevolence and humanity. As Benjamin Schwartz notes, *ren* does not refer to a static state of being in moral life; instead, it denotes a dynamic process of making: 'It is an existential goal which Confucius attempts to achieve for himself through his own self-cultivation. It is the result of a self effort which he believes can be taught to others. Again, like Socrates, he poses the simple question, "how can I make myself good [jen]"' (Schwartz 1985: 77). The most recognized authoritative answer provided by Confucius is *ke ji fu li*, which has been translated as 'curb your ego and submit to *li*' or 'self-disciplined and ever turning to *li*'. Here, *li*, another key notion in Confucian ethics, refers to rite, ceremony, manners and general deportment that bind together human beings and the spirits (see Schwartz 1985: 67–75). It is commonly translated in English as 'propriety'. Admittedly, the rich meanings of both *ren* and *li* have led to endless debates among scholars (Tu 1985). For my purposes here, however, suffice it to emphasize that *ren* represents the virtuous inner moral life and thus is mostly subjective, whereas *li* is manifested through a set of prescriptive virtues in human behaviour and thus is mostly objective. To reach the inner and existential goal of *ren*, an individual must cultivate herself to meet a set of objective requirements of *li* in social interactions of everyday life.

In this ethical reckoning, virtue equates with happiness, and how to make oneself virtuous (or good) constitutes the meaning of life. For the everyday life of ordinary people who lived mostly under a version of popular Confucian ethics that also took elements from other ethical sources such as Buddhism and popular religion, the process of *zuoren*, or self-cultivation, was guided by the moral principles of filial piety, reciprocity, sincerity, trustfulness, thrift and modesty, which in turn were worked on or played out through the interpersonal actions of *renqing* (human feelings), *mianzi* (face) and *guanxi* (networks). Individuals were motivated to work hard and to achieve higher goals, but the ultimate goal was to develop the family in daily life and glorify the ancestors in the universe of the spiritual life, as evidenced by the popular sayings *chuanzong jiedai* (continue the descent and connect the generations) and *guangzong yaozu* (glorify the ancestors). The individual male is important simply because he connects the past with the future in the long family line (Baker 1979), whereas the female is important mainly because of her reproductive capacity to achieve the same goal. All social and economic successes of an individual contribute to this goal, and, consequently, whenever there is a conflict between the individual interest and the interest of the family or kinship group, self-sacrifice is not only required but much anticipated.

The Communist revolution in 1949 attacked many aspects of traditional Confucian ethics through political campaigns, education and the economic construction of collectivization and nationalization. The individual was liberated from the all-encompassing social categories of the family, kinship and local community and was encouraged, or forced, to construct the new identity of a socialist citizen (Yan 2010). At the same time, however, the individual was also asked to sacrifice self-interest for a much higher goal, that is, the realization of Communism in China and the world. New collective virtues of impartiality and selflessness (*dagong wusi*) were promoted through socialist engineering programs; any attempts at self-improvement for other purposes were condemned as corrupt bourgeois thoughts or the remnants of the decaying feudalistic culture. The old virtue of working hard to glorify the ancestors and continue the family line was replaced by the seemingly new virtue of 'devoting one's entire life to Chairman Mao and the Communist revolution' (Cheng 2009; Madsen 1984). More than ever before, individual achievement was defined in collective terms. For example, any award recipient during the Maoist era (1949–76) had to state that the achievement was actually due to the leadership and the people, so much so that even in the early 1980s, when economic incentives were officially used to promote a new ethics of individual success, award recipients had to submit a large portion of the award to her or his work-unit or to share it with others.

The breakthrough came in the 1980s when Chinese individuals were called upon by the party-state to show more enthusiasm and to exert more energy to work harder and more creatively in the market-oriented economic reforms. Initially, the official call remained collectivist in nature, that is, to strengthen the nation-state by way of the modernizations of industry, agriculture, national defence and science and technology. But the accumulation of personal wealth rapidly became a legitimate pursuit, promoted by the official reform slogans such as 'to get rich is glorious' and 'let some people get rich first' (both of which are openly materialistic). As there was no longer a requirement to sacrifice for the collective or the nation, such as glorifying the ancestors or devoting oneself to the revolution, those people who became prosperous in the 1980s were successful individual entrepreneurs who were not members of a collectivity. In the official language, there was not even a ready term to call such individuals; hence the contradictory term *getihu* (literally individual-household) was coined. *Getihu* gained social recognition almost entirely by their newly accumulated personal wealth, and many earned the envious title of *wanyuanhu*, meaning a household with 10,000 yuan in net wealth. The moral influence of self-motivated, hard-working and prosperous *getihu* was amplified in the early 1990s with the party-state return to the market reforms, after a short detour since 1989, as seemingly everyone wanted to seize the new opportunities offered by the private sector and to become rich (see Tsai 2007). At the time, this national trend was called *xiahai*, meaning to jump into the sea of business and the market economy, and was captured by the popular saying '*shiyi renmin jiuyi shang, haiyou yiyi zai kaizhang*' (900 million out of the one billion population are businesspeople, whereas the remaining 100 million are to open their own businesses).

By the late 1990s, the zeal to make it big was further crystallized in the new imagery of *chenggong renshi*, or successful people, who often appeared in commercials and the mass media as fashionable, rich and confident individuals—mostly men but occasionally women as well. The most attractive part of this new cultural hero is that, as the cultural critic Wang Xiaoming sharply points out, it no longer represents an abstract and remote idealism; instead, 'it is embodied in a living and fresh man who enjoys the worldly life. It no longer requires you to sacrifice everything for a spiritual purpose; on the contrary, it promises you with the hypnotic power: you will have a car, a house, and much more money' (Wang 1998). However, the new cultural hero also suffers from the fear of being thrown out of the game, a loss of the basic perception of time and space caused by the penetration of business into private life and a general feeling of emptiness under the prevailing materialism (Liu 2002).

By focusing on the materialization of self-interest and the development of the individual, the new role model of successful people replaced the previous socialist morality of sacrificing oneself for Communism and implicitly further negated the traditional ethic of glorifying one's ancestors that had already been attacked by Communist ethics. More importantly, the new notion of successful people carries a clear and strong element of hierarchy; that is, successful people are above the common people and thus deserve more privileges and power. In the media and popular discourse, they are referred to as *ren shang ren*, literally meaning 'a person above other persons'.

It should be noted that the concept of *ren shang ren* is not new, as captured in the proverb '*chi de ku zhong ku, fang wei ren shang ren*' (only those who endure all harsh work can become a person above persons). This ethic of working hard to climb up the social hierarchy implies putting others down during the competitive process, as exemplified by the cutthroat contest of the imperial examination system. Yet in traditional China, the collective-oriented Confucian ethics of benevolence and propriety (*ren* and *li*) contained the highly aggressive spirit of becoming a person above persons and reoriented the individual towards the collectivism of glorifying one's ancestors. In the post-Mao reform era, there is no effective restraint—Confucian or Communist—to curb the newly awakened self-interested individual, and successful people, once realizing the goal of being a person above persons, are not shy about flaunting their power and privilege through conspicuous consumption, the abuse of power and unfair competition. In the late 1990s, government officials gradually became a new group of successful people due to their high salaries, job perks and, more importantly, political power to determine other people's life chances and opportunities. As a result, Chinese society became polarized (see Sun 2004: 1–136, 271–96). In such a society, being or becoming successful is crucially important for the individual because only a person above persons can have all the power and privileges, which will in turn accord the person dignity and social respect.

Of course, the imagery of successful people that Wang Xiaoming analyzed represents only a small portion of the Chinese population, although its influence is widespread. For those who are at the lower rungs of the society, the drive to strive may come from different sources. Many join the rat race to success because they do not want to bear the negative consequences of failure, such as the rural students described by Johnston in Chapter 3 (for another notable study of this phenomenon, see Kipnis 2001). Others choose to avoid the severe competition by revoking traditional values or they resist raising their self-expectation too high; but these individuals tend to be labelled as having an inferior *suzhi* (inner quality) and are typically cited as negative examples in the public discourse. The anthropologist Andrew Kipnis notes, 'As inequality becomes more visible, the anxiety generated by the possibility of falling behind increases competition to attain the trappings of *suzhi*' (2006: 310). In this sense, most striving individuals are driven by the fear of failure as much as by the drive for success, and the two work together to push the individual to strive, with or even without the chance to succeed.

Whereas the process of *zuoren*, or making oneself a moral person, by and large has been transformed into a process of making oneself a successful person, individual success is mainly measured by economic wealth and political power. This is partially true due to the legitimization of individual desires since the 1990s (see Rofel 2007), as wealth and power provide the shortest route to the satisfaction of desires. But the materialist understanding of success also derives from a crisis of beliefs caused by the rise and fall of Communist ethics (see Ci 1994; Wang 2002). In everyday life, for example, hot-ticket consumer durables, such as the well-known 'four big items' during the 1980s and 1990s, gauge the level of individual success and define individual identity (Yan 2009a: 207–42). One of the latest material indicators of success is home ownership, which has gained the moral meaning of defending one's personhood, as young people, especially young men, are not regarded as adults unless they own a private flat (L. Zhang 2010). In Chapter 10, Francesca Bray sheds new light on the study of ordinary ethics by introducing the theory and methods of science and technology studies (STS) and argues that more scholarly attention should be paid to the ethics of materiality and its dependence on an internal force of reflection and self-cultivation such as religion. The intriguing point is that under the strong influence of state developmentalism and global consumerism, material objects might have gained more weight in shaping the ethics of the striving individual in China.

ETHICAL PREDICAMENTS AND THE ENTANGLEMENT OF VALUES

The drive for success, while challenging both traditional Confucian ethics and Communist ethics, also creates moral predicaments for the individual, forcing her to choose between competing values, to judge right and wrong and good and bad and to take action accordingly. From Chapters 3 and 4, we have learned that new patterns in the parent–child relationship or in intimacy are deeply ethical as individuals must make moral judgements about what is good and how to achieve it. We also learned that the individual must take full responsibility for victories as well as for failures; yet we also see that many individuals are not comfortable with this individualization of responsibility because it requires too much individual effort and input. But, above all, it is a felt pressure of success, being it to marry an ideal husband or to make a lot of money, that drives the individual to work diligently and to reflect ethically. Why study hard? Why leave one's parents and home? Is it necessary to return home during Chinese New Year? Whom to trust and when? What constitutes the ideal femininity that makes a woman successful? Ultimately, the individuals in these two chapters all ask the same question: 'Where is *my* path out [*chulu*] to succeed and how do I get there?'

Although not presented always as explicitly as in Chapters 3 and 4, the ethics of the striving individual can be seen in one way or another in almost all the chapters in this volume. In Chinese schools, the meaning of success has been simplified to achieving good scores on tests, which translates into the focus of student curiosity and creativity only on things that will show up in tests (Fong 2004; Kipnis 2001). It is in this context that the naughty student Wu Hao—discussed by Chih-yuan Wang in Chapter 2—poses a serious ethical challenge to everyone in his school and a big question mark to the anthropologist: Is he a bad student, a bad person? He was judged to be bad by many fellow students and teachers because he disturbed the highly disciplined classroom. However, there are differences of opinion because Wu Hao is sincere and authentic—he speaks his mind and does what he likes. Yet, in the eyes of his ethics teacher, Wu has the dangerous tendency to become a man against society who will not succeed in the future and will ruin his entire family.

As Chih-yuan Wang suggests, the so-called good students share a lot in common with naughty students such as Wu, but the former can restrain themselves to fit the existing hierarchy, power and social expectations, ending up with a double-face or split-self, one inward/private and the other outward/public. This leads to a serious ethical question: What kind of striving individual is the Chinese school system producing?

The training for a double-face or split-self does not stop with the world of children; adults, especially successful adults, must be fully aware of the social expectations of the moral person and make special efforts to avoid causing negative feelings of envy. As Hui Zhang shows in Chapter 7, it is the ethical responsibility of the successful person to prevent the rise of envy in those less fortunate, and one of the main strategies to fulfil this responsibility is to cultivate good interpersonal relationships through gift-giving, meal-sharing, and other small favours, which is part of the *renqing* ethics. Once the sin of envy is aroused, however, the successful person who is the object of envy can defend herself or himself by blaming the envy on people of 'low quality' (*suzhi di*), which might also explain their unsuccessful lives in the first place. Either way, the ethics of avoiding envy results from the calculating actions of the individual who strives to achieve and defend success by all means. In this connection, the different strategies of family organization examined by Daniel Roberts in Chapter 9 reveal the same logic of the striving individual, that is, trying whatever works in order to succeed. Because of the windfall payments for land procurement, villagers in this rural community no longer need to worry about basic finances; instead, there is an emotional void that, once again, was created by young people leaving the village to seek better opportunities in the cities and the increasing commercialization of labour exchange. The flexibility of family organization is not new in itself, as Myron Cohen (1976) convincingly demonstrates in his classic study of the family in rural Taiwan during the 1960s. What is new to me, however, is the ethics of the individual in dealing with the pressures of success.

How to justify the moral worth of one's decisions and actions constitutes an important part of ordinary ethics; even a fourth-grade student feels compelled to defend his good moral characteristics, such as unselfishness and justness (see Chapter 2). However, in the real world of adults, individuals often find themselves in the ironic situation of being torn between competing or opposing values or coordinates of ethical reflections, which affects their agency and autonomy to make decisions or to take action. This renders judgement or self-judgement of one's moral standing quite complicated and often ironic. The main argument that Hans Steinmüller makes in Chapter 8 is that the use and refusal of irony are as ethical as other tropes of ethical reflection and discourse, but irony also serves as a means to produce a moral community because a mutual understanding of the ironies in question is required in the dialogue. Yet, implicitly, another common thread runs through almost all the ethnographic examples provided in this chapter: ironies are invoked when the individual fails to succeed due to an unexpected or uncontrollable external force, including the anthropologist's ironic encounter with the propaganda apparatus of the local Communist Party. Under the mask of irony, we can see the anxieties of success at work.

To support this observation, I cite from Stephan Feuchtwang's contribution to this volume (Chapter 12). When asked 'how and why do people where you came from talk about the famine', the informant, a county-level Communist cadre, said, 'Those who talk about it are those who have become wealthy. Those who have not succeeded, do not. Only when you are successful can your talk be influential. They boast that they have got over the hard times and of how different it is now, for them.' Is it not ironic that only successful people (defined as being wealthy) care about remembering the past suffering? Why? The key, according to this informant, is that their achievement has proved their capability to overcome the hard times, whereas the non-achievers cannot produce any proof of such capability.

In the introduction, Charles Stafford reminds us that the question of responsibility is a recurrent theme in this volume, a point with which I agree entirely; but I want to stretch this theme a bit further to include the ethical moments of irresponsibility. The most striking ethnographic example is presented by Jing Shao and Mary Scoggin in Chapter 13. One of their key informants, Zhongmin, was infected with HIV when he, along with hundreds of villagers in the region, repeatedly sold blood plasma to poorly regulated commercial blood-collection stations in the 1990s. His wife died of AIDS, as did two of his brothers, and another nine people in his extended family were also infected by the fatal virus. Yet Zhongmin was quite proud of himself for receiving romantic love from a much younger married woman, and he had unprotected sex with her. To justify his behaviour, Zhongmin insisted that his type of HIV virus transmits only through the blood, not through sexual encounters. The much deeper reasoning, as Shao and Scoggin reveal, is a rather influential Chinese ethical thinking that places the original cause of the HIV infection—being an innocent victim of others' errors or of one's own immoral behaviour, such as homosexuality or sexual promiscuity—above the absolute equal value over all individuals. In the case of Zhongmin and other rural victims of the commercial blood harvesting, 'exonerated of moral responsibility for their own infection, rightly or not, they have also found a way to distance themselves from the responsibility to prevent continuing the infections'.

Not in quite the same vein but also related to misfortune and victimization, Bright Gold, the main figure in Gonçalo Santos's ethnography (Chapter 11), bid on two decorative mirrors during a temple-sponsored charity auction. He did so to celebrate his recovery from a long illness and also to change his bad luck over the years, pretty much like the villager Liu Dawei (in Chapter 8) who wants to reverse his bad luck by building a new house. What makes Bright Gold remarkable is his refusal to settle his donation pledge after the ritual. He first refused to pay and then ridiculed the temple committee by suggesting payment with a traditional ritual currency, namely, 'spirit money', a particular kind of yellow paper cut into certain shapes. He cast doubt on the moral authority of the temple committee and announced his lack of belief in popular religion and the Taoist ritual.

Santos explains this case in terms of the conflict and contest between different ethical codes and of the complexity of social practices produced by individual responses to special circumstances. Yet Bright Gold's action and ethical reflection can also be examined in light of the responsibility theme that Stafford suggests. Is it not a rather simple and basic responsibility of the individual to deliver what she or he promises to deliver, especially the promise made to the public in a formal (and in this case also religious) occasion? Had Bright Gold had doubts about the moral authority of the temple committee and truly viewed the Taoist ritual as meaningless and useless superstition, why did he carefully choose the two mirrors that matched his personal situation and why did he bid to reverse his bad luck in the first place? Actually, I am not surprised by Bright Gold's inconsistency before and after the ritual, and I tend to believe that his inability to pay was because of his loss of financial power to his wife during his illness. What impressed me, however, was his open denial of a basic responsibility, the lack of a sanctioning force to punish his irresponsibility in the village community and the fact that he could escape all possible negative consequences and still keep the two mirrors after other people paid for his pledge.[7]

This leads me to think of the relationship between the ethics of the individual and the moral community at large. In his chapter on moral judgement, Stafford offers two insightful observations. First, villagers consistently make ethical decisions and moral judgements about themselves and one another in the context of ordinary life where no moral breakdown is necessary for ethical reflections. Second, villagers may judge others more generously because they know their fellow villagers almost as well as they know themselves, proving the widely recognized psychological finding about 'harsh to others, easy to one self' highly questionable (Chapter 6). Such a moral community, however, is currently under assault because the striving individual is urged, or pulled, to leave for possible wealth and success in the outside world, and the irresistible flow of information from outside undermines the previous consensus—moral and other alike. Consequently, mutual understanding based on a high degree of homogeneity and familiarity declines, and social distances and unfamiliarity grow. Once opened to competing moral values and individual choices, the sanctioning power of the moral community will decline as well, as shown in the case of Bright Gold in Chapter 11.

What remains intact in the changing moral landscape, however, are the family and the state that continue to function as the ethical pegs for the striving individual to attach to and to make sense of the meaning of life beyond material objects, albeit most of the time operating in different ways. Intriguingly, although the striving individual leaves the family in search of success and, once married, generally abandons the extended family structure in favour of the small and more affectionate conjugal family, the ideal of a family group containing all family members in harmonious relationships still shines as much as it did before the rise of the striving individual. As Roberts nicely puts it, individuals may strike out to adopt different ways of family management and organization, but they are working hard to realize the same dream. Evidently, the actual realization of this same dream varies greatly, shown by the different testimonies he cites in Chapter 9. Regardless of her/his actual behaviour in family relations, the striving individual invariably defines the process of making oneself a good person in terms of family harmony and happiness (see Chapters 3–6, 8, 9 and 11 in this volume).

By the beginning of the twenty-first century, the Communist ethics of sacrificing personal interests for the party-state and devoting oneself entirely to the revolutionary cause were long gone. Many people of the older generations viewed their past enthusiastic participation in or painful exclusion from the radical campaigns of social transformation, such as the Great Leap Forward or Cultural Revolution, with feelings of betrayal, failure, irony and the need to restore humanity (see Chapters 8 and 12), whereas youths simply do not care about knowing of the past or about Communist ethics at all. What is shared across generational lines, however, is a strange combination of distrust of government officials due to the widespread official corruption and at the same time high hopes of governmental protection of the individual's pursuit of success and happiness. As a result, how to make oneself fit better into the existing power and hierarchy structures while taking advantage of the opportunities accorded by the developmental state becomes another important part of ethical reflection and discourse in everyday life (see Chapters 2, 3, 7, 8 and 12).

Obviously, the striving individual in China is by no means free from the influence of the collective systems of morality and ethics that used to dominate the moral landscape in China; nor does the striving individual fully accept the individualistic ethics of autonomy, freedom and self-reliance. Rather, there is an entanglement of the traditional, the Communist and the individualistic moralities. In reality, the individual must strive to strike a balance—often on one toe, so to speak—between the conflicting values and to cope with the entanglements not only of different moralities but also of different behavioural patterns in practice. In the long run, ethical dilemmas and struggles come and go at the individual level, yet the predicament of value entanglement persists over time and cuts across generational lines. The case of old-age security in rural China provides a good example.

This issue attracted scholarly attention in the 1990s because of the rapid increase in empty-nest families in the countryside due to both out-migration of young villagers and, more importantly, the strong trend for the nuclearization of the family promoted by more independence-minded young couples. In the traditional Chinese family, the custom of a married couple to live with the husband's parents—post-marital co-residence—provided guaranteed care and support to the elderly; and the practice was backed up by the ethical notion of filial piety that, in addition to the basic duty to support the elderly, calls for the subordination of children to their parents and, by extension, to all senior kinsmen within the domestic hierarchy. As part of the effort to uproot patriarchal power in the family and community and to build a new socialist society of individual citizens, the party-state was critical of and actually attacked the notion of filial piety through marriage laws, political campaigns, education programs and policies during both the collective and post-collective periods. Liberated from the power of traditional kinship organization and influenced by the ideology of compulsive consumerism in a market economy, intergenerational reciprocity has clearly moved from the logic of delayed and generalized exchange to a much shorter-term, and more calculated, pattern of balanced exchange. The younger generation of villagers began to challenge the moral meaning of filial piety and the conventional model of elderly support, especially the custom of post-marital co-residence. In ethical discourse, although accepting it as an unavoidable family responsibility, the younger generation views elderly support as one type of exchange. As in other types of market exchange, one's efforts to support elders are measured by what one previously received. If the parents did not treat their children well, then the children have reason to reduce the scope and amount of reciprocity. Unfortunately, living under the planned economy system, most elderly in China did not have the chance to accumulate wealth and thus could no longer fulfil their traditional parental duties to pass down property to their married sons; consequently, they have little to exchange with their married sons in the new game of intergenerational reciprocity based on the new moral reckoning of balanced exchange rather than on the logic of filial piety. As a result, family disputes commonly occur, family division has come earlier and earlier and an increasing number of elderly people live in empty-nest families and feel that they are being treated unfairly (see e.g. Yan 2003; H. Zhang 2005).

The degree of the actual negative impact of the changing social practices on elder support varies from one place to another, with specific problems ranging from a lack of financial support to mental health issues deriving from moral confusion, loneliness and isolation among the elderly. A strong sense of moral decline existed among many villagers, including some village youth, throughout the 1990s. As the new practice became more common, however, an increasing number of elderly began to change their moral judgements about it; many no longer regard living alone as a shameful result of being abandoned by one's adult children, and some even view it as a way to maintain their own privacy and independence (Thøgersen and Ni 2008; H. Zhang 2005).

It is intriguing that although villagers have begun to perceive the new practice of elderly living alone as acceptable, the official and scholarly discourses focus more critical attention on this new practice, referring to it as a moral and social crisis. This is because China has 60 million people aged sixty-five or older living in the countryside (based on the 2000 census) and yet there is no social support system for them. In the foreseeable future, and despite official rhetoric about creating a rural welfare system, the government cannot afford to build a social support system for the elderly. From the perspective of the state, family support remains the only tangible resource (see Song 2006). At this point, the social basis of the perception of a moral decline in terms of support for the elderly has shifted from intergenerational conflicts among villagers to perceived structural changes in China's social support system among policy makers and scholars.

Responding to the rapid social changes in China, individuals must often make moral decisions about their own behaviour and moral judgements about others, many of which are complicated, confusing and, more often than not, the result of the entanglements of the old and new ethics. Elsewhere I discuss a case from Xiajia village in northeast China, where I have been conducting field research since the late 1980s. A couple in this village was admired by the villagers because their two daughters excelled in school; after graduating from college in 2003, the elder daughter landed an office job in Beijing and was able to support her younger sister in graduate school and buy her parents an apartment in the provincial capital. The family became the focal point of an ethical scandal when a middle-aged woman from Beijing came to the village and accused the elder daughter of destroying the woman's marriage. It turned out that the elder daughter was living in an apartment with a regular stipend provided by her boss, a married man who was twice her age. It was only by becoming his mistress, the villagers told me, that the elder daughter was able to send home so much money. Some regarded this as disgraceful and unacceptable, yet others praised the daughter for her devotion to her parents and her younger sister. How to make a fair moral judgement on her behaviour became a highly controversial issue and was often debated among my informants during my interviews (see Yan 2011).

The entanglement of different moralities and ethics also means that current changes in China's moral landscape are by no means mono-directional or single-dimensional. Although more and more Chinese individuals strive to succeed and to meet personal desires, others lament the decline of a collective ethics of responsibility, especially the loss of the meaning of life that was previously defined by collective interests, and they make an effort to preserve some collective values. Like Roberts in this volume, Hansen and Pang (2008) find in their field research that the harmony and prosperity of the family remains the ultimate goal among the young migrant workers even though they have left their parents to pursue their dreams of success in faraway urban areas. The sense of cultural belonging has grown stronger since the 1990s as more individuals, especially the rising middle class, want to showcase their Chineseness through lifestyles and public discourse; nationalism and consumerism have emerged together as the main threads to construct the world of meaning for most Chinese youth; and being patriotic has also become fashionable among young urban professionals (Gries 2004; Hoffman 2010; Jankowiak 2004; Rofel 2007). Moreover, individuals strive to pursue personal interests by way of the old collective ethics. For example, most workers who engage in rights assertion movements after they are laid off do so in accordance with the socialist value of industrial workers being the leading class of the new society (see Lee 2007). Returned overseas Chinese on a state farm refuse to privatize the collective farm because they do not see themselves as fit for the market economy. Quite interestingly, they resorted to the collective ethics and politics of patriotism to eventually win their battle (Li 2010).

Furthermore, individuals apply different moral logics that seem to be the most appropriate to a given case at a particular time. In a study of inheritance disputes in Shanghai, Davis (2004) discovers that when contesting family real estate, people first take into consideration the pathway by which the family obtained the property. If it is privately owned family property, or *sifang*, the logic of the family estate will be applied; if it is a residential unit allocated by the work-unit or rented from the city's real-estate bureau (*gongfang*), the logic of the regulatory state will be emphasized; if it is a commercial flat purchased after the Chinese housing reform (*shangpin fang*), the logic of the law of the market over-rules all other logics (Davis 2004).

Finally, the entanglements of different moral behaviours and ethical reasonings are further complicated by the remaining influence of a strong party-state that, at least at the level of the official ideology and the government-controlled public discourse, still demands the individual's submission to the party-state, both politically and ethically. According to this official ideology, the individual's autonomy and freedom are granted by the party-state, as are the achievements made by the individual by exercising her/his agency. Individual success, therefore, should be interpreted first and foremost as a successful result of state efforts, as represented by the leadership of state officials at various levels. For example, Zhou Yang, an 18-year-old skater, won the 1,500-meter gold medal during the 2009 Winter Olympics in Vancouver. At a press conference, the overjoyed young athlete opened her remarks by thanking her parents and expressing her wish that the gold medal will enable her parents to live a much better life (as she expected to receive a monetary award from the government). A deputy director of the State General Administration of Sports openly criticized Zhou Yang in the media for putting her parents ahead of the state: 'There is no problem to thank your father and mother. [You] should at first show gratitude to the state, place the state at the front, instead of thanking [your] parents and that was it' (*Liaowang guancha* 2010). What followed was even more interesting. On the Internet, most netizens disagreed with the official's criticism and supported Zhou Yang for putting parents ahead of the state, even though both Zhou Yang and her parents issued public apologies to the state. Eventually, Zhou received a large award as promised and bought a BMW X5 for her parents, but her ethical reflection on the entire ordeal remains unknown to the public.[8]

THE STRIVING INDIVIDUAL IN A CHANGING CHINESE MORAL LANDSCAPE

At this stage, the notion of the 'striving individual' becomes much clearer: the individual is driven by the urge to succeed or the fear of failure or the combination of both; in order to succeed or avoid losing out, the individual must be industrious, self-disciplined, calculating and pragmatic. Yet, because of the entanglement of different value systems and the Chinese political regime, to a great extent the striving individual is confined to the sphere of private life and to economic activities in the public sphere; success is mainly defined in materialistic terms. Individual autonomy and freedom, which constitute the key to ethics, have not been developed much beyond the pursuit of personal interests in the market competition. The striving individual has increasingly become apolitical and devoid of civic obligations (Yan 2003). These features set the striving individual in China apart from counterparts in contemporary Western societies, which Nikolas Rose (1998) refers to as 'enterprising individuals'.

Based on Foucault's notions of governmentality and the technologies of the self, Rose develops a theory on the contemporary regime of the self under 'advanced liberalism', namely, liberal-democratic polities in Western societies, in which the notion of the 'enterprising individual' or 'enterprising self' serves as a prism to look at the new self being invented along with the arrival of modernity. 'The enterprising self will make an enterprise of its life, seek to maximize its own human capital, project itself a future, and seek to shape itself in order to become that which it wishes to be. The enterprising self is thus both an active self and a calculating self, a self that calculates *about* itself and that acts *upon* itself in order to better itself' (1998: 154; italics in original).

In this connection, it is also interesting to note that the individualization thesis in European sociology examines much of the same process of radical change in the making of the contemporary self but with a radically different focus. In one of his earliest explanations of individualization resulting from modernity's dissolving impact on the foundation of industrial society, Ulrich Beck offers a tripartite definition:

[D]isembedding, *removal* from historically prescribed social forms and commitments in the sense of traditional contexts of dominance and support (the 'liberating dimension'); the *loss of traditional security* with respect to practical knowledge, faith and guiding norms (the 'disenchantment dimension'); and—here the meaning of the word is virtually turned into its opposite—re-embedding, *a new type of social commitment* (the 'control' or 'reintegration dimension'). (Beck 1992: 128; italics in original)

Although these three features of individualization can be found in both the objective domain of life situations and the subjective domain of consciousness (Beck 1992: 128), Beck and Beck-Gernsheim (2002) and others in this school of thought primarily focus on the objective domain, examining individualization as a transformative process in life situations and biographical patterns. In contrast, Rose (1998) takes a Foucaultian approach and focuses on the psychological domain, or the making of subjectivities.

On the surface, the striving individual in contemporary China resembles Rose's enterprising self and, to a great extent, is also experiencing patterns of social change similar to the individualization process in Western Europe. Like the enterprising self, the striving individual in China is a self-driven, calculating and determined subject who wants to better his or her life in accordance with individual plans, seeking to live 'a life of one's own' or a 'do-it-yourself biography' (see Beck 1992; Beck and Beck-Gernsheim 2002). This resemblance in the subjective domain has led a number of China scholars to examine the making of self-regulating subjectivity in light of the notion of the enterprising self through studies of job market and career development (Hanser 2001), white-collar professionals (Hoffman 2010), public culture and individual desires (Rofel 2007) and a Chinese version of neoliberal governance that involves a set of technologies of the self (Ong and Zhang 2008). The similarities in the objective domain, namely, changing life situations and biography patterns, enable other scholars to understand the rise of the individual and the individualization of Chinese society in light of the individualization thesis (Hansen and Svarverud 2010; Yan 2009a, 2010).

Yet there are also deeply rooted differences between the Chinese case and its counterpart in Western societies; chief among these is the absence of classic liberalism in the Chinese polity and consequently the unfinished task of emancipation politics. According to Rose, the enterprising self is born out of the presuppositions of the individual's natural rights of autonomy, freedom, choice, liberty and identity, which 'underpinning and legitimating political activity imbues the political mentalities of the modern West' (1998: 151). In a similar vein, the individualization theory identifies three preconditions for the wave of individualization in second modernity: namely, cultural democracy, the welfare state and classic individualism (see Bauman 2001; Beck 1992; Beck and Beck-Gernsheim 2002; Giddens 1991). In my mind, these are two sides of the same coin of a liberal-democratic polity that has been succinctly interpreted by Charles Taylor as a gradual yet consistent growth of a new moral order concerning how human beings should live together in a given society. In this new moral order, the basic liberal idea that the individual is naturally autonomous and a self-determining agent, and thus born with a set of individual rights, is widely accepted; various mechanisms have been created to limit the state's power in order to protect the individual (Taylor 2004). This consensus is equally important in most contemporary social theories in the West, but it is only viewed as a given because the politics of emancipation in Western societies has mostly ended and the new dominant form of politics is that of lifestyles, as opposed to that of life chances (Giddens 1991: 209–31).

In contrast, the Chinese party-state never accepted political liberalism after it took national power in 1949, and the post-Mao reforms have been geared towards maximizing the benefits of a market economy without political liberalization. Although the party-state has adopted many developmental strategies that were originally promoted by the liberal and neoliberal market-economy models, these strategies should not be confused with the fundamental principle in both political liberalism and first modernity in the West; that is, the individual, as the bearer of natural rights, stands out as the end instead of the means of political life (Taylor 2004). Gauging by this principle, we can clearly see that the presuppositions of the enterprising self, namely, individual autonomy, freedom, choice, rights and identity, remain the goal of emancipation politics in contemporary Chinese society, despite all the radical changes in social life; it follows that something important is missing if one applies the notion of the enterprising self to the Chinese case. This is why I prefer to call the newly emerged self in China the striving individual, because the notion does not rest on a set of values of liberalism but at the same time connects with a long-held image of the hard-working person in traditional Chinese culture (Harrell 1985).

Perhaps one of the most influential theoretical models in the new century is the critique of neoliberalism. Being perceived as a well-designed national and transnational project of loosening controls on the capital and enabling the triumph of global capitalism all over the world since the late 1970s, neoliberalism has been found responsible for many market-driven political and social changes in many countries. David Harvey's (2005) claim that neoliberalism is compatible with dictatorial regimes and can be instrumental for developmental states under authoritarian rule has been quite influential. Yet Harvey's followers tend to overlook a basic feature of neoliberalism in Harvey's own formula: that is, neoliberalism assumes that the individual is a naturally autonomous and self-determining agent whose rights and freedom are protected by the established political regime (see Harvey 2005). This brings us back to Giddens's notion of emancipation politics being replaced by identity politics, Taylor's narrative of how a new moral order is being established and Beck's three social premises of individualization, all of which were missing in the Chinese case, as I discussed earlier.

Taking into consideration the absence of political liberalism, and especially the protection of individual political rights and freedom, Ong and Zhang propose that China is developing a distinctive neoliberal configuration characterized by flourishing economic liberalism without political liberalism and thriving market individuation without political individualism (2008: 12). In my view, it is logically difficult to practice neoliberalism without political liberalism because the former derives from the latter and holds the autonomy and natural rights of the individual to be the core of its theoretical reasoning. Yet it is possible for a society to undergo an individualization process without political liberalism and classic individualism because this reconfiguration of social relations can be carried out by other mechanisms, such as state power and market incentives, as revealed in the Chinese case. In this regard, Beck's individualization thesis provides a much stronger theoretical framework to understand the Chinese case because it focuses on the structural changes in the individual–society–state relationship instead of on any political philosophy or ideological imperative. Yet Beck's theory also omits the subjective domain of the making of the new self, which, as indicated earlier, is the focus of Rose's endeavour with the notion of the enterprising self.

In light of the individualization theory of Beck, Bauman and others, yet at the same time emphasizing the important differences that set the China case apart from its counterparts in Western societies, I have tried to document a double-transformation of Chinese society, that is, the rise of the individual and the individualization of society through the structural changes of social relations, especially the individual–society–state relationship (Yan 2009a, 2010). The key to understanding the Chinese case is to treat it as a specific strategy to pursue modernity that was first explored among the Chinese elite during the turn of the twentieth century and later practiced at the societal level. A common thread in the discourse and practice of this double transformation is that the individual must bear more responsibilities and take proactive steps in order to achieve wealth and power for the family and the nation-state, which among ordinary Chinese are commonly referred to as the modernizations of the family and the Chinese country. Looking at the case of China through such a perspective, the double-transformation is actually a long process, originating with the early modernization attempts under the Qing empire in the late nineteenth century and cutting across the divide between the Maoist and post-Mao eras (see Yan 2010). What makes the thirty-plus years of the post-Mao era particularly noteworthy, however, is the impact of globalization and China's proactive integration into the global market.

As far as ethics and moral life are concerned, an important ethical shift has occurred in post-Mao China, that is, the shift from a collective ethics of duties and self-sacrifice to a more individual ethics of rights and self-development, thus radically changing China's moral landscape.[9] As I document elsewhere, in addition to the conventional moral life that helps to reproduce the social order, new ethics and moralities emerge— and are contested. This situation disturbs behavioural patterns in various ways, leads to complications in ethical reasoning and generates new ethical discourses and reflections. As a result, the moral landscape is full of new developments and new tensions at the same time (Yan 2009b, 2011). The ethics of the striving individual should be examined as part and parcel both of this changing moral landscape and of the individualization of Chinese society that underpins it.

NOTES

I owe special thanks to Charles Stafford and two anonymous reviewers for their insightful and very helpful comments on an early draft of this chapter. I am also grateful to the John Simon Guggenheim Foundation for the 2010 Guggenheim Fellowship, which enabled me to concentrate on the writing of a number of articles including this chapter.

1. Interestingly, the aesthetic of order—issues of harmony, balance and contrast—that Miller and his research team explore also has an inherent ethical dimension, especially when individuals attempt to make sense of their life by way of either action and discourse or the arrangement of material objects (see Miller 2009 and Bray's Chapter 10 in this volume).

2. Intriguingly, during the charity auction in rural Guangdong where decorative mirrors with auspicious Chinese characters are purchased, the most expensive is '*git-bohng*', or '*jie bang*', traditionally meaning to score number one in the imperial examination. (See Chapter 11 of this volume.)

3. These practices are not uncommon among migrant workers but have drawn little scholarly attention because they tend to be viewed as idiosyncratic behaviour by the individual. In her in-depth description of the pursuit of success by rural young women working in factories, Leslie T. Chang examines the various strategies employed by female migrant workers, including the frequent use of fake names, IDs and resumes. The night schools are designed to help these young women move up the social ladder, specifically to teach them how 'to lie their way up' (Chang 2008: 171–205). For a systematic account of the counterfeiting culture in China, see Y.J. Lin's (2011) *Fake Stuff*.

4. Both issues are extensively explored by Eona Bell in Chapter 5 of this volume. But because the people she studies live in different social and political contexts, I do not discuss her chapter here.

5. In two recent articles, I focus my analysis on the immorality of the striving individual and the dark side of the changing moral landscape; see Yan (2009b, 2011).

6. For an excellent study of Chinese work ethics motivated mostly by a willingness to sacrifice self-interest for the family group, see Harrell (1985).

7. Chapter 4 in this volume provides an example of the wish to avoid responsibility. While taking more responsibilities in their life course, ranging from helping parents to build a new house, contributing to a brother's marriage finances and taking care of one's own in the hostile urban environment to proving one's moral worth by finding a good husband, these young women dream of taking no responsibility at all in a perfect marriage. Fang notes that what many of these women look for in an ideal marriage is 'neither responsibility for taking care of the household following the traditional division of labor nor responsibility for being the main bread-winner in the household'. The indicator of success is 'being provided for in life by a man' and 'avoiding having to work hard' (see Fang, Chapter 4). It follows that perhaps only a rich man can provide all of this; this may explain why some young female migrant workers proactively seduce their Taiwanese bosses by knocking at the latter's doors at night.

8. Normally, it would not make much sense to buy such a luxury car because her parents—both retired workers—lived in a small city in northern China, but the ownership of a BMW X5 has long been regarded as one of the ultimate symbols of success in Chinese society.

9. Such an ethical shift seems to be a rather universal phenomenon. See Lipovetsky with Charles (2005).

REFERENCES

Baker, H. (1979), *Chinese Family and Kinship*, New York: Columbia University Press.

Bauman, Z. (2001), *The Individualized Society*, Cambridge: Polity Press.

Beck, U. (1992), *Risk Society: Towards a New Modernity*, trans. M. Ritter, London and Thousand Oaks, CA: Sage Publications.

Beck, U., and Beck-Gernsheim, E. (2002), *Individualization: Institutionalized Individualism and Its Social and Political Consequences*, London and Thousand Oaks, CA: Sage Publications.

Chang, L. T. (2008), *Factory Girls: From Village to City in a Changing China*, New York: Spiegel & Grau.

Cheng, Y. (2009), *Creating the 'New Man': From Enlightenment Ideals to Socialist Realities*, Honolulu: University of Hawai'i Press.

Ci, J. (1994), *Dialectic of the Chinese Revolution: From Utopianism to Hedonism*, Stanford, CA: Stanford University Press.

Cohen, M. L. (1976), *House United, House Divided: The Chinese Family in Taiwan*, New York: Columbia University Press.

Davis, D. (2004), 'Talking about Property in the New Chinese Domestic Property Regime', in F. Dobbin (ed.), *The New Economic Sociology: A Reader*, Princeton, NJ: Princeton University Press.

Fong, V. (2004), *Only Hope: Coming of Age under China's One-child Policy*, Stanford, CA: Stanford University Press.

Giddens, A. (1991), *Modernity and Self-Identity: Self and Society in the Late Modern Age*, Stanford, CA: Stanford University Press.

Gries, P.H. (2004), *China's New Nationalism: Pride, Politics, and Diplomacy*, Berkeley: University of California Press.

Hansen, M.H., and Pang, C. (2008), 'Me and My Family: Perceptions of Individual and Collective among Young Rural Chinese', *European Journal of East Asian Studies*, 7/1: 75–99.

Hansen, M.H., and Svarverud, R. (eds) (2010), *iChina: The Rise of the Individual in Modern Chinese Society*, Copenhagen: NIAS Press.

Hanser, A. (2001), 'The Chinese Enterprising Self: Young, Educated Urbanites and the Search for Work', in P. Link, R.P. Madsen, and P. G. Pickowicz (eds), *Popular China: Unofficial Culture in a Globalizing Society*, Lanham, MD: Rowman & Littlefield Publishers.

Harvey, D. (2005), *A Brief History of Neoliberalism*, Oxford: Oxford University Press.

Harrell, S. (1985), 'Why Do the Chinese Work So Hard? Reflections on an Entrepreneurial Ethic', *Modern China*, 11/2: 203–26.

Hoffman, L.M. (2010), *Patriotic Professionalism in Urban China: Fostering Talent*, Philadelphia: Temple University Press.

Jankowiak, W. (2004), 'Market Reforms, Nationalism and the Expansion of Urban China's Moral Horizon', *Urban Anthropology*, 33/2–3: 167–210.

Kipnis, A. (2001), 'The Disturbing Educational Discipline of "Peasants"', *The China Journal*, 46: 1–24.

Kipnis, A. (2006), '*Suzhi*: A Keyword Approach', *The China Quarterly*, 186: 295–313.

Lee, C.K. (2007), *Against the Law: Labor Protests in China's Rustbelt and Sunbelt*, Berkeley: University of California Press.

Li, M. (2010), 'Collective Symbols and Individual Options: Life on a State Farm for Returned Overseas Chinese after Decollectivization', in M.H. Hansen and R. Svarverud (eds), *iChina: The Rise of the Individual in Modern Chinese Society*, Copenhagen: NIAS Press.

Liaowang guancha (2010), '*Auyun guanjun xian ganxie fumu haishi guojia*' (Should the Olympic Gold Medalist First Thank Her Parents or the State?), 9 March. Available online: http://www.lwgcw.com/NewsShow.aspx?newsId= 3450 (accessed 25 October 2010).

Lin, Y.-C.J. (2011), *Fake Stuff: China and the Rise of Counterfeit Goods*, London: Routledge.

Lipovetsky, G., with Charles, S. (2005), *Hypermodern Times*, Andrew Brown (trans.), Cambridge: Polity Press.

Liu, X. (2002), *The Otherness of Self: A Genealogy of the Self in Contemporary China*, Ann Arbor: University of Michigan Press.

Madsen, R. (1984), *Morality and Power in a Chinese Village*, Berkeley: University of California Press.

Miller, D. (ed.) (2009), *Anthropology and the Individual: A Material Culture Perspective*, Oxford and New York: Berg.

Ong, A., and Zhang, L. (2008), 'Introduction: Privatizing China: Powers of the Self, Socialism from Afar', in L. Zhang and A. Ong (eds), *Privatizing China: Socialism from Afar*, Ithaca, NY: Cornell University Press.

Rofel, L. (2007), *Desiring China: Experiments in Neoliberalism, Sexuality, and Public Culture*, Durham, NC: Duke University Press.

Rose, N. (1998), *Inventing Our Selves: Psychology, Power, and Personhood*, Cambridge: Cambridge University Press.

Schwartz, B.I. (1985), *The World of Thought in Ancient China*, Cambridge, MA: Belknap Press of Harvard University Press.

Song, J. (2006), *Zhongguo nongcun renkou de shouru yu yanglao* (Income and Elderly Support among the Rural Population in China), Beijing: Zhongguo renmin daxue chubanshe.

Sun, L. (2004), *Zhuanxing yu duanlie: Gaige yilai Zhongguo shehui jiegou de bianqian* (Transition and Cleavage: Structural Changes in Chinese Society since the Reforms), Beijing: Qinghua daxue chubanshe.

Taylor, C. (2004), *Modern Social Imaginaries*, Durham, NC: Duke University Press.

Thøgersen, S., and Ni, A. (2008), ' "He is He, and I am I": Individual and Collective among China's Rural Elderly', *European Journal of East Asian Studies*, 7/1: 11–37.

Tsai, K.S. (2007), *Capitalism without Democracy: The Private Sector in Contemporary China*, Ithaca, NY: Cornell University Press.

Tu, W.-M. (1985), *Confucian Thought: Selfhood as a Creative Transformation*, Albany: State University of New York Press.

Wang, X. (1998), '*Banzhanglian de xiaoxiang*' (A Half-faced Portrait), reprinted in Wang, X. (2004), *Banzhanglian de Shenhua* (The Half-faced Myth), Guilin, China: Guangxi Shida Chubanshe.

Wang, X. (2002), 'The Post-Communist Personality: The Spectre of China's Capitalist Market Reforms', *The China Journal*, 47: 1–17.

Yan, Y. (2003), *Private Life under Socialism: Love, Intimacy, and Family Change in a Chinese Village, 1949–1999*, Stanford, CA: Stanford University Press.

Yan, Y. (2009a), *The Individualization of Chinese Society*, Oxford: Berg.

Yan, Y. (2009b), 'The Good Samaritan's New Trouble: A Study of the Changing Moral Landscape in Contemporary China', *Social Anthropology*, 17/1: 9–24.

Yan, Y. (2010), 'The Chinese Path to Individualization', *The British Journal of Sociology*, 61/3: 489–513.

Yan, Y. (2011), 'The Changing Moral Landscape', in A. Kleinman, Y. Yan, J. Jun, S. Lee, E. Zhang, P. Tianshu, W. Fei and G. Jinhua, *Deep China: The Moral Life of the Person, What Anthropology and Psychiatry Tell Us about China Today*, Berkeley and Los Angeles: University of California Press.

Zhang, H. (2005), 'Bracing for an Uncertain Future: A Case Study of New Coping Strategies of Rural Parents under China's Birth Control Policy', *The China Journal*, 54: 53–76.

Zhang, L. (2010), *In Search of Paradise: Middle-Class Living in a Chinese Metropolis*, Ithaca, NY: Cornell University Press.

INDEX

embezzlement, 128
embodied ethical practice, 5, 151,
    177–8
emotional intimacy, 10, 18, 95
emotional support, 158, 160,
    169
emotional wellbeing, 15, 169
emotions, and morality, 106
enculturation, 5, 19
    see also socialization
envy, 115–31 *passim*
    sin of being envied by others,
    115
    in Western tradition, 115, 129
    malicious, 125, 127
    of others, 115–16, 129–30
ethical acts, 7, 25, 109, 180, 242,
    252, 262
ethical choices, 18, 56, 278
    by children, 46, 49–53, 265
    by parents, 80–95 *passim*
    delegation to technology of,
    185
ethical codes, role of state in
    cultivation of, 125
ethical discourse, 279, 287
ethical responsibility of
    anthropologists, 256–7
ethics
    collective versus individual, 287
    explicit or implicit, 5
ethnicity, 80, 84, 94–5, 158
evil eye, 115

factories, lives of workers in,
    67–78 *passim*
failure, 14, 130, 134–5, 180, 224
    educational, 61

fear of, 272, 278, 282
    financial, 52
    moral, 210
family
    care of parents by children, 93
    ideal of, 134
    strategies of residence and
    support, 15, 85–90,
    154–69, 209–10
    see also grandchildren;
    grandparents; kinship;
    parents
fear, 68, 85
    of moral censure, 88
    of HIV/AIDS, 19, 242, 253
    see also failure, fear of
femininity, ethics of, 75–6, 78,
    266, 273
festivals *see* Chinese New Year;
    jiao festivals
Fong, Vanessa, 6, 20, 82
food
    and care of parents, 140, 162
    and historical judgement,
    239–40
    and hospitality, 107–11
    and reciprocity, 242, 246
    security, ethics of, 189
    sharing among children, 42
    temple offerings, 207
forgiveness, 12, 19, 111
Freedman, Maurice, 160
friendship, 11, 38, 42, 67, 71, 87,
    91, 123–4, 140–1, 147–8,
    164
    ethics of, 69
fundamental attribution error,
    102–5, 110

London School of Economics Monographs on Social Anthropology Series
Series Editor: Laura Bear

With over 70 volumes published since 1949, including classic work by Gell, Barth, Leach and Firth, the LSE Monographs now form one of the most prestigious series in the discipline of Anthropology. Presenting scholarly work from all branches of Social Anthropology the series continues to build on its history with both theoretical and ethnographic studies of the contemporary world.